A Short History of
Irish Literature

A Short History of Irish Literature

Seamus Deane

University of Notre Dame Press

Notre Dame, Indiana 46556

Contents

Preface

There are several histories of Anglo-Irish literature and many surveys of particular periods within the field. Even though there is a
perceptible uneasiness about the date of the emergence of this body
of writing and, even more, about the relation it bears on the one
hand to Gaelic and on the other to English literature, there is no
substantial dispute about the integrity of this literary tradition in the
English language. To describe this literature as 'Anglo-Irish' is by
now anachronistic, although 'Irish literature' is not without its perils
also. This is an inevitable problem in a colonial or neo-colonial
culture like ours, where the naming of the territory has always been,
in literary, geographical or historical contexts, a politically charged
activity. One of the aims of this book is to show how literature has
been inescapably allied with historical interpretation and with political allegiance. The Irish experience, in all its phases, has led to an
enhanced sense of the frailty of the assumptions which underlie any
working system of civilization and of the need to create, by a
persistent effort, the enabling fictions which win for it the necessary
degree of acceptance. Because of this, Irish writing has traditionally
been extraordinarily interrogative. It has moved between the
extremes of aestheticism – seeing literature as an end in itself – and
of political commitment – seeing it as an instrument for the
achievement of other purposes. Most of the great writers incorporate both attitudes within their work and they share with lesser
writers the conviction that the matter of Ireland is, *in parvo*, the
matter of civilization itself. It is only in a minority culture, acclimatized to discontinuity, that such a dream of totality can be regularly
entertained.

However, such matters cannot be dealt with in any detail in an
introductory volume which has no claim to the comprehensiveness
of a history or to the minuteness of a monograph. The need to
compress the material involved a number of exclusions. Gaelic
literature is, for instance, treated in a summary fashion, partly

because of my own deficiencies in that area, partly because the emphasis had to be on literature in the English language. Even then, there are omissions. Swift's poetry, the tradition of Irish oratory, Shaw's full career as a dramatist and polemicist as well as the work of a large number of modern and contemporary writers, are sacrificed for the sake of a continuous narrative in which some of the preoccupations I have mentioned are prominent. The same imperative led me to exclude Irish fiction of the eighteenth century. Henry Brooke and William Chaigneau are interesting figures, but their inclusion here would have taken me too far from the central story.

In effect, that story is about a literary tradition which has undergone a series of revivals and collapses, all of them centred upon an idea of Ireland. Sometimes the Ireland we speak of is an Edenic, sometimes it is a Utopian place. On other occasions, it is a rebuke to both. There is a consistent fascination with the discrepancy between the Irish world as imagined and the Irish world as it is, and this eventuates, time and again – in Swift, in Joyce, in Burke, in Standish O'Grady and many others – in a critique of the idea of authority. Authority and its legitimacy and effectiveness was always a matter of concern in Ireland, since it has only seldom proved its claim to either. But for writers, the questionable nature of authority has an especial charm, since there is, for an author, no more natural or, indeed, radical question. The interrogation of the status of an author as such is more likely to proceed when there are two prevailing conditions. One, is that the author is uncertain about his true audience; and second, that the author is uneasy with the very medium of communication. Both these conditions prevail in Ireland for writers of both English and Irish and their reality is exhibited in the fluctuating state of the Irish publishing industry. To be an Irish writer in English for a predominantly Irish or for a predominantly English audience is an ambiguous fate, overcome only by those few who manage to be both. A more thorough exploration of these ambiguities leads to strange, experimental and subversive enterprises, like those we associate with, say, Swift, Beckett, Flann O'Brien, George Moore, Joyce and, in a tributary fashion, with the translators who play such an important role in the endless negotiation between the two languages and between the competing interpretations of history which are so often involved with them. Linguistic unease lends itself to formal experimentation, although, equally, it can lead to *naïveté*, clumsiness and a degree of introverted provincialism. All of these features are strongly pronounced in the literature discussed here.

Finally, there is another kind of exclusion which merits observation. The exemplary instances are Congreve and Sterne. It is, naturally, with some reluctance that I omit writers of such quality, both for their own sakes and because of the compatibility between their work and some of the masterpieces of the Irish tradition. It would be easy to associate Congreve with Farquhar and, by extension, Wilde and the long line of Irish comic dramatists. Sterne is often invoked as a forerunner of Joyce, because of the degree of his formal experimentation. Yet, attractive as these associations are, they seem to be ultimately insubstantial. Both writers belong without any stress or strain to the English tradition and their Irish background is more peripheral than central to their literary achievement. There are many authors of Irish extraction whose relation to Irish writing is unimportant or non-existent. The Brontës are a case in point; so too is Robert Graves; and even Hazlitt has an Irish element in his family background. There is no point in pursuing these ghostly affiliations in the biography unless they are realized in some pronounced and substantial form in the writings. It has not, therefore, been my concern to claim for the tradition of Irish writing authors who are much more naturally understood in the English context. This is not to say, of course, that the problem is unreal or that the relationship between the two cultures is ever anything less than close as well as strained. This is an introduction to a literature in which ambiguity and tension of this kind has been transmitted into art more memorably and effectively than they have been in any other Irish enterprise.

1 The Gaelic background

The art of writing came to Ireland with Christianity in the fifth century. The new Christian communities, gathered together in monastic settlements, brought Latin culture into contact with a Gaelic civilization which had a long and rich oral tradition. Although the relationship between the new Christian clergy and the old professional class of learned men, dominated by the poet (*file*), was at first uneasy, the incorporation of the pagan and Christian elements was remarkably peaceful and comparatively swift. The flowering of this Christian and Gaelic culture in the sixth and seventh centuries in the Irish monasteries led to the ninth-century Irish missions to Europe and the conversion of the Germanic peoples to Christianity. But the Viking invasions, begun in 795, had already begun to weaken the fabric of the monastic civilization. By then, the basic materials for our understanding of pre-Christian Ireland had begun to accumulate as the result of a compromise between the clerical scribes and the poets of the old dispensation. It was traditionally the poet's function to preserve traditional lore (*senchas*) in relation to places, families, customs and laws. The monastic scribes were concerned to incorporate this material into the system of Christian belief. In doing so, they recorded the origin stories of Irish history and the great sagas – the Ulster Cycle, centred on Cu Chulainn, the Fenian Cycle centred on Finn Mac Cumhaill, the Cycle of the Kings, including the story of Mad Sweeney, and the Mythological Cycle and the group of Immrama or Voyages. All of these were written down in Irish, thus making it the oldest of European vernacular literatures and, as a consequence, the literature which uniquely blends the old pagan and the new Christian worlds. Much of this material was written down in the sixth or seventh centuries and was copied over and over again thereafter. Although no manuscript in the Irish language dates from earlier than the twelfth century, there is no doubt that the great mass of poems, sagas, annals and genealogical accounts derives from the pre-Christian Gaelic tradition.[1]* The endurance of this literature in the Irish imagination is attested by the fact that Thomas Kinsella published his translation of the *Táin Bó Cuailnge (The Cattle-Raid of Cooley)* in 1969; Paul Muldoon's poem 'Immram' in *Why Brownlee Left* (1980) is an adaptation of the *Immram Mael Duin*, an early Christian adaptation of a pagan story; and Seamus Heaney's *Sweeney Astray* is a version of the medieval *Buile Suibhne*, a tale based on traditions going back to the seventh century. Instances like these could be multiplied in twentieth-century Irish writing. John Montague's *The Faber Book of Irish Verse* (1976) is an anthology stretching from the sixth century to the present day, with modern translations of the early material.

The reconstruction of the pre-Christian history of Ireland is recorded in the *Lebor Gabhala* or *Book of Invasions*, the creation of centuries of accretion, adaptation and reorganization of earlier records into a political and Christian narrative, which justified the predominance of the Gaelic civilization in Ireland and traced its origins back to Adam. The central tale of the Ulster Cycle, the *Táin Bó Cuailgne*, preserved in three recensions, of which the twelfth-century *Book of Leinster* version is the most coherent, is the national epic of the Gaelic world. It tells the story of the great Ulster warrior, Cu Chulainn, who single-handedly held up the army of Queen Maeve's Connacht men while the rest of the Ulstermen lay under a spell which rendered them inactive. This story was to be resurrected again in the late nineteenth century by Standish O'Grady and Lady Gregory. Cu Chulainn was thence to become one of the heroic atavars of Yeats's poetry. But the stories and legends attached to his name remained part of the Irish folk imagination long after the destruction of Gaelic civilization and long before the Irish revival's reincorporation of them in modern literature. He is the epitome of the heroic spirit in Irish literature. The other great Irish hero, Finn Mac Cumhaill, the central figure in tales and poems, which had been transcribed since the eighth century, displaced Cu Chulainn from his central position with the appearance in medieval times of a work known as *Agallamh na Seanórach (Colloquy of the Ancient Men)*, the work of an unknown thirteenth-century genius. The stories of Finn (or Fionn) and the

---

*Superior figures refer to the Notes at the end of chapters.

fianna, the wandering band of warriors and hunters whom he led, were expanded and developed in prose sequences containing metrical insets. These insets in the *Agallamh* developed into the Ossianic lays, poems or ballads in which Oisın, one of Fıonn's companions, is the interlocutory figure who brings the pagan Fıonn and the Christian St Patrick together in a series of exchanges which embody the different world views of the two dispensations. The form of the lays is in itself conciliatory and the tone, for the most part, courteous. The opposition between the two worlds is brightly but not starkly contrasted. The culture is discovering through these tales and poems a way of preserving both pagan and Christian elements as integral parts of itself. In later centuries the tales continued to be extended and elaborated, both in formal literature and in the oral tradition. Europe rediscovered Fıonn and his companions in the eighteenth century through the publications of James MacPherson, whose *Fingal* (1762) and *Temora* (1763) were claimed as translations of poems written by Ossian (the Scottish form of Oisin) in the third or fourth century. Thus Fionn became one of the Celtic heroes of Romanticism long before Cu Chulaınn was retrieved for the Irish revival at the close of the European Romantic era. But the first coherent formulation of the Fionn Cycle, although its materials belonged to Gaelic Ireland, was a product of the new culture which had arrived with the Normans in 1169, a date equivalent in Irish history and literature to 1066 in England.

Irish lyric poetry began in the ninth century with the monastic scribes, many of whom would insert in the margins of the Latin treatises they were transcribing lyrics on occasional subjects – the song of a blackbird, the sunlight flickering on the pages of the manuscript, a bell ringing on a windy night. In the ninth century this lyrical impulse was sharpened by the ascetic devotionalism of a reform movement, which gave to the severe life of the hermit monk an enhanced prestige and a closer intimacy with the natural world in which he spent his solitude. The exile willingly undergone by the missionary monks also bred a poetry of longing for the beloved native place, most famous of which are the poems attributed to (but not possibly written by) St Colmcille, who Christianized Scotland and northern England and lamented the homelands of Gartan and 'angel-haunted' Derry, which he would never see again. Such personal themes, also found in the Latin poetry of the monks, do not form part of the repertoire of the older metrical tradition of verse. It was dominated by historical and mythological themes, passages of praise for warriors and chieftains, genealogies and the lore of sacred places. Such verse was in many ways more distinct from poetry proper than from prose, but its cultivation inevitably nurtured technical skills and ritual forms of great complexity. When these converged with the Latin forms learned by the scribes, most especially as the traditional *file* or poet disengaged from the role of historian, lawyer and encomiast, there emerged a body of poetry remarkable – and almost untranslatable – in its formal perfection. The mixture of religious and secular themes and the intense personal cadence of this poetry is sustained even into the lyrics, which were inset in the prose sagas, although not many of these preserved their full integrity in their passage from the oral to the written tradition. The more personal poetry was written in what were called the new metres (*nua-chrutha*), derived from the Latin hymns of continental Europe. These were syllabic, but the Irish poets refined the rhyme patterns and introduced elaborate alliterative ornaments native to the old tradition. From the ninth to the seventeenth century Irish poetry continued to develop its immense technical resources – rhyming quatrains, tercets and strophes of rhyming couplets, line end and internal accentual rhyme, and many other features which gave primacy to the aural enjoyment of a strictly organized poem – although it also exercised these within conventional limits. After the Norman invasion had begun to be absorbed, the schools of bardic poets began to flourish under the patronage of Norman or Gaelic lords, producing masses of formal verse in the family poem-books (*duanaire*), as well as less formal verse, which is generally valued more highly by modern readers. The specifically clerical and monastic influence receded and the starkness of the heroic literature was softened in its detail as the European conventions of romance literature were increasingly absorbed along with the other aspects of Anglo-Norman culture.[2]

The bardic schools predated the Norman invasion, although their organization is perhaps definitive from the twelfth century only. Under the kingship of Brian Boru in the tenth century, the centres of Irish learning had moved from the eastern seaboard to the monasteries of Clonmacnoise and Terryglass on the Shannon. In these great centres of learning the earlier literary and historical tradition was redefined and consolidated and became, in effect, the responsibility of hereditary literary families. Brian Boru's victory at the Battle of Clontarf (1014) was construed in the eleventh century as a victory by the High King of Ireland over foreign invaders – in this case, the Norse. But the Norse were by then already a minor element in the complicated and war-torn Irish polity. Brian Boru's court codified the rules of Irish metrics and rhetoric and subsequent antiquarian movements enhanced the retrospective impression that Ireland was and always had been an independent and centralized culture. But it was the Normans who brought the political reality of centralization with them. The European impact of their arrival had been anticipated by the arrival of the continental religious orders, led by St Malachi, who founded the Cistercian monastery of Mellifont in the Boyne valley in 1142. They were followed by the Franciscans. These orders became increasingly absorbed into the Gaelic civilization, recruiting many of their members from the dominant literary families. Although the Anglo-Norman invaders were also absorbed into the Gaelic polity, their insistence on the distinction between themselves and the Gaels, originally based on their boasted superiority in civilization, became a critical mark of identity for them after 1560, when the Reformation and subsequent political developments in England brought to Ireland a new invasion of settlers whose religion was Protestant and whose aim was dominance over the whole country at the expense of the Gaelic as well as the Norman, now the Old English, element.[3]

Between 1200 and the end of the sixteenth century, there were four languages in use in Ireland – Irish, Norman-French, Latin and English. The only literature of enduring quality was produced in Irish, although there are historically interesting poems in Middle English like *The Land of Cokaygne*, a satire in rhymed couplets. The Irish poetry may be divided into three general kinds – court poetry, love-poetry and ossianic lays, this last group being part of the elaboration of the Finn Cycle mentioned earlier. The love poetry is deeply marked by the impress of the European *amour courtois* and is practised both by the Norman aristocracy and by the professional poets. The court poetry, often in praise of a patron, was technically the most sophisticated, composed in strict versification (*dan díreach*) by highly trained professionals, who observed certain procedures even in the composition of their works. In their window-less rooms, in darkness, they produced a formal, hieratic poetry, which was then recited to music in the presence of the poet to the patron by the bard. One of the finest of the thirteenth-century poets, Giolla Brighde Mac Con Mighde, defined the function of this poetry when he declared that

If poetry were to be extinguished, my people,
If we were without history and ancient lays
Forever. . .
Everyone will pass unheralded.[4]

Poetry was both heroic history and a witness to the continuity of both family and race. Up to the late sixteenth century it was able to preserve this function, as it had done for a thousand years before, because the Gaelic civilization still retained the capacity to accommodate itself to the disruptions and invasions which had characterized the country's history. This capacity could only be sustained, however, as long as some system of patronage was permitted, and that itself depended upon the existence of at least a degree of respect for the Irish culture on the part of the dominant invading group. With the Reformation and the arrival of the New English, that disappeared. Irish poetry was cut loose from the social and economic anchorage in which it had ridden out the worst of the preceding political storms. Both Old English and New English were, for different reasons, thereafter intent on either Anglicizing the old culture or, failing that, destroying it completely.

The Norman conquest had from the beginning formulated a defence of its attempted subjugation of Ireland. Giraldus Cambrensis had accompanied Prince John to Ireland in 1184 and produced, as a result, two famous works, *Topographia Hibernica*, an account of the history, geography and wonders of Ireland, and *Expugnatio Hibernica*, an account of the conquest itself. Cambrensis introduced the distinction between the barbarous Irish and their civilizing conquerors which was to form a permanent part of the ideology of conquest and domination for succeeding centuries. Throughout the stormy period of the Norman settlement, various attempts were made to affirm this distinction and to keep inviolate the stronghold of Anglo-Norman rule, the area around Dublin known as the Pale, from Gaelic influence. The *Description of Ireland* (1577) by Richard Stanihurst (1547–1604), contributed to Holinshed's *Chronicles*, makes the same point in its discussion of the penetration of the Irish language into the Pale:

. . . this canker took such deep root, as the body that before was whole and sound was by little and little festered and in a manner wholly putrified . . . it is not expedient that the Irish tongue shall be so universally gaggled in the English Pale: because that by proof and experience we see, that the Pale was never in more flourishing estate than when it was wholly English, and never in worse plight than since it hath enfranchised the Irish.[5]

Later in the same work he attributes the Irish lack of civility to the absence of universities, teachers, preachers and all such aids to culture. Yet, despite the violence of the sixteenth century and the growing religious and racial polarization in Ireland and in Europe, the Gaelic poets, locked in their traditional attitudes, seemed to be unaware of the growing threat to them and the culture which they conserved. In fact the culture also lived and would continue to live in the oral tradition of songs, laments, lays and ballads, but the professional poets were more vulnerable in that they relied on the survival of a complex system which distinguished them as a caste. Once they lost that distinction, the literature they created lost its specific function and disappeared with them.

Thus it was only in the seventeenth century that Gaelic literature began belatedly to organize itself against the powerful new aggression of Tudor violence and propaganda with its strident Protestant rejection of anything Catholic. The New English put forward proposals for a complete military subjugation of the country as a necessary precondition of its conversion to the reformed faith. Edmund Spenser, who spent eighteen years (1580–98) of his life in Ireland in the service of the English Crown, gave an effective summary of New English attitudes and policies in his *A View of the Present State of Ireland* (1596), in which he defended the severity of the measures taken in Munster against the native population and advocated the complete extirpation of the Irish kinship and legal systems as a prelude to the civilizing of the degenerate and barbarous Irish. In 1622, Archbishop James Ussher provided Spenser's arguments with historical support in *A Discourse of Religion Anciently Professed by the Irish and Scottish*, in which he attempted to prove that the Church of St Patrick had been restored to its former purity by the new established reformed religion. He provided the Protestant planters with a crude predestination theology which seemed to justify their presence in Ireland as a providential attempt to rescue the Catholics from their benighted state or to reveal that it was no more than a proof of their outcast condition. By the time Ussher wrote, Gaelic civilization had begun to die from the top down.[6]

The beginning of the end came on Christmas Day, 1601, at the

Battle of Kinsale, when Lord Mountjoy's English army defeated the Irish force under Hugh O'Neill. After the Elizabethan wars, of which Kinsale was the culmination, the conditions which had sustained the production of classical Irish literature disappeared. Just before its extinction, the bardic school had a brilliant autumnal flare in the poetry of Eochaidh Ó hEoghusa and Tadgh Dall Ó hUiginn. One of Ó hEoghusa's poems, his lament for the plight of his patron, the great warrior Hugh Maguire of Fermanagh, as he marched off with O'Neill to Kinsale, where he was killed, gained renewed fame in James Clarence Mangan's translation of the nineteenth century, *O'Hussey's Ode to the Maguire*:

> Where is my Chief, my Master, this bleak night, mavrone!
> O, cold, cold, miserably cold is this bleak night for Hugh;
> Its showery, arrowy, speary sleet pierceth one through and through,
> Pierceth one to the very bone.

By 1607, the leaders of Gaelic Ireland had despaired and, in the famous Flight of the Earls, had fled to the continent, leaving their people without political leadership. Many scholars also emigrated and were trained as priests in the continental seminaries where they at last learned the lesson their experience should have taught them – that the collision which had destroyed their world was a part of the great dispute between Reformation and Counter Reformation in Europe. The need for a Catholic revival through the Irish language was plain. The result was a series of publications, theological, historical and literary, designed to reach the mass of the Irish people and to mobilize them against the Protestant enemy. The Franciscan college of St Anthony at Louvain was the centre of this new effort. The spread of printing, which led to the arousal of national feeling over all of Europe, ensured that this new polemical literature would be visibly different from the old manuscript tradition and the politically innocent attitudes which it had sustained. In addition, colloquial Irish rather than the learned Irish of the bardic schools was used; the didactic purpose of these new Counter-Reformation works could not be achieved otherwise. The new missionary effort also used the same argument as Archbishop Ussher had deployed on behalf of the Reformed faith, namely that the Church of St Patrick had embodied the spirit of Counter-Reformation Catholicism and that the Irish, in adopting the new militant spirit, were conforming to their most ancient traditions. Since the population was largely illiterate, many of the new practices and prayers were communicated in verse. This helped to break even more thoroughly the exclusivity of the bardic schools.

Devotional literature, modelled on continental works and adapted to Irish conditions and purposes, was directed at both clergy and laity who had some knowledge of Catholic doctrine and were in need of some introduction to the differences between its tenets and those of Protestantism. Verse summaries of these treatises made their contents accessible to a wider audience. Among the most famous of these new prose works were Antoin Gearnon's *Parrthas an Anma* (*Paradise of the Soul*) of 1645, Florence Conry's edition of *Desiderius*, also known as *Sgáthán an Crábha ıdh* (*The Mirror of Faith*) of 1616 and, in 1618, Aodh Mac Aingil's *Scáthán Shacramuınte na haıthrıdhe* (*The Mirror of the Sacrament of Penance*). The most remarkable of this group of revisionist historians and religious reformers was Geoffrey Keating (c. 1570–c. 1650). A priest, poet and historian, Keating attempted to explain the defeat of Catholic and Gaelic civilization and to provide a millenarian hope that the day of the Gael would come again after the crisis had passed. In his *Trí bıor-ghaoıthe an bháıs* (*The Three Shafts of Death*) he made a parallel between the Viking and the English invasions, attributing the temporary success of each to the decline of Gaelic civilization from its original and stern perfection. The three shafts of death, by the sword, famine and plague, all of them recently suffered, were God's punishment on a race that needed to repent and undergo a spiritual revival which would restore it eventually to its former eminence. In his synthetic history, *Foras feasa ar Éırınn* (*The History of Ireland*) he conflated the old stories of the origins of the Gael, the children of Mil, and refuted the charges of barbarism which various writers such as Stanihurst, Spenser, Sir John Davies and Fynes Morison had made. Although this was a crucial work of historical definition for Gaelic Ireland, Keating could be accused of having made a serious tactical error in failing to distinguish between the Old English attitude, represented by the Catholic Stanihurst, and the New English attitude of the Protestant writers. Stanihurst was against the military conquest of Ireland; he favoured what was in effect a peaceful policy of diplomatic suasion and education which would convert the native Irish to English civility. Gaelic Ireland, both in its political leadership and in its propaganda, was consistently maladroit in its failure to recognize the possibility of exploiting, for its own advantage, the Old English separation from the authorities in London and from the New English administrations in Dublin. Nevertheless, the destruction of the Gaelic polity proceeded apace. After the Flight of the Earls, many poems on the subject appeared, dominated by grief at this departure but often insinuating too that the Earls had abandoned the cause they should have defended. Keating's poem *Om Sceol Ar Ardmahagh Fail* (*At the News from Fal's High Plain*) is characteristically bitter against the 'trash' of the newly arrived English settlers and the weakness of the leaders who had surrendered the North, the last bastion of the Gaelic world:

> At the news from Fal's high plain I cannot sleep.
> I am sick till doom at the plight of its faithful folk.
> Long have they stood as a hedge against hostile trash,
> But a lot of the cockle has grown up through them at last.

Yet throughout the seventeenth century the Gaelic poets, particularly Keating himself, Píaras Feirítéar, Padraigín Haicéid and Dáibhí Ó Bruadair, found themselves torn between the demands made by the ideology of the Catholic Reformation, with its notions of papal supremacy and rejection of heretical rulers, and the requirements of the constantly shifting Irish political situation in which the survival of all that they represented was continuously in question. They therefore gave their loyalty to the Stuart cause after the accession of James I in 1603, in the hope that a Catholic monarchy would ultimately redress the wrongs of the Elizabethan wars. It is doubtful that they ever wholly reconciled themselves to the erosion of the Gaelic nobility and of their own position, even though they did on many occasions make strategic overtures to the new landowners, seeking from them a patronage which they would repay by giving in return a respectable and ratifying ancestry. The strains of such a position, or series of positions, were grievous indeed. Crises like that of the Catholic rebellion of 1641 and the ten years of war that followed, climaxing in Cromwell's terrifying and punitive campaign of 1649–50, tended to drive the poets into a desperate opposition to the English subjugation of the country and back upon the increasingly frail hope that either Providence would intervene to save them or that France would send a military expedition to restore the Stuarts. The shock of the Cromwellian campaign was devastating. The Irish and the Old English were now completely dominated by the New English, their religion was abhorred, their music proscribed, their possessions reduced. Disease, famine and emigration followed upon the military campaigns. The three shafts of death, of which Keating had written, struck the Irish in mid-century and again during the Williamite wars in the late 1680s. After that, little could survive and the settlement of 1688–91 reduced the aristocratic Gaelic civilization to an immiserated peasant culture. As a result of the Cromwellian confiscations and the enforced exodus of the native Irish to Connaught beyond the Shannon, the English language penetrated more deeply and thoroughly than ever before and the Irish language receded to an unprecedented degree. Even in these conditions, the Gaelic poets still tried to cling to a hope of redemption that would be granted after a long exercise of endurance. Fear Dorcha Ó Meallain closes his poem *An Dibirt go Connachta* (*Exodus to Connacht*) thus:

> People of my heart, stand steady,
> don't complain of your distress.
> Moses got what he requested,
> religious freedom – and from Pharaoh.
>
> Identical their God and ours.
> One God there was and still remains.
> Here or Westward God is one,
> one God ever and shall be.
>
> If they call you 'Papishes'
> accept it gladly for a tile.
> Patience, for the High King's sake.
> *Deo Gratias*, good the name!
>
> God who art generous, O Prince of Blessings,
> Behold the Gael, stripped of authority.
> Now as we journey Westward into Connacht
> old friends we'll leave behind us in their grief.[8]

Such resignation was unavailable to the two great poets who endured the disasters of the century, Dáibhí Ó Bruadair (c. 1625–98) and Aogan Ó Rathaille (c. 1675–1729). Ó Bruadair, reduced to field labour after the loss of the patronage of the Fitz-Gerald family, turned with an implacable bitterness on both conqueror and conquered, seeing both as debased and philistine people among whom no poetry could survive. The native Irish, especially the peasantry for whom he had his caste's contempt, seemed to him a sorry lot, stumbling in broken English in their speech, vulgarizing the poetry of the professionals in their songs. The power of his poetry derives in part from the sour perception that his civilization had destroyed itself:

We ourselves have buried the summer at last.

Aogán Ó Rathaille's bitterness is no less pronounced, but he, even more than Ó Bruadair, conveys the sense of a deep mutilation both of his own culture and sensibility. In the last year of his life he wrote his most famous poem *Cabhair ní Ghairfeadh* (*No Help I'll Call*). All hope has gone. No Spanish fleet, no restoration of lands or privileges is in sight; the last of his traditional patrons, the McCarthys, is gone. For him too, death is a blessing. Better to sleep with the Gaels of the old dispensation than stay alive in this nightmarish dispossession.

I will not stop now — my death is hurrying near;
now the dragons of the Leamhain, Loch Lein and the Laoi are
    destroyed.
In the grave with this cherished chief I'll join those kings
my people served before the death of Christ.[9]

Two hundred years later, in 'The Curse of Cromwell', Yeats wrote of

. . . an old beggar wandering in his pride?
His fathers served their fathers before Christ was crucified.

The deliberate echo from Ó Rathaille comes aptly from the great modern poet, who was also preoccupied by the extinction of an aristocracy, although Yeats is of course referring to the descendants of those by whom Ó Rathaille's culture had itself been destroyed. Yeats is also akin to Ó Bruadair and Ó Rathaille in his attacks on the vulgarity and ignorance of his fellow Irish, who neither appreciate the craft of poetry nor the glory of language but instead affect the fashions and attitudes of their conquerors, thereby betraying one of the reasons for their defeat – the lack of confidence in their own culture. In the end, the repeated invasions which had given Irish history its peculiar dynamic also led to the repeated attempt in literature to fashion myths of recovery or cede to the tragic recognition of culture's failure. This was ultimately to be as true of Anglo-Irish as it was of Gaelic literature.

The destruction of the Gaelic order had, as one of its consequences, the enhancement of the oral tradition. With the loss of aristocratic privilege, the poets were forced to survive among the people, as hedge school masters, as people whose learning, removed from its natural context, manifested itself very often as anachronistic pedantry. But the formal skills of the learned tradition enriched the oral tradition, and it in turn invigorated those skills with the passion and spontaneity which had always been among its most enviable possessions. Some of the most memorable songs and poems of the seventeenth and eighteenth centuries are by unknown authors, yet all of them have a structural and linguistic sophistication unique in Western folk-poetry. Their themes are the usual concerns of any community – love, grief at parting, lament for death, drinking, hymns. The verse becomes increasingly accentual rather than syllabic, although there can be little doubt that a long tradition of accentual verse preceded the eighteenth century. Some of the best-loved and most enduringly remembered of the Gaelic poets flourished in this period. Chief among them is Eoghan Rua Ó Súilleabháin (1748–84), known simply as Eoghan Rua or as Owen of the Sweet Mouth. He extended the millenarian hopes of the previous century in his development of the *aisling* or dream poem, which Ó Rathaille had established as a specific form. In this kind of poem, the poet dreams of a fair lady who comes to him in a vision. She represents Ireland and speaks of the day when she will be rescued from her misery by help from beyond the seas. It is a poetry still based on the Irish hope of a return of the Stuart line of English kings, reduced in the eighteenth century to the possibility of the restoration of Bonny Prince Charlie, the grandson of James II, to the English throne. This predominantly Scottish hope of restoration died after the extinction of Scottish Gaeldom in the rebellion of 1745. Ó Súilleabháin's *Ceo Draíochta* (*A Magic Mist*) is one of the last notable poems in which the return of the Stuarts is joyfully anticipated. Yet this poetry is less an expression of an unrealistic hope than it is an expression of a permanently rebellious attitude towards the existing order. In Ulster, where the Gaelic poets were in an even more exposed position than in the Munster where the aisling was born, the visionary woman may appear without a

message of hope, merely with a plea to join her in the eternal silence
of the Gaels of Tyrone. Art Mac Cumhaigh (1738–73) provides in
Ur-Chill An Chreagain (*The Churchyard of Creagan*), one of the
best-known laments for the loss of the O'Neills and the cold com-
pensation of a promised burial in his native Creggan, in Armagh. In
the last stanzas the visionary woman speaks and the poet answers:

'Since the wreck of the tribes at Eachroim and, O, by the Boinn
– Ir's people, those princes that readily welcomed sages –
better come to our dwellings, and I by your side each noon,
than John Bull's arrows endlessly riddling your heart.'

'O pleasant sweet princess, if you're fated to be my love,
a compact – a promise – ere I take the road West with you:
though I die by the Sionainn, in Man, or in mighty Egypt,
bury me under this sod with Creagan's sweet Gaels.'[10]

Nevertheless, the poetry survived. As literature, its existence was
vestigial. As part of the oral tradition, it remained strong. Its chief
prospect of survival was in English translation or in a revival of the
Irish language itself. The nineteenth and twentieth centuries were
to offer both, although the conditions in which these offers were
developed almost killed the language more effectively than any
planned campaign of extermination could have done. The translations were important but were also, in important respects, mutila-
tions. The revival of the language was a noble ambition, which
quickly degenerated into a series of political gesturings. Yet, in the
receding tide of the old tradition, poets managed to find ways of
accommodating themselves either to the near-derelict system of
patronage or to the richer support provided by the general community, in which respect for the status of the poet was still a reality.

As additional proof of the improbable survival of Gaelic poetry
into the late eighteenth century, two of the language's greatest
masterpieces appeared. *Cuirt an Mhean Oiche* (*The Midnight
Court*), a 1000-line poem by Brian Merriman, a County Clare
schoolteacher and farmer, is Gaelic's most renowned comic poem.
Its headlong energy and its bawdy eloquent humour are redolent of
the Courts of Love poems of the Middle Ages and forcibly remind
the reader that Irish poetry had not been affected to any serious
degree by the European renaissance. It therefore lacks that subtle
tone of civility, which can degenerate into the pallidly genteel,

which distinguishes the literature which received the impress of the classical renaissance. Merriman's poem is close to the spirit of the folk poetry of the West, much less literary than the poetry of Munster. It is a parody of the aisling poem because, in this instance, the poet's vision is of a giant, raw-boned woman, Aoibheall, Queen of the fairies of Thomond. The Court is an assembly of women who protest at the behaviour of men in marrying old women for money and leaving the young starved of affection and sexual pleasure; they also attack clerical celibacy and finally decide to punish men for their failure to please women. Just as they begin to carry out the punishment of binding and flaying the poet himself, he wakes up on the hillside where the vision had first come to him. The satiric power of the work is beyond the reach of translation, but one sample will give some sense of its vigour: a young woman is speaking of her unsatisfactory marriage to an old man whom she has cuckolded:

> We knew from the start, and this maggot as well,
> not warmth nor affection nor love in the least
>   could catch him this noble pearl of women,
> but her desperate need, crying out for comfort.
> It was gloomy doings, the nightly joy
>   – oppression and burden, trouble and fright:
> legs of lead and skinny shoulders,
> iron knees as cold as ice,
> shrunken feet by embers scorched,
> an old man's ailing, wasted body.
> What handsome woman would not go grey
> at the thought of being wed to a bundle of bones
> that wouldn't inquire, not twice in the year,
> was she half-grown boy or meat or fish?
> – this dry cold thing stretched out across her
> surely and spent, without power or bounce.
>   O what to her was a lively hammering
> hard as the devil, and twice a night!

The other great poem was by a woman, Eibhlín Dhubh Ní Chonaill, *Caoineadh Airt Uí Laoghaire* (*Lament for Art O Laoghaire*). It is so much a part of the folk tradition that parts of it may be traditional material from long-rehearsed keenings over the dead. But it is essentially her poem, an outburst of grief at the murder of her husband, Art O'Leary, by the bodyguard of the High Sheriff of Macroom, County Cork, one Abraham Morris. The poet was one of the famous O'Connell family of Derrynane, County Kerry, and an aunt of the Liberator, Daniel O'Connell. The incident took place in 1773. The various sections of the poem correspond to the keening of Eibhlin at separate times after the shooting – the first over her husband's dead body at the site of the murder, another after his body had been prepared for burial, another when the remains were transferred to a second burial ground, and so on. Even in translation the passion of her grief is unmistakable. She remembers everything about him and each memory sharpens the pain. Yet, throughout, the poem retains a discipline and measured rhythm; it does not disintegrate into tears, it consistently matches grief with eloquence. There is no greater love poem in Irish.

> My steadfast friend!
> I didn't credit your death
> till your horse came home
> and her reins on the ground
> your heart's blood on her back
> to the polished saddle
> where you sat – where you stood . . .
> I gave a leap to the door,
> a second leap to the gate
> and a third on your horse.
>
> I clapped my hands quickly
> and started mad running
> as hard as I could,
> to find you there dead
> by a low furze-bush
> with no Pope or bishop
> or clergy or priest
> to read a psalm over you
> but a spent old woman
> who spread her cloak corner
> where your blood streamed from you,
> and I didn't stop to clean it
> but drank it from my palms.[11]

While this 'Hidden Ireland' struggled for survival, the Protestant nation, now willing to describe itself as Irish, assumed to itself the rights, stretching back to Norman times, which had previously been claimed by the Old English. On this basis they demanded a degree of independence from England, claiming that the country's prosperity suffered so badly from Whitehall legislation that the process of bringing the gifts of civilization to the Catholic masses – a prelude to their final conversion to Protestantism or to enlightenment principles – was being seriously delayed. The Protestants of the established Church were further worried about the large numbers of Northern dissenters, increased by another influx of Scots in the aftermath of the Battle of the Boyne. But most of these arguments faded in the face of any proposal to restore to Catholics their civil rights, especially when these proposals came towards the end of the century during the French Revolution. The Catholics, it appeared, were as liable to be Jacobins as Jacobites. In fact, the Protestant patriot or colonial nationalist position was impossibly contradictory because it sought independence from an England upon which it was entirely dependent, for the simple reason that the whole plantation policy had failed in its aim of bringing the Catholics into the zone of civilized society. After two centuries of plantation, war, confiscation and penal legislation, the Catholics had neither prosperity nor the reformed religion. Nor had the Protestants security. The great rebellion of 1798 proved that beyond doubt. Suddenly 1641 seemed very close again.

When the Catholic Committee was formed in 1760 to agitate for Catholic relief from the myriad penalties they groaned under, that was in itself the sign of a certain resurgence of energy. But the antiquarian movement in which they were also involved, and which was powerful enough to lead to the first Celtic revival, was a subtler and more successful manoeuvre. By 1789 Charlotte Brooke's *Reliques of Irish Poetry* had been published, and the organizers of the Belfast Harp Festival of 1792 asked Edward Bunting to take down the airs which were being played there by the last of the Irish harpers. By proving to an English-speaking audience that Ireland had a long and sophisticated culture in literature, music and other arts, the Irish Catholic Committee and its supporters were advancing their claims to social and political parity. They were turning the planter argument that they were barbarians back on its sponsors and claiming that a proof of past civility was sufficient to warrant present political liberty. Indeed, many Protestants, either individually or through the Royal Irish Academy, supported these antiquarian researches because they also were pleased to find that their own idea of being Irish and different had a great deal of historical evidence in its favour. But in 1790, the Reverend Edward Ledwich turned a very bleak enlightenment eye on the fictions surrounding early Irish history in his *Antiquities of Ireland*. Ledwich had realized that the Celtic revival had political implications which could be dangerous to the Protestant interest. As in the seventeenth century, no research into the past could be innocent. The result was always going to be the formation of an official or semi-official myth which would lend credence to the claims of one political or religious grouping.[12]

There was a further complication. The various forms of artificial respiration on Gaelic culture had no hope of ever reviving it as such. It was well and truly dead by the end of the eighteenth century. But as an idea or as an ideal, it continued to live. Yet its ultimately distinguishing feature, its language, was effectively destroyed as a living force by the mass of the Catholic people with whom that language had been identified for a millennium. The reason was simple. English was needed to survive either within or outside the country. Moreover, as the Catholic population became politically conscious under O'Connell's leadership in the nineteenth century, they became more devoted to English as the language, through the use of which they could win reform and improvement. Thus it is with some sense of initial surprise but final understanding that we must recognize that the fortunes of the Gaelic civilization passed out of Catholic hands in the eighteenth century and into the possession of predominantly Protestant intellectuals and antiquarians. For them the old language and culture was valuable because through its recovery they could realign themselves with the past of the country they lived in and (decreasingly) governed; because through it they could more effectively proselytise the Catholic Irish of the West and, finally, they could find in its revival a powerful counter to the egalitarian mass democracy which it was in the interest of the Irish Catholics to realize. The fear of anglicization became an obsession among some of the most influential Protestant intellectuals and writers in the nineteenth century, Thomas Davis and W. B. Yeats among them. By the close of the century, Douglas Hyde, the founder of the Gaelic League in 1893, was to become the unwitting sponsor of a theory of both cultural and political separatism. By preaching the de-anglicization of Irish culture, he managed to persuade his audience that Irish independence was a political as well as a linguistic ideal. In the early twentieth century, the idea of the integral spirit of an ancestral and revived Gaeldom had become the informing energy in the mind of Patrick Pearse, the leader of the 1916 rebellion. From that point forward, Gaelic civilization and Catholicism renewed their ancient alliance, and Protestantism, especially in the North of Ireland, returned to its former fidelity to both England and English culture.

Notes

1 For this and for much else in this chapter see the following: Proinsias MacCana, *Celtic Mythology* (London, 1970); Robin Flower, *The Irish Tradition* (Oxford, 1947); Myles Dillon (ed.), *Early Irish Society* (Dublin, 1959); Gerard Murphy, *Saga and Myth in Ancient Ireland* (Dublin, 1961), *The Ossianic Lore and Romantic Tales of Medieval Ireland* (rev. ed. Dublin, 1971); Douglas Hyde, *A Literary History of Ireland* (rev. ed. New York, 1967); Aodh de Blacam, *Gaelic Literature Surveyed* (rev. ed. New York, 1974, with new chapter on the twentieth century by Eoghan O hAnluain); Patrick Power, *A Literary History of Ireland* (Cork, 1969).

2 James Carney (ed.), *Early Irish Poetry* (Cork, 1965); Sean Mac-Reamoinn (ed.), *The Pleasures of Gaelic Poetry* (London, 1981); Eleanor Knott, *Irish Classical Poetry* (Dublin, 1960).

3 See Donncha O Corrain, *Ireland Before the Normans* (Dublin, 1972); D. A. Binchy, 'The Background of Early Irish Literature', *Studia Hibernica*, I (1961), pp. 7–18.

4 Translation by Seamus O'Neill in 'Gaelic Literature', in *Dictionary of Irish Literature*, ed. Robert Hogan (Dublin, 1980), pp. 18–64.

5 Quoted in St John D. Seymour, *Anglo-Irish Literature, 1200–1582* (Cambridge, 1929), p. 184.

6 See Nicholas Canny 'The Formation of the Irish Mind: Religion Politics and Gaelic Irish Literature 1580–1750', *Past and Present*, no. 95 (May, 1982), pp. 91–116; Brian O Cuiv, 'The Irish Language in the Early Modern Period', in *A New History of Ireland*, eds. T. W. Moody, F. X. Martin and F. J. Byrne, vol. III (Oxford, 1976), pp. 509–45.

7 Sean O Tuama and Thomas Kinsella, *An Duanaire 1600–1900: Poems of the Dispossessed* (Dublin, 1981), p. 84.

8 ibid., p. 104.

9 ibid., p. 167.

10 ibid., p. 181.

11 ibid., pp. 203–4.

12 Cf. Oliver MacDonagh, *States of Mind: A Study of Anglo-Irish Conflict 1780–1980* (London, 1983, 1985), pp. 1–14, 104–25.

2 The formation of the Anglo-Irish literary tradition, 1690–1800

The Glorious Revolution of 1689 in England, completed by 1690 in Ireland, gave the New English settlers complete authority over the Catholic Irish and the Old English, the descendants of the Anglo-Norman invasions of the twelfth century. This predominantly Anglican Ascendancy was in some respects supported and in others opposed by the other non-Catholic groupings within the island, the most important of which was the largely Presbyterian Scots settlers in the North of Ireland. The Irish Dissenters – those who did not conform with the beliefs and practices of the Anglican Church of Ireland – were distinct, therefore, from the English Independents. Their hostility towards Roman Catholicism did not preserve them from the animosity of the Anglican Ascendancy, which effectively disbarred them from full civil rights and political power, even though their humiliation was limited when compared to the organized degradation of the Roman Catholics by the Penal Laws, a series of measures passed between the 1690s and 1720s with the aim of removing property, education and religious practice from this disaffected and overwhelmingly numerous grouping. Politically, therefore, the term 'Anglo-Irish' refers to the New English propertied class, which controlled Ireland from 1690 to the middle of the nineteenth century. In literature, however, the term is more hospitable, referring both to the literature produced by that class and to the literature produced by others who were neither Anglican nor descended from English settlers. The fact that the literature is written in the English language by people of Irish birth and connections is by itself almost enough to admit it into the Anglo-Irish fold, although there are even then exceptions – like William Congreve and Laurence Sterne – who modify the usefulness of this criterion. From the seventeenth century, Anglo-Irish literature displays affinities with the Gaelic, English, Scottish and European cultures which make it distinct and at the same time reveal its precariousness as a specific and independent tradition. In the eighteenth century, it may be said to have achieved that independence, although, as in the political field, the independence was never secure or unambiguous.

The political and economic subordination of Ireland in this period had fearful consequences. Famine and emigration reduced a fast-growing population, which had become dependent on the cultivation of the potato as its staple food. Northern Presbyterians emigrated in large numbers to America where they were to play a central role in the War of Independence. The Catholic aristocrats had long since departed for the Continent, leaving the peasantry without political leadership but with an ineffectual dream of a day of Jacobite restoration, brought from France or Spain in the form of a military invasion. The central Anglican Ascendancy also lost many of its most gifted members to London, the metropolitan centre where power and fame were to be had. In fact Ireland could export little but its people and its rents. As a consequence, its intellectual life decayed along with its economy. Catholics were educated in the Irish colleges in France, Spain and Italy; Dissenters went to the Scottish universities, particularly Glasgow; and the Anglicans pursued their careers in London. Yet, from the end of the seventeenth century, there was an incipient awareness among this part of the Protestant Ascendancy that there was, intellectually as well as economically, a specific Irish interest which was not identical with the English interest. Increasingly stimulated by the selfishness and insolence of Whitehall's attitudes, this awareness finally developed into a consciousness of the necessity for a measure of independence from England, even though this was always tempered by a recognition of Protestant Ireland's dependence on her in the event of a rebellion or invasion. Successive English administrations pursued policies which eroded the position of the Protestant garrison, with such unwitting effectiveness that it drove that garrison to the point of risking its security for the sake of its integrity. It was a complex process, fertile in the production of ambiguous and contradictory attitudes towards the relationship between England and Ireland. The reasons for the failure of the Glorious Revolution to provide in Ireland the relative peace and harmony which had been its consequence in England could be endlessly disputed. But it was beyond dispute that Irish experience was profoundly affected by a sense of insecurity and crisis. This displays itself in the writings of the Irish expatriate writers in London – Swift, Burke, Goldsmith and Sheridan. Swift and Burke in particular expended much of their energy as writers in attacking the various forms of corruption, political and intellectual, which robbed established authority of its traditional appeal and reduced it instead to the exercise of despotic and unprincipled power. They had seen too often the ill-effects of the system of political patronage, which provided for Englishmen of small competence positions of large responsibility in the conduct of Irish affairs. Bad in itself, this jobbery had the further consequence of so discrediting government and morality that it left them vulnerable to the attacks of those radicals and liberals whom Swift and Burke, in their different ways, regarded as dangerous fanatics and visionaries. Increasingly, in the case of each writer, these men were regarded as the greater threat.

Since Dissenters, of the Irish or English sort, had a natural interest in attacking the established order, which excluded them from full participation in civil life, their writings often had and were understood to have a political import, whatever their ostensible subject. The strangest and most notorious of the Irish dissenting radicals in the early eighteenth century was John Toland (1670–1722), an Irish-speaking Catholic from Donegal who repudiated his religion and went to Glasgow to become a radical Presbyterian and, after a year in Holland and one in Oxford, settled in London where he gained a reputation as a freethinker (he was the first European writer to be so called) and a passionate supporter of the Hanoverian succession to the English throne. Swift, Bishop Berkeley and Burke all attacked him as anti-Christian, as a sceptic and a deist, although Burke's dismissal of him in 1790 is influenced by the fact that deism had by then gained especial notoriety because of the association between it and French Enlightenment thought. (Both Voltaire and d'Holbach admired Toland.) The book which made Toland famous was his first; *Christianity not mysterious* appeared in London in 1696, the year Swift embarked on *A Tale of A Tub*. Toland visited Dublin the following year when the Irish House of Commons ordered the book to be burnt and recommended the arrest of the author. Toland departed with some speed to England, leaving behind him a furore that was to have repercussions in Irish intellectual life for half a century.[1]

The sensation caused by Toland's book was especially fierce in Dublin because the Irish Anglican establishment, and particularly its conservative wing, saw in it a threat to religious belief and to the political practices allegedly sanctioned by it. The assumption, for instance, that there was a natural relationship between the proper form of Christian belief and the right to political power was not safe if Toland's implication – that Christianity had been rendered mysterious for the many by the few who wished to justify illicit political authority – was allowed. The truth of Revelation, Toland argued, had been communicated by Christ in such a way it could be verified by reason. Anything beyond verification was superstition and nonsense:

Could that Person justly value himself upon being wiser than his neighbours, who having infallible Assurance that something call'd *Blictri* had a Being in Nature, in the mean time knew not what this *Blictri* was?[2]

Toland, who was a friend of Locke, brought Locke's *Reasonableness of Christianity* (1695) to his aid in his attempt to formulate a rational, anti-authoritarian form of religious belief. The effects were twofold. In the first place, he stimulated Irish Anglicanism to formulate its own conception of the relationship between reason and belief. This was a contributory cause to the efflorescence of Irish intellectual life in the early part of the century, dominated in philosophy by Bishop Berkeley (1685–1753), whose *Alciphron* (1732), a dialogue attacking freethinking, contains clear references to Toland. In the second place, Toland's book begins the consolidation of the alliance between Lockean rationalism and Northern Presbyterianism, which was to be such a potent political force throughout the century. Rationalism in religion, toleration, and hostility to established authority became revolutionary ideas in the 1790s and were part of the common heritage of Ulster Presbyterians and United Irishmen.

Toland's later writings confirmed the suspicions which his first book had aroused. *Letters to Serena* (1704), addressed to the sister of George I, *Adeisidaemon* (The Man Without Superstition) of 1709 and *Nazarenus, or Jewish, Gentile and Mahometan Christianity* (1718) as well as the highly eccentric *Pantheisticon* (1720) were all variations on his unorthodox, even heretical, attitudes towards Christianity and showed his increasingly syncretic inclination towards pantheism, a word which he coined. Politically, he became a more and more fervent supporter of the Hanoverian cause, breaking with Robert Harley, the Earl of Oxford, in 1710 over the proposed peace treaty with France, the very issue on which Harley recruited Swift to write his famous pamphlet *The Conduct of the Allies* (1711), designed to mobilize public opinion behind the new policy. Toland proclaimed himself a true Commonwealth man, an inheritor of the seventeenth-century English republican tradition and saw himself and his compatriot, Robert, later Viscount, Molesworth as true defenders of ancient liberty against contemporary despotism. Molesworth's *An Account of Denmark* (1694), an analysis of the circumstances which led to the extinction of freedom there in 1660, is rightly considered to be an important work in this radical tradition. But Molesworth, whose estates had been sequestered by James II, although no friend of depotism, was a convinced Anglican and a privy counsellor to the monarch on two occasions. He remained part of the Irish Protestant establishment, on its liberal wing, and was never an outsider like Toland. Thus Toland could be attacked by conservative Anglicans like Swift, Archibishop King, Bishop Edward Synge and Bishop Berkeley, and still find, within that group, support from men like Molesworth and William Molyneux, liberals who retained their affection for the anti-authoritarian republican and Lockean traditions who, nevertheless, remained apart from the more radical developments given them by a man like Toland. It is, finally, characteristic that Toland should have also been a pioneer in the various attempts in this century to provide some account in English of the fading Celtic civilization. His *A Critical History of Celtic Religion* appeared posthumously in 1740, although its influence was not felt until the early nineteenth century, when it was reissued.

It was inevitable that disputes about religious belief should have complicated repercussions in Ireland, where political discrimination was founded upon religious differences. Anyone who, like Toland, threatened to dismiss the importance of religious differences was also seen to be issuing a threat to the whole political system. Archbishop William King of Dublin demonstrated the link between political and philosophical writing in this period in a particularly clear manner. In 1691 he published his *State of the Protestants of Ireland* in which he justified the rebellion of Irish Protestants against James II of England and blamed the Catholics for having backed the wrong horse and thereby brought deserved punishment on themselves. For it was obvious that 'either they or we must be ruined'.[3] In 1702 he published *De Origine Mali (On the Origin of Evil)*, a defence of the view that those who have lost a position of supremacy must have committed some folly or evil, and those who have gained such a position must have done something pleasing to a god who has rewarded them. The two works are mutually supportive defences of the new Protestant dispensation.

Toland was the first to test these defences; a fellow Ulster Presbyterian, Frances Hutcheson, was the next.

Hutcheson (1694–1746) was a member of a group of intellectuals which formed under the patronage of Viscount Molesworth in the 1720s. The Molesworth Circle revived the spirit of toleration and enlightened rationality which the controversy over Toland had almost destroyed. Molesworth's pamphlet *Some Considerations for the Promotion of Agriculture and Employing the Poor* (1723) and a collection of essays and letters, originally published in the *Dublin Journal* in 1726, and reprinted in London in 1729 under the editorship of the poet James Arbuckle, were characteristic of the Circle's latitudinarian sympathies. But Hutcheson's first important work, *An Inquiry into the Original of our Ideas of Beauty and Virtue* (1725), gave the Circle its classic formulation of its central beliefs. As Toland had carried Locke into the centre of Irish philosophical dispute, Hutcheson brought the name of the Third Earl of Shaftesbury into a similar prominence. Like Shaftesbury, he proclaimed that it was possible to be moral and to act morally without religious belief. From there he went on to portray the recognition of the good in ethics as analogous to the recognition of the beautiful in aesthetics. Hutcheson left Dublin in 1729 to become professor of moral philosophy at Glasgow, where he developed Shaftesbury's thought into an early version of benevolent utilitarianism. Among his students was Adam Smith; Thomas Jefferson was one of the many Americans whom he attracted by his liberal doctrines of representative government, colonial independence and social justice:

The Characteristick of *Despotick Power*, is this, 'That it is solely intended for the Good of the Governors, without any *tacit Trust* of consulting the Good of the *Governed*.' Despotick Government in this sense, is directly inconsistent with the Notion of Civil Government.[4]

Although Hutcheson is best remembered now as the founder of the Scottish school of philosophy in the eighteenth century, his importance in Ireland still rests on the new emphasis he gave to the principle of toleration and to the consequent erosion of the religious basis for the Penal Laws. His blending of religious, political and aesthetic issues in a new vision, 'a classic expression . . . of the new optimistic creed'[5] was to be brilliantly modified by the young Edmund Burke in his early writings into an exposition of a powerful and renovated traditionalism. It is strange to see how deeply

Hutcheson and Burke were involved in the American Revolution because of their hostility to that species of colonial misgovernment which they had observed and experienced in Ireland. But the belief in colonial autonomy was not in itself an eccentric conviction for liberal Irish Protestants who had been forced to recognize the need for it in the drastic conditions of eighteenth-century Ireland. It had first been proclaimed by William Molyneux in his famous pamphlet *The Case of Ireland Stated* (1698), an important, if flawed, statement of the relationship between the local and central legislatures in an imperial system. The English Commons ordered it to be burned; it was reprinted ten times in the next 90 years and was especially influential in the Thirteen Colonies prior to the War of Independence. The flaw in Molyneux's argument was central. It consisted of his exclusion of the *'Antient Irish'* from the political nation. He was arguing 'the Cause of the whole race of *Adam*', for Liberty as 'the Inherent Right of all *Mankind*'.[6] But he was seeking the ratification of the right to power of an exclusive group. This was a fatal weakness. The new Ascendancy had to make a principle of permanent exclusion a feature of its version of colonial nationalism. When this proved unacceptable to Whitehall, it had no choice but to give up on the idea of national independence.

Nevertheless, until the choice was forced at the end of the century, the Anglo-Irish insisted on their distinctness as a people with a unique destiny in a country close to but profoundly different from England. Their politics, their literature and their philosophy achieved a remarkable prominence because of the high tension generated by the paradoxes of their position and the sense of insecurity which haunted it. In the writings of Swift and Burke, we see the formation of a literary tradition which was dominated by an ideal of a stable and traditional civilization and, to an equal extent, by the experience of an unstable and disrupted country. In searching for the language and the literary modes which would most effectively register this contrast, they inaugurated a tradition in which language is rarely reconciled to fact, but is instead always in the condition of transcending or humiliating fact, implying that the mind can never be wholly at home in a world which has shown itself unamenable to desire or intelligence. The failure of political and economic circumstance, the failure of the English colonial mission in Ireland, is at the heart of the great Anglo-Irish enterprise in literature. This is represented most tragically and powerfully in the figure of Jonathan Swift, the most legendary presence in the whole tradition and the writer in whom the experience of dislocation is most effectively transmuted into a literary technique which transfers that dislocation to his reader. Anglo-Irish writing does not begin with Swift, but Anglo-Irish literature does.

Most of the works we have discussed so far achieve much of their sometimes polemical effect by insinuating a solidarity between author and reader as persons of common sense and civility. The full resources of this technique seem to have been only dimly appreciated by them, for when we come to Swift we find that this gentlemanly contract between reader and writer can be exploited for satiric purposes to a subversive and disturbing degree. Swift (1667–1745) was born a few months after his father died, leaving him dependent on the support of his uncle. This stimulated the first of the many resentments, which he bore for the rest of his life, and the anger which he felt at his maltreatment and enforced poverty while he was a student at Trinity College because of his uncle Godwin's miserliness, reinforced by his menial position in the house of Sir William Temple at Moor Park in England, where he had gone in 1689 to escape the troubles which had broken out in Ireland in that year, made him an ideal candidate for the articulation of Irish resentment at her dependent position in the British system. For him, as for many of his class, this inferior position was all the more galling after the Union between England and Scotland in 1707, especially as they considered Ireland to have been much more faithful to the English cause than Scotland had ever been. Swift wrote a pamphlet on this occasion, *The Story of the Injured Lady*, which was not, however, published until the year after his death. The pamphlet is an allegory of Ireland's betrayal by England and her abandonment for another, Scotland. It is the first of seventy-five pamphlets by Swift on Irish affairs. Twenty-three were unpublished in his lifetime. The bulk of them were written during the years 1709 and 1738, during which period he visited England no more than four times. Like Molyneux, Swift would have preferred a Union on equal terms with England. But seeing that this was, from Whitehall's point of view, unattractive or impossible, he turned his attention to the improvement of the existing system. From the Irish point of view, this was sorely needed. From the English Woollens Act of 1698, which effectively destroyed one of the central industries in the Irish economy, to the Declaratory Act of 1719 and the controversy over Wood's halfpence in 1722, the Irish parliament was constantly reminded of its impotence in the face of Whitehall.

Although it was mollified to some extent by the passage of severe laws against both Catholics and Dissenters, it became evident that any attempt to assert independence was going to involve a constitutional crisis and the arousal of national feelings which would have to discriminate between Ireland's wish to be distinct from England as an autonomous kingdom and the wish to be separate from her as an independent nation.

Swift's first important work, *A Tale of A Tub* (not published until 1704), was an attack upon corruption in religion and learning. It was not welcomed by his clerical contemporaries and has had a mixed reception in later times as a ribald, if brilliant, exposure of the excesses of the new learning, of Catholicism and of evangelical Protestantism. The indecency of the *Tale* offended Queen Anne and her advisors and certainly hindered Swift's chances of promotion in the Church, even though he was defending Anglicanism as a happy middle way between the extremes of the other religions. The religious part of the satire was written between 1695 and 1699 when the newly-ordained Swift held the prebend at Kilroot, outside Belfast, in a fiercely Dissenting neighbourhood. During these years there was an influx of new Presbyterian settlers from Scotland, sufficiently large to disturb the Anglican sense of security in Ireland and sufficiently assured to question more strongly than ever the disabilities which they suffered under law. Swift was to remain hostile to Dissenters, English and Irish, and to any move towards the relief of their position. As for the Catholics, he was soon to dismiss them, even in Ireland, as a threat to the state; yet, despite sympathy for their impoverished plight, he remained very much a member of his class in regarding their exclusion as necessary to the security of Protestant property and as an appropriate response to their superstitious and uncivil state. The new learning seemed to him a much more serious threat and he missed no opportunity to associate it – however unfairly – with the various forms of dissent, with fanaticism and even with deism or atheism. At times, indeed, as in *An Argument against abolishing the Christian Religion* (1711) he attacks freethinkers like Matthew Tindal and John Toland – 'the great Oracle of the Anti-Christians' – by claiming that their radical arguments against Christianity are no more than ploys for the re-establishment of Popery:

For supposing Christianity to be extinguished the People will never be at ease till they find out some other Method of worship; which will as infallibly produce Superstition, as this will end in Popery.[7]

Dissent, according to this reasoning, leads to deism, which leads to the collapse of Christianity and thence to the reintroduction of Popery. It is a characteristically Swiftian vicious circle. All his enemies are despatched together; the extreme of reason leads to the emergence of superstition. Yet it is difficult to be sure that this is no more than a satiric reduction. The tone is also tinged with anger and fright.

All of Swift's writings draw some of their force from his ability to simplify complex issues in such a manner that he intensifies his polemical vigour and obliterates troublesome discriminations. Thus he makes a basic and traditional distinction between reason and imagination on the grounds that reason leads to truth, which is widely shared and accepted, while imagination leads to fantasies and delusions, the product of individual minds given over to eccentricity and fanaticism. In this he is following in the steps of earlier groups, such as the Anglican Rationalists. But Swift exploits the distinction more ruthlessly and brilliantly to the point at which he is expounding the claims of common sense against innovatory intelligence. This profound anti-intellectualism is finally disheartening, for it shows in Swift an extraordinarily intense desire to defend the status quo, to prohibit change and to assert an ideal Anglican perfection against the corruptions of the actual state of affairs. Yeats was later to claim that Swift, along with Burke and Berkeley, was manifesting an essentially Irish hostility to the modern world in his attacks upon the Royal Society and the new speculators and scientists it sponsored. But it would be closer to the point – while admitting some similarity with Burke and Berkeley – to say that Swift's fear of modernism was very much of a piece with the fear his contemporaries had shown in the face of Toland's *Christianity not mysterious*. It was in effect a fear of the political effects of the principle of toleration, which would be a necessary consequence of the flattening of religious distinctions. As a Christian priest, he disliked any secularizing trends; but as an Irish Protestant Anglican he feared the disruptive consequences they could have on the settlement of 1688.

Swift's writings are, therefore, based on a complex principle of exclusion. Outside the temperate zone, where the majority of humankind resides, live the tropical monsters of the Dissenting, individualistic imagination. They come in many forms – Presbyterian zealots, Catholic fanatics, deists, freethinkers, experts, experimenters, astrologers, corrupt politicians. The danger they represent is enhanced by their affectation of normality. So Swift satirizes them not only by ventriloquizing their voices and opinions but also by exposing the false nature of the implied solidarity with the reader which they exploit. In a satire of vertiginous energy like the *Tale*, the effect can be bewildering. The reader becomes so acclimatized to the deceits of the rhetoric that it is difficult to be sure when a 'true' or normative voice is speaking. Irony is the dominant mode, but where does it diminish or disappear (if it disappears) in a passage like the following, from Section IX of the *Tale*, 'A Digression concerning the Original, the Use and Improvement of Madness in A Commonwealth'?

For, the Brain in its natural Position and State of Serenity, disposeth its Owner to pass his Life in the common Forms, without any Thought of subduing Multitudes to his own *Power*, his *Reasons* or his *Visions*; and the more he shapes his Understanding by the Pattern of Human Learning, the less he is inclined to form Parties after his particular Notions; because that instructs him in his private Infirmities, as well as in the stubborn Ignorance of the People. But when a Man's Fancy gets *astride* on his Reason, when Imagination is at Cuffs with the Senses, and common Understanding, as well as Common Sense, is kickt out of Doors; the first Proselyte he makes, is Himself, and when that is once compass'd, the Difficulty is not so great in bringing over others; a strong Delusion always operating from *without*, as vigorously as from *within*.[8]

This is a portrait of a fanatic, but it is also a caricature. The basic figure of the brain in its natural and then unnatural position is in itself comic, even though the development of the figure is precise and telling. But the question remains – is this an avowal by Swift of his own opinion or is it the adopted voice of one of his many personae? On a larger scale, his use of allegory in the development of the double parable, which lends the *Tale* its admirably disciplined form without at all subduing its richness, also places the reader at a disadvantage. The allegory is a satirical ploy but, sustained as it is, it permits no confidence on the reader's part about the distinction between literal truth and figurative distortion, which the work nevertheless seems to point towards as a necessary and critical distinction. Still, there is no room for doubt that the zealot, bound within his own world of inner conviction, estranged from the actual world of 'common Forms' and yet determined to impose his own will upon it, is the type of all that Swift disliked and feared. From this figure to the more complex and subtle representation of Gulliver and the lethally rational economist of *A Modest Proposal* (1729), the family resemblance is striking. It is also in its way shocking, for it reveals in Swift an obsessiveness not exceeded by any of his monomaniac victims. This in itself is a symptom of the unchanging nature of Swift's opinions throughout all the vicissitudes of his career as a churchman, political pamphleteer and formulator of the rights of Ireland against England.[9]

A Tale of A Tub, *The Battle of the Books* and the *Discourse Concerning the Mechanical Operation of the Spirit* were Swift's early masterpieces. Before they were published, he had entered on his first political crusade with *A Discourse of the Contests and Dissentions between the Nobles and Commons in Athens and Rome* (1701), written on behalf of the Whigs to whom he now looked for favourable financial arrangements for the Irish Church. By 1708, it had become clear that these would not be granted save at the price of toleration for the Dissenters. Swift thereafter gravitated towards the Tories, the High Church party, and had become so closely identified with them that he was inevitably involved in their ruin on the death of Queen Anne in 1714. In 1713 he had been installed as Dean of St Patrick's Cathedral, Dublin – a post which disappointed him grievously, as he had hoped for preferment in England. He visited London in 1726 and 1727; but from 1714 until his death in 1745, Swift lived and worked in Ireland. As the author of *Gulliver's Travels* (1726), *The Drapier's Letters* (1724) and *A Modest Proposal* (1729) he achieved great fame. Although he continued to write with great force into the mid-1730s (the first *Collected Works* published in Dublin in 1735), Swift's life thereafter is a sad tale of disappointment, frustration and illness, culminating in three years of insanity and near-silence.

As an Irish pamphleteer, Swift began with suggestions for remedying the distorted relationship between Ireland and England, especially in economic affairs, but ended in despair, convinced that Irish apathy and English greed formed a combination which neither Reason nor Nature could defeat. His first sally into Irish politics was *A Proposal for the Universal Use of Irish Manufacture* (1720), in which he advised the Irish to boycott English imports of cloth and to concentrate on the consumption of their own goods. This was, in part, a response to the Declaratory Act of 1719 which asserted Ireland's dependence on England. It was also an attack on the economic exploitation of Ireland which had been affirmed as a policy by the Woollen Acts of 1699, itself a caustic reply to Molyneux's pamphlet of the previous year. The Irish Tories were at last discovering a patriotic voice. The famous statement – made with characteristic indirection, partly to escape prosecution, partly to create the ironic distance between speaker and proposition, which Swift measured with such disturbing precision – so often quoted to prove Swift's patriotic credentials, reads:

I heard the late Archbishop of *Tuam* mention a pleasant Observation of some Body's; *that* Ireland *would never be happy 'till a Law were made for* burning *every Thing that came from* England, *except their* People *and their* Coals: I must confess, that as to the former, I should not be sorry if they would stay at home; and for the latter, I hope, in a little Time we shall have no Occasion for them.[10]

But eleven years later, in *The Answer to the Craftsman*, an entirely disillusioned Swift is bitterly recommending the destruction of the Irish economy by a set of reverse proposals:

I ADVISE likewise, that no Commodity whatsoever, of this Nation's Growth, should be sent to any Other Country, except *England*, under the Penalty of high Treason; and that all the said Commodities shall be sent in their natural State, the Hides raw, the Wool uncombed, the Flax in the Stub; excepting only Fish, Butter, Tallow and whatever else will be spoiled in the Carriage. On the contrary, that no Goods whatsoever shall be imported hither, except from *England*, under the same Penalty: that *England* should be forced, at their own Rates, to send us over Cloaths ready made, as well as Shirts and Smocks to the Soldiers and their Trulls; all Iron, Wooden, and Earthen Ware; and whatever Furniture may be necessary for the Cabins of Graziers, with a sufficient Quantity of Gin, and other Spirits, for those who can afford to get drunk on Holydays.[11]

In the interval between these two tracts, Swift lost confidence in the possibility of remedying the economic terms of the relationship between the two countries. His efforts to educate both Irish and English into a sense of the realities of the economic position made it clear that the position of the Protestant garrison in Ireland was hopeless unless there was an alteration in the constitutional relationship between it and the English Parliament.

But Swift could not go so far as to recommend this. Instead, in a manner reminiscent of Toland, Molesworth and Molyneux, he lamented the failure of the Protestant Irish to secure the liberties left to them by 1688 and the despotism of the English in traducing the principles of that Revolution in their treatment of their own people in Ireland. As with all the Irish writers of this century, the dominant emotional tone is one of nostalgia and regret for an opportunity lost, a civilization betrayed, a country ruined. The tenderness of this standard classical motif – *quantum mutatus ab illo* – does survive in some of Swift's most ferocious pages and it lends to them, as to much of Burke's later writings, a tragic tone rarely found in English literature of the period. We often find, though, that Swift's tragic effects are generated by the contemplation of absurdities so systematically developed that they have the form of reason without its substance. It is a vacuous world he exposes to us:

This is the sublime and refined Point of Felicity, called, *the Possession of being well deceived*; the Serene Peaceful State of being a Fool among Knaves.[12]

That could be applied, with uncomfortable directness, to the position of the Irish Protestant whom Swift saw was being compelled to acquiesce in his own ruin. Yet, although he tried to rally his compatriots into organized protest against their lot, he was thereby endeavouring to conserve the established system, or his own ideal version of it, rather than undermine it. His dislike of radical groups opposed to established forms within a state was unwavering. Anabaptists, Huguenots, Socinians, Arminians all received his condemnation. In 1708, he had written in *The Sentiments of a Church-of-England Man*, the clearest statement of his Whig faith in the Revolution and his Tory affection for the Church, of the dangers of schism in the State:

When a *Schism* is once spread in a Nation, there grows, at length, a Dispute which are the Schismaticks. Without entering on the Arguments, used by both sides among us, to fix the Guilt on each other; it is certain, that in the Sense of the Law, the *Schism* lies on that Side which opposeth it self to the Religion of the State . . . And I think it clear, that any great Separation from the established Worship, although to a new one that is more pure and perfect, may be an Occasion of endangering the publick Peace; because, it will compose a Body always in Reserve, prepared to follow any discontented Heads, upon the plausible Pretexts of advancing *true Religion*, and opposing Error, Superstition, or Idolatry. For this Reason, *Plato* lays it down as a Maxim, that *Men ought to worship the Gods, according to the Laws of the Country*; and he introduceth *Socrates*, in his last Discourse, utterly disowning the Crime laid to his Charge, of *teaching new Divinities*, or Methods of Worship. (II, 11–12)[13]

In his role of Irish patriot, Swift does not offer himself as a focus for dissent against the State. Instead, he presents himself as the representative of the 'common forms' of reason and nature against the English faction within the Irish state which was destroying its very being. Had the Irish parliamentarians, so many of whom were willing to trade their votes with Dublin Castle on any given occasion, raised their eyes from the narrow world in which they were ensnared, they might have seen something more real than the chimerical problems of their insulated politics:

I should wish the Parliament had thought fit to have suspended their Regulation of *Church* Matters, and Enlargements of the *Prerogative* . . . and, instead of those great Refinements in *Politicks* and *Divinity*, had *amused* themselves and their Committees, a little, with the *State of the Nation*. (IX, 16)[14]

The issues were large indeed:

Were not the People of *Ireland* born as *Free* as those of *England*? How have they forfeited their Freedom? Is not their *Parliament* as fair a *Representative* of the *People* as that of *England*? And hath not their Privy Council as great or a greater Share in the Administration of Publick Affairs? Are they not Subjects of the same King? Does not the same *Sun* shine on them?[15]

This was the voice of the Drapier.

The Wood's Halfpence controversy which led to the writing of *The Drapier's Letters* is too well known to bear much repetition here.[16] But it may be said that the patent, granted to the Englishman William Wood to mint a copper coinage for Ireland, managed to embody three characteristics of English rule in Ireland in a memorable form – corruption, insolence and exploitation. Swift responded by producing a series of pamphlets, *The Drapier's Letters*, in which he assumed the persona of a Dublin tradesman in his attack upon the unfortunate Mr Wood and on the policies of the Prime Minister, Robert Walpole, and King George I. In the famous fourth letter 'To the Whole People of Ireland', he refers to Molyneux's attempt to oppose 'Truth, Reason and Justice' against the 'Love and Torrent of Power';

Indeed the Arguments on both sides were invincible; For in *Reason*, all *Government* without the consent of the *Governed is the very Definition of Slavery*: But in *Fact*, *Eleven Men well Armed will certainly subdue one Single Man in his Shirt*. But I have done. For those who have used *Power* to cramp *Liberty* have gone so far as to Resent even the *Liberty of Complaining*, altho' a Man upon the Rack was never known to be refused the Liberty of *Roaring* as loud as he thought fit.[17]

In the fifth letter, addressed to Lord Viscount Molesworth, the author of *An Account of Denmark*, the Drapier congratulates himself on having been saved from prosecution by the Dublin Grand Juries:

. . . which hath confirmed in me an Opinion I have long entertained, That, as Philosophers say, *Virtue is seated in the Middle*, so in another Sense, the little Virtue left in the World is chiefly to be found among the *middle* Rank of Mankind, who are neither *allured* out of her Paths by *Ambition*, nor *Driven* by *Poverty*.[18]

'The Whole People of Ireland' meant, in effect, the English people in Ireland. Swift quotes Wood's surprise at the insolence of the Irish in refusing his coin and adds

. . . where, by the Way, he is mistaken; for it is the *True English People of Ireland*, who refuse it; although we take it for granted, that the *Irish* will do so too, whenever they are asked.[19]

In brief, Swift was defending this exclusive view of the Irish nation on the basis that the English in Ireland were being treated by Whitehall as though they too were, like the Irish, a conquered people. But Swift's status among later nationalist writers and commentators was established at the expense of this important discrimination. He neither deserves it nor would he have desired or comprehended it. Yet the idea of a specific Irish nation, maltreated by England and demanding justice for itself, was forced upon him by the exigencies of his class's humiliated situation in the 1720s. It was an idea that could easily migrate across the boundaries of sect and class.

Swift composed *Travels into Several Remote Nations of the World* by Lemuel Gulliver during his engagement with the Wood's Halfpence controversy. Published in London in 1726, it is his masterpiece. Although the controversy left its mark in the work – particularly in Book III where it is allegorized as the episode of the Flying Island and Lindalino in a sequence of five paragraphs which were omitted from all editions, including the first, until 1899 – neither Irish nor English political references are central to its melancholy preoccupation with the protean fertility of human pride and its degenerative effects upon society. Gulliver begins as ostensibly normal and finishes as clearly abnormal. A man of apparent common sense is transmogrified into a monomaniac. The volume of commentary on this work is awesome, but for the present purpose we need only look at one issue, although it is central. The fourth book of the *Travels* is traditionally regarded as the most disturbing because it exhibits (or seems to exhibit) Swift's hatred for and disgust at mankind in the memorable fiction of Gulliver's tragic and enforced choice between the rational and clean horses, the Houyhnhnms, and the filthy and degraded humans, the Yahoos. His first biographer, the Earl of Orrery, and his friend, Patrick Delaney, initiated the long sequence of attacks and repudiations of this 'insult upon mankind' which, in the nineteenth century, was explained as the result of incipient madness. The debate still goes on. Yet if we assume that Swift was doing no more than presenting us with the traditional Christian view of human nature as essentially corrupt and prone to evil, we can see how characteristic an attack the *Travels* would be on that rational and benevolist view of human nature and its capacity for infinite improvement which had been expounded by his compatriots, Toland and Hutcheson, and in England by Locke and Shaftesbury. In other words, *Travels* decisively affirms man's limitations and implies, with equal force, his need for the protection and guidance of religion. In that light, it is a masterpiece of Anglican Christian literature, given especial force by the embattled position of the Irish Anglicans whom Swift was defending against the dangerous Laodicean rationalism of the Enlightenment. As in the political field, Swift was to be adopted for different purposes by people of strongly opposed views. John Wesley calls on the support of Book IV's portrayal of human nature against the benevolists in *The Doctrine of Original Sin* (1756), while the utopian benevolist William Godwin found the Houyhnhnms to be a description of 'men in their highest improvement'.[20] The point remains that Swift, because of his rhetorical strategies, is open to a variety of interpretations, which seem diverse and extravagant in relation to the conventional and narrow views which he held. This is not to say that the ferocity of his convictions should be undervalued. It was their abiding characteristic and it seems proper that this intensity should have been the prerogative of a beleaguered, if powerful, minority's greatest writer.

Swift's anger increased as he got older and more intimately acquainted with the state of Irish affairs. *A Modest Proposal* (1729), written in the year Burke was born and Hutcheson left Dublin for Glasgow, is a culminating satire on the mind of the expert and a lament for the failure of common sense reforms in Ireland. Where Nature and Reason have been defeated, Madness rules. The impossibility of creating even a minimal prosperity in Ireland, assured by the economic policies of England and the dependent constitutional position of Ireland, is finally accepted. The consequences of this acceptance were beyond the imagination of Swift to conceive. But the analysis of the dilapidated state of a nation, which had almost forty years of peace and English government in its immediate past, found no better voice than that of the engagingly polite and reasonable monster who speaks in these pages:

Some Persons of a desponding Spirit are in great Concern about that vast Number of poor People, who are Aged, Diseased, or Maimed; and I have been desired to employ my Thoughts what Course may be taken, to ease the Nation of so grievous an Incumbrance. But I am not in the least Pain upon that Matter; because it is very well known, that they are every Day *dying*, and *rotting*, by *Cold* and *Famine*, and *Filth*, and *Vermin*, as fast as can be reasonably expected.[21]

What is being satirized here is not merely the mercantilist theory of economics. The optimism of those who, like Mandeville in *A Fable of the Bees* (1723), argued for the social uses of selfishness in economic affairs, appears utterly absurd when placed beside Swift's version of the famine-ridden Ireland of the late 1720s. Swift could see no solution, from the political point of view. Morally, what he saw was sufficient ground for a pessimism of the sort which the Enlightenment did much to weaken – the pessimism of a mind possessed by the prevalence of sin and corruption and of the degeneracy of the human race from its original condition. Swift and Molyneux had, in their unwitting ways, begun to identify what was later to be understood as colonialism. They simply could not regard Ireland as a colony. It was an integral and central part of the Empire. Colonies were elsewhere, across oceans, not across St George's Channel. Swift, however, did see that whatever the political name for it might be, the human cost was appalling. His first biographer, the Earl of Orrery, claimed that the fourth book of *Gulliver's Travels* gives a view of human nature which 'must terrify, and even debase the mind of the reader'.[22] Swift himself, writing to his friend Thomas Sheridan in 1725, tells him to

expect no more from man than such an animal is capable of, and you will every day find my description of the Yahoos more resembling.[23]

Cannibalism, filth, extremism, hypocrisy, injustice, apathy, stupidity – the list of human error and foulness is endless; the prospects of improvement remote.[24]

Anthony Collins was the deistic writer who best represented the ironic mode much favoured by those who were of like mind. In the year 1729, when Swift's *A Modest Proposal* appeared, Collins published *A Discourse concerning Ridicule and Irony in Writing*, in which he attacked the solemn and grave defenders of conventional religion:

Contempt is what they, who commonly are the most contemptible and worthless of men, cannot bear nor withstand, as setting them in their true Light, and being the most effectual method to drive Imposture the sole Foundation of their Credit, out of the World.[25]

He goes on to cite Swift as a master of this procedure, 'one of the greatest droles that ever appear'd upon the Stage of the world';[26] yet he recognizes that Swift was a supporter of the High Church party. Voltaire, who took so much from the deistic writers and who made a point of citing Toland, in particular, even though he seems to have read very little of him, never quite understood Swift's loyalty to Anglicanism and assumed that his writings had a more subversive intent than they pretended to have. But Swift was, in many respects, a man and mind subverted rather than subversive. Ireland enriched his rhetoric and undermined his beliefs. In the end, he appeared to himself to have become one of his own foolish projectors, a man preaching improvement to a doomed people. 'Satire', he once said, 'is a sort of glass, wherein beholders do generally discover every body's face but their own'.[27] By the close of his career in Ireland, Swift was beginning to see his own reflection in his reformist writings. The Irish world would not be mended, but the Irish writer would be transmogrified in his attempt to improve it.

Edmund Burke (1729–97) is generally regarded as one of the most important of the eighteenth century's political thinkers. Yet, for all the power and coherence of his achievement, he has had remarkably little effect upon his own country, failing to achieve the popular reputation of Swift, even though he went far beyond Swift in his recognition and advocacy of the measures required to heal the poisoned relationship between Ireland and England. At the same time, Burke, like Swift, found the intractability of the Anglo-Irish political problem to be connected in a way neither could quite specify with the great intellectual struggle of the age, that between the conserving forces of historical tradition and the galvanizing energies of organized freethinking, utopian radicalism. Although Burke had much closer bonds with the Irish Catholics – his mother and his wife were of the oppressed faith – and deeper sympathy with their plight than Swift, his central political preoccupation on the subject of Ireland was the preservation of his country as an integral and central part of the British Imperial system.[28] He had no enthusiasm for the legislative independence achieved in 1782, and even less for the idea of Union, which became a reality soon after his death. Ideas of a proto-nationalist kind – the imposition of a tax on absentee landlords, the Swiftian recipe for the consumption of home-produced goods – belong to the undergraduate Burke, the debater who formed the club which later became the Trinity College Historical Society. These soon evaporated after he left Ireland for England in 1750. When he returned, eleven years later, as personal secretary to W. G. Hamilton, Chief Secretary for Ireland, he began a thorough study of the Penal Laws which led to his *Tracts Relative to the Laws Against Popery in Ireland*, part written in 1761, possibly continued for some years afterwards, but never published during his lifetime. Five years before, in 1756, Burke had published his first book, *A Vindication of Natural Society*, an ironic attack on the theory of natural religion then associated with the name of Lord Bolingbroke, Swift's friend and political ally in the last years of the reign of Queen Anne. Bolingbroke's defence of natural against revealed religion was part and parcel of the deistic controversy which had been initiated by Toland's *Christianity not mysterious* in 1696. It is appropriate that these early writings had their origins in theological and sectarian disputes, dating from the past century, and that Burke's attention should be directed towards an analysis of their political and social consequences. The disastrous effects of the Penal Laws and of deistic thought upon political life were for him exemplary instances of the hostile forces which it was his duty to combat for the rest of his career. The irony that both of them originated in the Ireland of the 1690s seems to have escaped him. Like Swift, he was a prisoner of the origins of the Irish settlement of that decade, almost preternaturally alert to the forces which threatened its survival. As late as 1790, in *Reflections on the Revolution in France*, Burke was contrasting the success of the French *philosophes* in their own country with the failure of the freethinkers in England:

Who, born within the last forty years, has read one word of Collins, and Toland, and Tindal, and Chubb, and Morgan, and that whole race who called themselves Freethinkers? Who now reads Bolingbroke? Who ever read him through?[29]

It is the name of Toland that stands out here, the originator of that 'race', a compatriot of Burke's, born into that Catholic nation which Burke was to say, over and over, would be radicalized by oppression.

Burke's *Tracts* are themselves an instance of the revival of the consciousness of the Irish Catholics in this period. His friends, Charles O'Conor and John Curry, formed the first Roman Catholic Association in 1757; in 1758, Curry published his *Historical Memoirs of the Irish Rebellion of 1641*, a work in which the Protestant Ascendancy view of the past century's history was challenged. By 1760 the Catholic Committee had been formed to express the desire of the emergent Catholic middle classes for social justice. But this was also the period which saw the outbreak of the agrarian violence in Ireland, the first phase of which climaxed in the judicial murder of a Catholic priest, Father Nicholas Sheehy, in 1766 – an outrage which Burke never forgot.[30] It seemed to him the characteristic crime of a faction which, in the name of English law, brought shame on English justice. Like the execution of the Maharajah Nandakumar in 1775 in Warren Hastings's India, it was a symptom of a deep-rooted systematic oppression, which had to be terminated in the interests of both justice and prudence. Between 1761 and 1764, at the outset of his political career, Burke saw the cruel oppression of the Irish Catholics and observed how it was enforced by the Protestant Ascendancy. He also saw the emergence of the Catholic movements for reform through constitutional appeal and pressure, and for resistance through acts of organized violence. He realized even then that the peaceful constitutional method would never be successful when faced with the punitive prejudices of the Ascendancy. Over the next thirty years it became increasingly clear to him that the solution to the Irish problem lay in the removal of that Ascendancy which had been established in the first place to preserve the English connection, which was so dear to Burke in itself and, in his view, so necessary to the welfare of Ireland. Thus he was faced with a problem which, difficult in itself in even the most ideal circumstances, became tragically insoluble in the years after the outbreak of the French Revolution and leading up to the Irish Rebellion of 1798. The intractability of the Irish situation was finally borne in upon Burke as it had been on Swift. In each case, the ultimate remedy – a complete reappraisal of the settlement of the 1690s – was not imaginable, at least in part because it would have as its cause and effect the release of the illicit energies of utopian, fanatic, abstract visionaries, whose aim would be to uproot the historically established order of things. The classic revolutionary tract of Irish republican nationalism – Wolfe Tone's *An Argument on behalf of the Catholics of Ireland* (1791) – was addressed to the Irish Protestant Dissenters. The Anglicans he regarded as politically ineducable and morally calloused. This alliance between the two excluded groups, between the two extreme factions caricatured in *A Tale of A Tub*, was precisely what Burke always feared, for it was an alliance proposed on revolutionary principles. The race of English deists, founded by Toland, had been transformed into the French *philosophes* and now was being transmuted again into the new Irish cabal of the United Irishmen. The projectors had finally won a disastrous victory.

In the third of his *Letters on a Regicide Peace* (1796), Burke declared:

Never was there a jar or discord between genuine sentiment and sound policy. Never, no never, did Nature say one thing and Wisdom say another. Nor are sentiments of elevation in themselves turgid and unnatural. Nature is never more truly herself than in her grandest forms.[31]

Forty years earlier, in his *A Philosophical Inquiry into the Origin of our Ideas of the Sublime and the Beautiful*, he had made a similar claim:

Men often act right from their feelings, who afterwards reason but ill on them from principle . . .[32]

This treatise on aesthetics, thought to have been written while Burke was still at Trinity College, is an important formulation of Burke's political theory of 'dread' or reverence. He is careful to distinguish this from the plain fear of tyranny, on the one hand, and the agreeable feelings which arise from a sense of rational control on the other. There is a salutary power of fear which is rooted in a fear of a power beyond us:

. . . the notion of some great power must be always precedent to our dread of it. But this dread must necessarily follow the idea of such a power, when it is once excited in the mind. It is on this principle that true religion has, and must have, so large a mixture of salutary fear; and that false religions have generally nothing else but fear to support them.[33]

While it is perfectly true that this description of the emotions attendant upon the Sublime anticipates a great deal in the Gothic and Romantic literature of the latter part of the century, it is also an extension of Bishop Berkeley's attack upon the limitations of the Lockean theory of meaning. For Berkeley, the secular implications of the notion that language enabled us to achieve rational control over the universe had to be dispelled. He attacked this position in *The Principles of Human Knowledge* (Dublin, 1710) and in *Alciphron, or the Minute Philosopher* (1732) by insisting that the mysteries of religion, for instance, were understood because they aroused in men feelings of awe, fear and reverence. This is part of the Irish establishment's attack on Toland and the Deists. Burke is the inheritor of this too, and much that seems original or even eccentric in his thought appears much less so when he is seen against that background. Moreover, the powerful role given to emotion, mystery and religion by both Berkeley and Burke contrasts very sharply with the placid, even smug, benevolist interpretation of the aesthetic and ethical issues raised by Francis Hutcheson in his *Inquiry into Beauty and Virtue* (1725), the only other important aesthetic treatise of the century in Ireland. In every field there was a radical difference between the Irish Anglican and Dissenting traditions. In Swift, Berkeley and Burke, the Anglican view insisted upon the limitations of human reason and the frailty of human nature, even to the point of enhancing the power of feeling to a position of dominance (while still differentiating it from emotionalism). The Dissenting view stressed man's rational capacities, the essentially unmysterious nature of the world and the human capacity for goodness and improvement. This standard collision between the traditional and the Enlightenment attitudes had its own peculiarly Irish dimension.

Yet while this must be remembered, Burke's view of the Irish situation was governed by the fact that he was a member of an English political party, the Rockingham Whigs. The great crusades of his career, on American Independence, on India and on the French Revolution, are developments of attitudes which were formed in and by Ireland, but they enlarged the range of his vision to the point where he was able to articulate these attitudes in terms of general political and moral principles. America helped him to define the relationships between the imperial power and its colonies more trenchantly than he had ever been able to achieve in the Anglo-Irish situation; India compelled him to formulate the idea of cultural integrity and its intimate connection with historical evolution with a degree of force which he had only briefly attained in his *Tracts on the Popery Laws* in relation to Ireland; France compelled him to provide a comprehensive defence of traditional society against the twin enemies of abstract rationalism and universal cosmopolitan benevolence, neither of which had developed to any comparable degree in Ireland. Yet, as he turned to Irish affairs again in the last years of his life, Burke was reviewing his country's plight in the light of a philosophy which had first been formed by it, however greatly it had expanded since his departure in mid century. Although the European and imperial application of Burke's thought makes it appear much less limited than that of Swift, the categories which sustain it are similar and the circumstances which moulded it have their origins in the 1690s. By the 1780s those circumstances had altered so much that the attitudes born of them had reached a point of crisis and, through Burke, of redefinition. With him, the formation of the Anglo-Irish cultural and literary identity reaches completion.

The central change in those circumstances was brought about by the effect of the French Revolution on the policies of the English government towards the Irish Catholics. By 1792, Pitt and Dundas had determined to make concessions to them which would have the effect of almost entirely dismantling the Penal Laws. This, of course, threatened the security of the Protestant Ascendancy in Ireland. Curiously, it is in that year that the very term 'Protestant Ascendancy' is first coined as a description of a system of privilege based on the interests of one group, which defined itself in politically sectarian terms.[34] That is to say that the theological differences between Protestantism and Catholicism had entirely given way to a political distinction between them. It was this distinction which the Irish Protestants were determined to preserve, even at the cost of excluding Catholics altogether from political life. This bigotry cost them dear. It alienated them from the English government and it finally alienated Burke from them. Although he had seen that government's policy wavering between the indifference of cruelty and the cruelty of indifference for more than forty years when the Catholic issue was raised, he now recognized that a confrontation was inevitable. His son Richard was agent to the Catholic Committee in Dublin, and through him he was kept closely informed of the events in Ireland. The resistance of the Protestant middle classes and landed interests to Catholic concessions, the radicalism of the Belfast Presbyterians, led by the Anglican Wolfe Tone, and the increasing resentment of the Catholics, between the granting of the first concessions to them in 1793 and the final dashing of their hopes in 1795, were known to him in great detail, although his tragic view of Irish affairs in his last years was no doubt influenced by the death of his son in 1794 and by the débâcle of his friend and patron Fitzwilliam in the next year.[35] From the publication of his *Reflections on the Revolution in France* (1790) to *A Letter On the Affairs of Ireland* (1797), Burke's vision of Europe and of Ireland rests on the conviction that the ruin of civilization is imminent because of the folly and pride of men who have lost the capacity for reverence and, with it, the wisdom of natural feeling. The rupture with tradition is as complete as it is deliberate:

I defy the most refining ingenuity to invent any other cause for the total departure of the Jacobin republic from every one of the ideas and usages, religious, legal, moral, and social, of this civilised world, and for tearing herself from its communion with such studied violence, but from a formed resolution of keeping no terms with that world. It has not been . . . that these miscreants had only broke with their own government. They made a schism with the whole universe, and that schism extended to almost everything great and small.[36]

The ferocity of Burke's denunciations of the Protestant Ascendancy, of the Jacobins, and of Warren Hastings and his minions, has
laid him open to the charge of being hysterical and even insane in
the last years of his life. The historian Froude claimed that when
Burke at last took up Ireland's cause in earnest, 'it was with a brain
which the French revolution had deranged'.[37] But his attacks on
these groups were of a piece with his famous outburst of 1773 when
he spoke in the House of Commons in support of toleration for the
Dissenters. In the first two months of that year he had visited Paris
and gone to the leading salons, where he heard the conversation of
the *philosophes*. He was startled to find that atheism had advanced
so far in French society. Thus, in his speech, he turned to atheists as
a group and distinguished them from others, like the Dissenters:

The most horrible and cruel blow, that can be offered to civil society, is
atheism. Do not promote diversity; when you have it, bear it; have as many
sorts of religion as you find in your country; there is a reasonable worship in
them all. The others, the infidels, are outlaws of the constitution; not of
this country, but of the human race. They are never, never to be supported,
never to be tolerated.[38]

The atheist denied the assumptions upon which society was tacitly
based. So too did the Jacobin; and, in his own way, so did the
Protestant zealot in Ireland. In his second letter to Sir Hercules
Langrishe, written in 1795, Burke explained the connection:

I think I can hardly overrate the malignity of the principles of Protestant
Ascendancy, as they affect Ireland; or of Indianism as they affect these
countries, and as they affect Asia; or of Jacobinism as they affect all Europe
and the state of human society itself. The last is the greatest evil. But it
readily combines with the others, and flows from them. Whatever breeds
discontent at this time, will produce that great master-mischief most
infallibly. Whatever tends to persuade the people, that the *few*, called by
whatever name you please, religious or political, are of opinion that their
interest is not compatible with that of the *many*, is a great point gained to
Jacobinism.[39]

There is no inconsistency in these positions, nor is it necessary to
attribute hysteria to the pronouncements of a man who analysed the
French Revolution and the Irish problem more penetratingly than
anyone else of his generation. In his clarification of the connection

between international radical freethinking (Jacobinism) and local bigotry (Protestant Ascendancy), he demonstrated the moment at which Irish Protestantism bifurcated into Irish Republicanism, on the one hand, and Orangeism (founded in 1795) on the other.

Drawn by his devotion to the British Constitution, to the Glorious Revolution, the Whig settlement in Ireland and his idea of a Christian society, Burke gravitated steadily throughout his life towards a conception of 'that narrow scheme of relations called our country, with all its pride, its prejudices and its partial affections'.[40] In other words he contributed towards that cultural nationalism which, in the eighteenth century, was closely associated with the various antiquarian movements (interest in the Gothic, in the Middle Ages, in ballads and folk music) and had a profoundly conservative and reverential attitude towards history and its deposits of manners, habits, customs and monuments.[41] Burke's chief importance in the history of that movement is in his dramatic representation of revolutionary and radical thought as the natural opponent, even antithesis, of this new nationalism. The idea that a nation had what he called a 'moral essence' which was a guarantee of its spiritual survival even in the midst of revolutionary ruin and dilapidation was an ambiguous one in Irish circumstances, although it was originally applied by Burke to the old France which had been displaced by the new.[42] But in calling in the old world of antiquarian sentiment and complexity to redress the imbalance created by the new world of the Enlightenment and the Revolution, Burke was unwittingly providing the Protestant Ascendancy, which he so despised, with a means of access to the Catholic tradition and the Catholic population that was otherwise forbidden to them. Within forty years of Burke's death, the Celtic revival in Ireland was well under way. The Irish had found by then that one way of overcoming the recent wounds of the past was by recovering the idea of a once and future Irish kingdom – an ancestral presence and a beckoning hope. Although this is part of the history of nineteenth-century Irish literature, it is also a direct, if largely unacknowledged, part of Burke's heritage also.

Even more directly, the writings of Burke's last seven years have left a deep imprint on later Irish literature. The imagery of his late work survives even into the present century, sometimes with its political implications still intact. The ruined building, representing anything from the Tuileries palace in Paris to the British Constitution, the unruly Jacobin mob, the defenceless Christian or Royal

family, the counterposed image of the revolutionary cabal or con-
spiracy, the atheistic salon or Revolutionary Club, the debased
currency, the alchemical experimentation in politics, the abstract
furies of ideologues and their theatrical, utopian illusions, the tide
of violence and the loosening of anarchical forces upon a once
cultured and civilized community – all of these images, in an almost
infinite variety of permutations, dominate Burke's late pamphlets,
speeches and letters, as they also dominate Irish writing into the age
of Yeats. Important too is the conviction that Ireland represents, *in
parvo*, the great historical events of the world. For it was a country
which had been transformed by the three great revolutions of the
century – the Whig Revolution of 1688, the American Revolution
of 1776, the French Revolution of 1789. From the Battle of the
Boyne in 1690 to Grattan's parliament in 1782 to the Rebellion of
1798 and the Act of Union, which closed the century and this era of
Irish politics, Ireland had been engaged in a desperate attempt to
articulate for itself a cultural identity which would reinforce and
even validate the political fate, which it had in part chosen and had
had in part foisted upon it. Protestant Ireland formed the basis of a
new literature in English but in doing so defined the antipathies and
tensions which ensured its own disintegration as a political entity.
Burke's role in this process is central. Yet without consideration of
the part played in this long formative and tragic process by Swift, by
the deistic Toland and the 'patriot' political pamphleteering of
Molesworth and Molyneux, by the Irish theologians and
philosophers, whose disputes created the climate in which Berkeley
and Hutcheson could produce their very different philosophies, we
would be at a loss to account for the power of Burke's writing. The
emergence of a form of cultural nationalism from the Anglo-Irish
minority seems, in some ways, inevitable. But it was a slow and
painful emergence, darkened always by the political shadows which
it brought with it, especially for a Protestant minority, which found
itself increasingly beleaguered by events and ended by finding itself
disowned by its greatest political intelligence. In such anomalous
circumstances, the tradition began.

Notes

1   On Toland, see J. G. Simms, 'John Toland (1670–1722), A Donegal
    Heretic', *Irish Historical Studies* XVI, no. 63 (March, 1969), 304–20;
    Norman L. Torrey, *Voltaire and the English Deists* (New Haven,

1930), reprinted (New York, 1960), pp. 12–25; Franco Venturi, *Utopia and Reform in the Enlightenment* (Cambridge, 1971), pp. 49–55, 57–62, 64–7; Caroline Robbins, *The Eighteenth Century Commonwealthmen* (Cambridge, Mass., 1959); F. Heinemann, 'John Toland and the Age of Enlightenment', *Review of English Studies* XX (1944), 135–45; Ernst Cassirer, *The Philosophy of the Enlightenment* (Boston, 1955), pp. 171–2; David Berman, 'The Golden Age of Irish Philosophy', in *A History of Anglo-Irish Writing* (forthcoming, Dublin, 1986).

2 *Christianity not mysterious, or a Treatise shewing that there is nothing in the Gospel contrary to reason nor above it and that no Christian doctrine can be properly call'd a mystery* (London, 1696), p. 133.

3 *State of the Protestants in Ireland* (London, 1691), p. 239.

4 *Inquiry Concerning Moral Good and Evil* (4th ed., London, 1738), pp. 297–8.

5 T. O. Wedel, 'On the Philosophical Background of *Gulliver's Travels*', *Studies in Philology* **23** (1926), 434.

6 *The Case of Ireland's being bound by acts of parliament in England, stated* (Dublin, 1698), reprinted with an introduction by D. G. Simms and an afterword by Denis Donoghue (Dublin, 1977), pp. 34–5.

7 *Prose Works of Jonathan Swift*, ed., H. Davis (Oxford, 1939–68).

8 ibid., I, p. 108.

9 Oliver W. Ferguson, *Jonathan Swift and Ireland* (Champaign, Illinois, 1962); J. C. Beckett, *The Anglo-Irish Tradition* (London, 1976), pp. 143–5.

10 *Works* IX, p. 17.

11 *Works* XII, p. 176.

12 *Works* I, p. 110.

13 *Works* II, pp. 11–12.

14 *Works* IX, p. 16.

15 *Works* X, p. 31.

16 *The Drapier's Letters*, ed. H. Davis (Oxford, 1965); A. Goodwin, 'Wood's Halfpence', *English Historical Review* **51** (1936), 647–74; J. M. Treadwell, 'Swift, William Wood, and the Factual Basis of Satire', *The Journal of British Studies* XV, no. 2 (1976), 76–91; W. B. Ewald Jr, *The Masks of Jonathan Swift* (Oxford, 1954).

17 *Works* X, p. 63.

18 *Works* X, p. 90.

19 *Works* X, p. 66.

20 Quoted in I. Ehrenpreis, *The Personality of Jonathan Swift* (London, 1958).

21 *Works* XII, p. 117.

22 *Remarks on the Life and Writings of Dr. Jonathan Swift* (London, 1752), p. 184.

23   *The Correspondence of Jonathan Swift*, ed. H. Williams, 5 vols (Oxford, 1965).

24   Cf. Denis Donoghue, *Jonathan Swift: A Critical Introduction* (Cambridge, 1969).

25   *Discourse*, p. 7.

26   Quoted in Torrey, *The English Deists*, p. 30.

27   *The Battle of the Books*, Preface; *Works* I, p. 140.

28   Thomas D. Mahoney, *Edmund Burke and Ireland* (Cambridge, Mass., 1960).

29   *The Works of the Right Honourable Edmund Burke*, 8 vols (London, 1881), II, p. 361.

30   See his *Letter to a Peer of Ireland on the Penal Laws* (1782); *Letter to Sir Hercules Langrishe* (1792); *Letter to William Smith* (1795).

31   *Works* V, p. 278.

32   *Works* I, p. 86.

33   *Works* I, p. 99.

34   W. J. McCormack, *Ascendancy and Tradition in Anglo-Irish Literary History from 1789 to 1939* (Oxford, 1985).

35   Fitzwilliam, sent over as Lord Lieutenant, rashly promised more reforms than he could deliver. He raised hopes and saw them dashed.

36   *Works* V, p. 215.

37   J. A. Froude, *The English in Ireland in the Eighteenth Century*, 3 vols (London, 1881), II, p. 231.

38   *The Parliamentary History of England*, ed. W. Cobbett and J. Wright, 36 vols (London, 1806–20), XVIII, p. 432.

39   *Works* VI, p. 58.

40   *Works* V, p. 268.

41   A. B. C. Cobban, *Edmund Burke and the Revolt against the Eighteenth Century* (2nd ed., London, 1960); 'Edmund Burke and the Origin of the Theory of Nationality', *Cambridge Historical Journal* II (1926), 36–47; J. G. A. Pocock, 'Burke and the Ancient Constitution: A Problem in the History of Ideas', *Cambridge Historical Journal* III (1960), 125–43.

42   *Works* V, p. 220.

3 The Celtic revival, 1780–1880

In the sixth of *Peter Plymley's Letters* (1807–08), Sydney Smith, like Edmund Burke some forty years earlier, attacked the English view of the Irish as a turbulent people:

Before you refer the turbulence of the Irish to incurable defects in their character, tell me if you have treated them as friends and equals? . . . Nothing of all this. What then? Why you have confiscated the territorial surface of the country twice over: you have massacred and exported her inhabitants: you have deprived four fifths of them of every civil privilege: you have at every period made her commerce and manufactures slavishly subordinate to your own: and yet the hatred which the Irish bear to you is the result of an original turbulence of character, and of a primitive, obdurate wildness, utterly incapable of civilization.[1]

Smith's advice to the English government was forthright – conciliate the Irish Catholics by restoring to them their full civil rights, even if this has to be done at the expense of the brutal Orange tyranny, and thus render Ireland safe from French invasion. It is not necessary to go far in Irish literature to find material to support Smith's view of the situation. The hatred of England and the recourse to French aid against her oppression find their classic exposition in *The Autobiography of Wolfe Tone*, which covers the years 1763–98. As leader of the United Irishmen, Tone, inspired by the French Revolution, had defined his republican ambition in the famous formulation of 1791:

To subvert the tyranny of our execrable Government, to break the connection with England, the never-failing source of all our political evils, and to assert the independence of my country – these were my objects. To unite the whole people of Ireland, to abolish the memory of all past dissensions, and to substitute the common name of Irishman in place of the denominations of Protestant, Catholic and Dissenter – these were my means.[2]

The circumstances of the decades in which Tone and Smith wrote were so drastic that their ideas of revolution or reform seemed hopelessly impracticable. The novelist, William Carleton, born in 1794, had vivid memories of what Ireland was like at the turn of the century:

Merciful God! In what a frightful condition was the country at that time. I speak now of the North of Ireland. It was then, indeed, the seat of Orange ascendancy and irresponsible power. To find a justice of the peace *not* an Orangeman would have been an impossibility. The grand jury room was little less than an Orange lodge. There was then no law *against* an Orangeman, and no law *for* a Papist. I am now writing not only that which is well known to be historical truth, but that which I have witnessed with my own eyes.[3]

Yet, despite all the political disasters of the last decade of the eighteenth century – the dashing of Irish Catholic hopes of reform, the rise of Orangeism, the fomenting and quelling of the rebellion of 1798 and the Act of Union in 1800 – the conception of Ireland as a culturally distinct and coherent nation had already begun to take shape. The turbulence and wildness attributed to the Irish, their intractability to the requirements of 'civilization' and even their sectarian divisions began to enter into a new ideology of Irish cultural nationalism, carefully denuded, especially after 1798, of the doctrinal, revolutionary elements introduced by Tone and so savagely attacked by English writers like Coleridge and Southey or by Irish Ascendancy journalists like John Wilson Croker.[4] It is customary to take the fateful year 1789 as the beginning of this strange recrudescence of national feeling. In that year, Charlotte Brooke published her *Reliques of Irish Poetry*.

The first Celtic revival was Welsh and Scottish in its origins, not Irish. James Macpherson's famous 'translations' from the Gaelic, beginning with the *Fragments of Ancient Poetry* (1758), followed by *Fingal* by 'Ossian' (1762), *Temora* (1763) and *The Works of Ossian, the Son of Fingal* (1765), inaugurated a vogue for the primitive and the Celtic, which fused with the new appreciation of the Sublime (formulated by Burke in 1757). Despite Dr Johnson's repudiation of Ossian, these forged translations achieved respectability and fame with the help of critics like Hugh Blair and a variety of imitators.[5] A much more scholarly work, Evan Evans's *Specimens of the Poetry of the Ancient Welsh Bards* (1764) was outshone in popular esteem by Ossian, although it was welcomed by Thomas Percy, later Bishop of Dromore and founder member of the Royal Irish Academy, known to history for his *Reliques of Ancient English Poetry* (1765), the three volumes of which were added to in the editions of 1767, 1775 and 1794. Charlotte Brooke's volume is an important document in the history of primitivism as a literary movement, but it had an especial importance in Ireland because of the political condition of the country at that time. Even before the achievement of legislative independence in 1782, antiquarian research had begun to make its contribution to the notion of a specifically Irish cultural identity, attractive to the Anglo-Irish as much as to the native Irish in that era. It was a politically powerful notion, for it brought together on the cultural plane, at a sufficiently removed distance in time, groups which were hopelessly divided from one another in the present. Charlotte Brooke's god-father, Sylvester O'Halloran, had reacted to the Ossian uproar by publishing *An Introduction to the Study of the History and Antiquities of Ireland* (1772), a preparation for his important *General History of Ireland* (1778); the military engineer and surveyor Charles Vallancey began, in the same decade, to pursue his strange researches into the connection between the ancient Irish and the ancient Carthaginians, setting off that series of contrasts between a destructive imperial-Roman-England and a devastated-but-surviving Ireland-Carthage, which was to have such durability in Irish writing. The *Proceedings of the Royal Irish Academy* had a special section for Antiquities; amateur scholars like Charles O'Conor and Edmund Ledwich, politicians like Sir Laurence Parsons, all brought some offering to the new shrine of cultural nationalism where the new gods of Language and of War presided, converting the old accusations of crudeness in speech and turbulence into symptoms of natural spontaneity and of valour.[6] What the Irish state lacked in political and social cohesion, the Irish nation was ready to supply.

It is appropriate that the origins of this idea of the nation should be rooted in such motley source materials. Translations, often inaccurate; historical theories, often eccentric; versions of primitivism, often sophisticated; antiquarianism, often politically motivated: these were the characteristic formative elements in the constitution of a new literature which sought to find in culture the basis for what Tone called 'the common name of Irishman' without extending this into the political realm, where the threat of revolutionary separatist republicanism lingered, a repressed but residually powerful force. The influence of Burke's attack on the French Revolution as a speculative and barbarous theory of politics, destructive of anti- quity, local affections and loyalties, and his support of the Irish Catholics against the hard-line Protestant junta, provided Anglo-Irish literature with a style of liberal conservatism which supplanted Tone's radical and Painite approach. Ironically, it was the Romantic rediscovery of Ireland's past through the Gaelic language which confirmed the authenticity and the appeal of this conservatism. The language of the Catholic masses, which O'Connell was to teach them to abandon, became a point of entry, for an influential sector of the Ascendancy, to the nationalism which they and their class had effectively suppressed. Few went so far as to learn the language, but many came to respect it as a sort of Romantic ruin, all the more attractive in the political landscape which emerged after the Act of Union because it was clothed in nostalgic associations, having become the symbol of a lost culture rather than the reminder of a rebellious one. Along with the language of the Gaels there was their music. The traditionally close link between music and poetry, which found expression in the popular ballad in eighteenth-century Ireland, was an article of faith among the sponsors of primitive poetry.

In 1786 Joseph Cooper Walker produced his *Historical Memoirs of the Irish Bards*. Six years later, in Belfast, there was a famous gathering of harpers, which had as its aim the revival of 'The Ancient Music and Poetry of Ireland'. The prospectus for the meeting asserted

An undertaking of this nature will, undoubtedly, meet the approbation of men of refinement and erudition in every country. And when it is considered how intimately *The Spirit and Character of A People* are connected with their national poetry and music, it is presumed that the Irish patriot and politician will not deem it an object unworthy of his patronage and protection.[7]

Wolfe Tone was in attendance at some of the sessions, although he does not seem to have had the proper patriotic response – 'The Harpers again. *Strum strum* and be hanged'.[8] The most important figure there was Edward Bunting, who wrote down the music he heard at this, the last gathering of its kind. The result was his *General Collection of Ancient Irish Music* (1796) in which sixty-six airs were recorded. In 1809, the second series of this work added another seventy-five, many of them collected by Bunting in travels in the West. An expanded edition came out in 1840, with valuable additional material on Irish music, some of it contributed by Sir Samuel Ferguson and George Petrie, two important names in the next generation. Between them, Charlotte Brooke and Bunting provided the seminal works for the Irish version of the Celtic revival. She introduced her English-speaking audience to Gaelic poetry, by publishing the originals with accompanying translations. Bunting began the recovery of a vanishing musical tradition and supplied, at a very tense moment in Irish history, an example of the old native music, which could be adapted to contemporary circumstances by another kind of translation – that is, by lending to the old airs new lyrics in the English language. This was an opportunity which Thomas Moore was to exploit with incomparable skill.

Between 1807 and 1834, Moore published the *Irish Melodies* in ten separate numbers. Six volumes of *National Airs*, collected from various European countries and embellished by Moore's lyrics, were published between 1818 and 1827. The lyrics were not published apart from the music until 1821. Moore was right to resist this separation, for his poems simply do not survive it. In addition, outside Ireland they do not survive the political conditions which initially gave them their appeal. In a well known letter to Sir John Stevenson, the composer who collaborated with him on the *Melodies*, Moore wrote:

Thus our airs, like too many of our countrymen, for want of protection at home, have passed into the service of foreigners. But we are come, I hope, to a better period of both politics and music; and how much they are connected, in Ireland at least, appears too plainly in the tone of sorrow and depression which characterises most of our early songs. – The task which you propose to me, of adapting words to these airs, is by no means easy. The poet, who would follow the various sentiments which they express, must feel and understand that rapid fluctuation of spirits, that unaccountable mixture of gloom and levity, which composes the character of my countrymen, and has deeply tinged their music.[9]

Moore had reasons to feel the connection between music and politics. The Belfast festival of 1792 was among them; but much more strongly felt was the death of his Trinity College friend, Robert Emmett, executed for his leadership of the abortive 1803 outbreak in Dublin. Three famous lyrics commemorate him but, more importantly, all of Moore's best lyrics are haunted by one refrain – that of loyalty to the betrayed. The treachery of time, which steals beauty, friends, hopes, is overborne by the fidelity of the tender heart, which retains the pristine force of the first, youthful commitment. It is, indeed, a sentimental theme, but in Moore, and in Moore's Ireland of the nineteenth century, it is also a political theme. The fidelity is given not only to Robert Emmett, but also to Ireland and its long litany of lost causes, from Kinsale to Vinegar Hill, from the parliament of James II to that of Grattan. It is, of course, true that Moore transformed the Gaelic airs into drawing-room songs; that he bequeathed to Irish verse in English a combination of metrical virtuosity and an idiom of limp, even simpering, nostalgia, from which it took almost a century to recover; that Hazlitt was right to say that Mr Moore 'converts the wild harp of Erin into a musical snuff-box'.[10] Yet, for all the faults that can be readily ascribed to this Whig pamphleteer who sang so many songs for so many suppers, his importance cannot be denied. He was a minor poet but a major phenomenon.The synthetic and artificial element in his work is its most important feature. The strange confections of Walker, Brooke, O'Halloran and others found their literary fulfilment in the *Melodies*. The injustice done to the Gaelic originals, in poem or in melody, was less important than the fact that it was only through such a determined emasculation of them that the political power of their appeal could be mobilized. Moore 'refined' Gaelic music and made it thereby an acceptable literary property, both to the English and to the Irish. As he expressed it in his 1807 letter to Stevenson:

That beautiful air, 'The Twisting of the Rope' . . . is one of those wild and sentimental rakes which it will not be very easy to tie down in sober wedlock with poetry. However . . . the design appears to me so truly national, that I shall feel much pleasure in giving it all the assistance in my power.[11]

Irish writers, like Gerald Griffin or Charles Kickham,[12] would have agreed. Irish nationalism was not a natural growth. It had to be invented. Moore put Ireland in the sentimental limelight in an unprecedented manner. After 1798 and the Union, this was an amazing achievement. The England that responded to him was the England which made Sydney Smith enraged by her callousness and stupidity in Ireland. But Moore sowed there the seed of the idea that Ireland was ungovernable because she was 'Celtic'. That was to have later and profound repercussions.

Moore's patriotism was by no means unconscious. His *Memoirs of Captain Rock* (1824) and *The Life and Death of Lord Edward Fitzgerald* (1831) are indictments of British misrule. But his strongest effects are achieved in lyrics where there is no satire or anger. A uniform emollience of nostalgic feeling is preserved in language of an extreme conventionality. Structurally, the lyric is always neat, a little plot with an expected denouement. But with the music, the simple-mindedness of the language and the structure is converted to simplicity, as in the elegy for Emmett:

> Oh! breathe not his name, let it sleep in the shade,
> Where cold and unhonour'd his relics are laid;
> Sad, silent and dark, be the tears that we shed,
> As the night-dew that falls on the grass o'er his head.
>
> But the night-dew that falls, though in silence it weeps,
> Shall brighten with verdure the grave where he sleeps;
> And the tear that we shed, though in secret it rolls,
> Shall long keep his memory green in our souls.

Moore knew no Irish. But he had perfect command in the narrow range of English in which he wrote. Others, like J. J. Callanan, who did know Irish and had some conception of the intricacies of the Irish poetry he translated, could be stimulated by the original beyond the decorous dreariness of his usual English. But, in general, there is nothing of distinction in Preston, Drennan, Furlong and others.[13] James Hardiman, the editor of *Irish Minstrelsy* (1831), complains in his foreword of the 'vulgar ballads' of the last 150 years which have 'displaced the native lyrics so effectually' that the memory of the originals has disappeared.[14] However, he did not do a great deal to improve the situation with the translations he printed in the second half of his own volume. In fact, there was a great deal more energy and life in the popular ballads, especially those dealing with 1798, than in the very literary translations, many of them made by people who had little sympathy with the Gaelic civilization and even less knowledge of the people who belonged to it. But translations had become the standard means by which Anglo-Irish literature was to transform itself into a national Irish literature. Until a translator of genius appeared, Tom Moore was the only writer who could demonstrate in an unforgettable way the potency of the combination of the old Irish with the contemporary English culture. Hardiman's book was the occasion for this translator's appearance on the scene. Sir Samuel Ferguson's articles on the problems of translation from the Gaelic appeared in the *Dublin University Magazine* (1834), along with over twenty versions by Ferguson himself of poems printed in Hardiman.[15] With these articles and translations, the Celtic revival advanced deeply into Ireland.

Between 1832 and 1850 Samuel Ferguson contributed over ninety items to periodical publications like *Blackwood's Magazine* and the *Dublin University Magazine*. Some of them were essays, some poems. Most of the essays were reviews of books of Irish interest; most of the poems were translations or redactions of Gaelic originals. His *Lays of the Western Gael* appeared in 1865, his translation, in five books, of a Gaelic epic, *Congal*, came out in Dublin and London in 1872, his *Poems* in 1880. In 1897, *Lays of the Red Branch* combined the volumes of 1865 and 1880, with some rearrangement of the sequence. This posthumous volume (Ferguson died in 1886) may be regarded as one of the important early works of the Irish revival. Ferguson was an Ulster Protestant, a fervent believer in the Union, and a cultural nationalist who believed in a specific national identity, for which the Union was a safeguard. For those, like O'Connell, who regarded the repeal of the Union as a necessary preliminary to the achievement of full nationality, he had nothing but contempt. This, for him, was nothing more than Jacobin fury, leading to a plebeian, Catholic demagogic wilderness, the triumph of what he called in 1834 'a perverse rabble'. In an essay of 1840, in the *Dublin University Magazine*, he announced his *credo*:

What we have to do with, and that to which these observations properly point, is the recovery of the mislaid, but not lost, records of the acts, and opinions, and condition of our ancestors – the disinterring and bringing back to the light of intellectual day, the already recorded *facts*, by which the people of Ireland will be able to *live back*, in the land they live *in*, with as ample and as interesting a field of retrospective enjoyment as any of the nations around us.[16]

It seems now that Ferguson contained within himself many of the contradictions which made the survival of his class and its political philosophy impossible. A nationalist who was a unionist, a

Protestant preaching intellectual freedom to the Papists whom he held in contempt, a utilitarian who wished to revive a version of romantic Ireland, a believer in the people who defended the supremacy of a caste. But the case is more complex than this array of contradictions would imply. In the first place, cultural nationalism and the defence, either of the Union or, before 1800, of the link with Britain, was not all anomalous. The patriot movement of the eighteenth century, of which Ferguson was an inheritor, had given its fidelity to this combination. And the expatriate groups, the absentee intellectuals, led by Burke, had looked to the conciliation of Catholic and Protestant through a policy of voluntary concession to Catholic claims as the only means of preserving the integrity of the British imperial system, with Ireland as a natural and central part of it. For them, it was the only political arrangement which would allow Ireland to play its part in the European concert. The alternative, separation, seemed ominous to Britain, especially during the Revolutionary and Napoleonic wars, and stifling for Ireland, since at best it might revert to a provincial insularity. No doubt there was a measure of special pleading in all this, since the link with Britain also assured the Ascendancy that its power and privilege, the product of slaughter and confiscation, would remain secure. But, given that, a man like Ferguson recognized after the Union that security had been bought by the Ascendancy at the expense of integrity. He wished to re-establish a basis for that integrity and found, in his search for it, that the permanent risk in conceding to Catholic claims, whether political or cultural, was the risk of Protestant exclusion or extinction from the remodelled nation. Like his forebears and his descendants, his view of Ireland was coloured by the recognition that the Catholic majority could be defeated over and over again and still remain a powerful presence in the land. The Protestant minority, on the other hand, could only lose once.

In the second place, by shifting the dispute over Catholic claims to the level of culture, Ferguson was not trying to dodge an intractable political problem. Instead, he was seeking to solve it through culture. The constitutional rearrangement brought about by the Act of Union was for him as final a settlement for Ireland as 1688 had been for England. In order to preserve it, he considered that there must be created, through literature, a feeling of mutual compatability between Protestant and Catholic, which would lead to the deeper civilization of both. The policy of concessions, however reluctantly yielded, to the new Catholic nation created by O'Connell seemed bound to produce instead a polarization of the two groupings, the effect of which would be to threaten the Union itself and to deny the possibility of mutual enrichment between the opposing groups, thereby leading to a vulgarization of the national consciousness, which had been so recently born in the last century. He had the sublime confidence to believe that a careful interrogation of Ireland's past would finally elicit from the Irish people an admission of the cultural unity which lay below the divisions which separated them.

Thus he attacked James Hardiman's *Irish Minstrelsy* because it claimed Gaelic Ireland as an exclusively Catholic possession. With one or two modifications, the claim was justified. But Ferguson set out to make it untenable. In this he succeeded. That in itself is a measure of his achievement and of his importance, not only for Yeats, Synge and others, but for the future history and literature of the island. The Antrim and the Belfast he came from had recently been the birthplace of the United Irishmen. Ferguson recognized that there, under Cave Hill and in the Glens, there existed two civilizations, Anglo-Irish and Gaelic. It was his ambition to bring them together without taking Tone's Jacobin path. But in the remarkable essay of 1833, published in the ultra-unionist *Dublin University Magazine*, 'A Dialogue Between the Head and the Heart of an Irish Protestant', Ferguson confronts the dilemma in which his life's ambition left him. On the one hand, there is the necessity of the Irish Protestant's retaining his independence and refusing sympathy to the Catholic cause; that is the head speaking. On the other, there is the heart's claim:

I love this land better than any other. I cannot believe it a hostile country. I love the people of it, in spite of themselves, and cannot feel towards them as enemies.[17]

The head too had claimed as 'our birthright, . . . the love of Ireland'. But could he love an Ireland which could not, or would not, love him? The answer was yes, but only on condition that the word Ireland was transformed to mean something other than Popery and potatoes. Once Catholics could have revealed to them their true identity as Celts, and Protestants could discover their true role, which was to absorb into modern, civil forms the fire and passion of that Celtic heritage, then the new Ireland could emerge. The Catholic would be liberated from the ignoble 'spiritual thraldom' of

his religion and the Protestant would be freed from the 'civil degradation' he had suffered from the British government. In their twin
freedom, they would discover the sweet mutuality of authentic
nationalism. Although many unkind things might be said of the
candid bigotry and the ingenuous hopefulness of Ferguson's opinions, his vision has the attraction and the generosity of that of Tone
or, even more, of Pearse, to whom he is strikingly (and Ferguson
would feel) appallingly similar.

Ferguson recognized and realized in his own work the connection
between antiquarian scholarship and popular appeal, which
Bunting and Hardiman had inaugurated with their own collections
and which Moore had, in his view, exploited. The ancient music and
the poetry of Ireland provided some of the materials for the formulation of a tradition. Ferguson added to these the rich, if confused,
element of legend and epic, so vaguely adumbrated by Macpherson
in his Ossian poems. A more exacting scholarship in the pursuit of
source material and a more demanding standard of accuracy in its
translation were for him the instruments of his literary-political
ambition. Ireland's heritage was to be mobilized for the sake of
Ireland's present. Among the early results of his labours were lyric
poems, translated from the Irish into an English which bore the
stress of the other language in its relatively unfamiliar patternings of
assonantal music, anapaestic rhythms and, above all, in its freedom
from the polite tearfulness of Moore. Here is the opening stanza of
his translation, *Cashel of Munster*:

> I'd wed you without herds, without money, or rich array,
> And I'd wed you on a dewy morning at day-dawn grey;
> My bitter woe it is, love, that we are not far away
> In Cashel town, though the bare deal-board were our marriage-bed
>   this day![18]

Another well known example is *Ceann Dubh Dilis* (*Dear Black
Head*), an old Irish song, translated so:

> Put your head, darling, darling, darling,
>   Your darling black head my heart above;
> Oh, mouth of honey, with the thyme for fragrance,
>   Who, with heart in breast, could deny you love?
> Oh, many and many a young girl for me is pining
>   Letting her locks of gold to the cold wind free,

For me, the foremost of our gay young fellows;
  But I'd leave a hundred, pure love, for thee!
Then put your head, darling, darling, darling,
  Your darling black head my heart above;
Oh, mouth of honey, with the thyme for fragrance,
  Who, with heart in breast, could deny you love?[19]

Something of the original's 'languishing but savage sincerity',[20] as he called it, is caught here and in as many as a score of other lyrics. But Ferguson fell victim in his longer poems to a characteristically Victorian fustian, which he mistook for 'dignity'. *Congal* (1872) is particularly unfortunate in this, yet it is an important poem historically. For it uses Irish historical material (Cath Mighe Rath, the Battle of Moyra, conflated with Fled Dun na nGed, The Feast of the Fort of the Geese, dating from the twelfth to fourteenth centuries, first printed, with a translation, by John O'Donovan in 1842), to produce an historical image of great resonance in later literature – the image of a pagan hero, Congal, defeated by the new force of Christianity, represented by King Domnal. Congal becomes the prototype of the Celtic hero defeated by an ignoble, but triumphant, civilization. He is at once a Protestant and also a nationalist figure, later to be rewritten as Parnell, Cuchulainn and, in another guise, as the Artist subdued by mediocrity. This laborious attempt at an epic poem, along with his version of the Deirdre legend and the long narrative poem *Conary*, constitutes one part of Ferguson's legacy to the Revival. History, legend and myth, converted into poetry through translation, became part of an imaginative possession, a deep hinterland implying a long tradition, which was to provide Yeats with the stimulus he sought in the 1880s and 1890s. Beside this popularized and more than faintly amateur attempt to recover the ancient past, there was an already established body of professional scholarship, associated with the names of Petrie, O'Curry and O'Donovan in Ireland, and the great German philologists who, since Zeuss's *Grammatica Celtica* (1853), made such an enormous contribution to Celtic studies, as well as with Renan and later de Joubainville in France. Thus, from mid-century, Irish literature's close association with scholarship was confirmed, although its readiness to convert scholarly materials to its own purposes, sometimes with a bogus display of learning, sometimes with a frankly political purpose, also becomes characteristic. But literature also stayed closely in touch with the popular tradition of music and ballad. The political circumstances of the time ensured that this also meant a close and readily recognized intimacy with political issues. Yet the mid-century also brought with it the disaster which completely changed everything – the Great Famine of 1845–7. Ferguson was so shaken by the British government's callousness in the face of this catastrophe that his faith in the Union wavered for a time. He failed to see that the effect of the Famine on his own project was to make what had been a programme for a future Ireland into an anachronistic but nostalgically appealing scheme for a lost Ireland. The Gaelic civilization and the Anglo-Irish civilization, which he had wanted to bring together, were both entering on the last phase of their existence in the late nineteenth century. The repercussions of this double death were to resonate, not in his work, but in that of Yeats.

Of the seven million Irish people who emigrated to the United States between 1740 and 1922, something close to one and a half million emigrated in the disastrous decade 1841–51.[21] Almost a million died from starvation and disease. With the disappearance of these people, the Irish language went into an irrecoverable decline. Only a quarter of the population was Irish-speaking after 1851. The death of the living language and the awakening of antiquarian and scholarly interest in it overlap. Organizations like The Gaelic Society (1807), The Hiberno-Celtic Society (1818), The Archaeological Society (1840), The Ulster Gaelic Society (1830) and The Celtic Society (1845) were interested in the translation of Irish into English, rather than in its revival. When The Ossianic Society (1853) declared its aim to be the publication of modern and therefore more accessible texts, instead of the ancient literature, it gained little support. Among those whose aims were the revival of the language rather than its adaptation into English for the sake of Unionism, the most prominent was John O'Daly, the publisher of *Reliques of Irish Jacobite Poetry* (1844), *Irish Popular Songs* (1847) and *The Poets and Poetry of Munster* (1849, second series, 1860). As the Famine began, John O'Donovan published his *Grammar of the Irish Language* (1845) and O'Daly, in the following year, his *Self Instruction in Irish*. But the combination of scholarship and popular appeal did not work for the language as it did for the literature in English. The audience for the language was almost destroyed; the audience for the literature was very far removed from the people O'Daly tried to reach with his penny collections. He said of Hardiman's collection, expensively published in two volumes, that it was published in such a manner, as to put it entirely out of the reach of the parties for whom such a work should be intended, I mean, the *Irish peasantry*.[22]

The near-extinction of the peasantry and of their language enhanced the value of both as literary properties. There were other consequences, which had a profound political and literary impact.[23] O'Connell's repeal movement died before 1848 was over. Both it and the Young Ireland movement were replaced by Fenianism, a secret, revolutionary society which was to carry on the Jacobin tradition of Tone, relying now on Irish-American rather than on continental support for its success. In John Mitchel, Fenianism found a powerful voice for its hatred of the British government which had, as Mitchel believed, committed the crime of genocide against the Irish people. His *Jail Journal* (1854) and *The Last Conquest of Ireland (Perhaps)* (1860) became classics of Irish revolutionary literature, reintegrating Irish writing with the radical separatist tradition from which it had been so carefully disengaged since the early days of the Union. Mitchel's undying bitterness made the rhetoric of Repeal, which had seemed so outrageous to Ferguson, appear anodyne indeed. After six years exile as a transported felon, Mitchel arrives in New York to find the new Irish-American nation:

The very nation that I knew in Ireland is broken and destroyed; and the place that knew it shall know it no more. To America has fled the half-starved remnant of it; and the phrase that I have heard of late, 'a new Ireland in America', conveys no meaning to my mind. Ireland without the Irish — the Irish out of Ireland — neither of these can be *our country*. Yet who can tell what the chances and changes of the blessed war may bring us? I believe in moral and spiritual electricity; I believe that a spark, caught at some happy moment, may give life to masses of comatose humanity; that dry bones, as in Ezekiel's vision, may live; that out of the 'exodus' of the Celts may be born a Return of the Heracleidae.[24]

By 1860, the vengeful message is addressed in part to the Americans. In the last paragraph of *The Last Conquest of Ireland (Perhaps)*, Mitchel declares

The subjection of Ireland is now probably assured until some external shock shall break up that monstrous commercial firm, the British Empire; which, indeed, is a bankrupt firm, and trading on false credit, and embezzling the goods of others, or robbing on the highway, from Pole to Pole, but its doors are not yet shut; its cup of abomination is not yet running over. If any American has read this narrative, however, he will never wonder hereafter when he hears an Irishman in America fervently curse the British Empire. So long as this hatred and horror shall last – so long as our island refuses to become, like Scotland, a contented province of her enemy, Ireland is not finally subdued. The passionate aspiration for Irish nationhood will outlive the British Empire.[25]

This was a militarism which meant more than the valour of Congal, Cuchulainn and the Red Branch Knights. Literary violence and political violence were bound to fuse eventually. In doing so, they would destroy the Union.

The Famine made it impossible for cultural nationalism to remove itself entirely from revolutionary politics. Twenty-five years later, with the disestablishment of the Irish Church in 1869 and Gladstone's first Land Act of 1870, the process of disintegration began for the Ascendancy. Yeats was born in 1865, the year of Ferguson's *Lays of the Western Gael*. Ferguson's Gaels lived in the dim west of antiquity; the modern Gaels lived in the western cities of Boston, Philadelphia and New York. The two classes or peoples Ferguson and Yeats sponsored so fervently in their poetry – Catholic Celts and Protestant Ascendancy Irish – were about to depart from the scene. The peasantry who remained in Ireland eventually became smallholders of land. The Ascendancy found it increasingly difficult to hold what remained. Sectarian division had also deepened as a result of the proselytizing actitivies of Protestant evangelicals during the Famine,[26] with the result that Irish national feeling became increasingly identified with the Catholic majority. Literature became the last stronghold of the Ascendancy, although the subjection of literature to political purposes by the Young Ireland and the Fenian movements inclined Yeats and others to believe that the Ascendancy was also the last stronghold of literature.

Before Parnell, before *Congal*, the tradition of the lost leader was well established in Ireland. Since the early seventeenth century there had been a line of military heroes, from Hugh O'Neill to Robert Emmett. The 1840s supplied three new heroes, figures who caught the popular imagination, and yet were not military. Thomas Davis died at the age of thirty-one in 1845; the great O'Connell died in 1847; James Clarence Mangan died in 1849. Davis, a Protestant, founded *The Nation* newspaper with the help of two Catholic friends, Charles Gavan Duffy and John Blake Dillon, in 1842. For the five years from 1840 to 1845, he preached to the Irish on a variety of subjects, from education, to music, to painting, to the virtues of Repeal. Most of all, he preached the Fergusonian doctrine of cultural unity, although Davis would have been willing to take this one step further towards political independence. He was a great popular educator, the vitalizing force in O'Connell's Repeal movement and, after its failure, in the process of politicizing the Irish song tradition. His attacks on the philistine utilitarianism of English civilization and the contrasting spirituality of the Irish supplied Yeats with one of his more monotonous, if occasionally powerful, themes. Davis stressed the Irish capacity for nobility of spirit in order to counteract the current British view of them as little more than ramshackle drunkards or, in times of political crisis, savage and simian creatures who were beyond the pale of what Lecky carefully called 'the law as it was administered in England'.[27] But, more importantly, Davis's campaign was directed against the effects of O'Connellism. Ferguson and he were at one on this. T. W. Rolleston, writing in 1889, put the case admirably:

No imaginable political success could have compensated, in his eyes, for the habits of cant, imposture, slavishness, and injustice which he saw the agitation of O'Connell was tending to engender, and which he opposed, even to the length of encountering the mighty orator before the Repeal Association, with unwavering determination.[28]

On that famous occasion, memorably described by Malcolm Brown, O'Connell reduced Davis to tears while his friend Dillon literally spat blood. O'Connell struck unerringly at the Ascendancy claim to form a new Ireland out of the materials of the old:

There is no such party as that styled 'Young Ireland' (hear, hear). There may be a few individuals who take that designation on themselves (hear and cheers). I am for Old Ireland (loud applause). 'Tis time that this delusion should be put an end to (hear, hear, and cheers). Young Ireland may play what pranks they please. I do not envy them the name they rejoice in, I shall stand by Old Ireland (cheers). And I have some slight notion that Old Ireland will stand by me (loud cheers).[29]

The attack is the more telling because Davis was, in so many ways, hopelessly naive. But he did recognize that the achievement of Irish nationality depended on the successful alliance of the political supporters of O'Connell and the educated classes who read or wrote for the *Dublin University Magazine*. To preserve Ireland from British utilitarianism, 'the whole horde of Benthamy',[30] counter measures had to be taken. These were, first, the Repeal agitation and second, Literature and Education. Like Ferguson, Davis believed 'culture' to be the central agency in the formation of a new politics. But he returned again and again to the notion that cultural separation from imperial and industrial England was a precondition of success in the enterprise. To remain attached to London was a form of slavishness disguised as cosmopolitanism. This was an important and a new note. Davis, in deflecting the charge of provincialism by calling its opponents shallow cosmopolitans was again anticipating one of the obsessions of the Irish revival while clearly marking the distance travelled since Charlotte Brooke imagined the British and Irish muses as

sweet ambassadresses of cordial union between two countries that seem formed by nature to be joined by every bond of interest and amity.[31]

The contrast with what Davis wrote in 'The Library of Ireland', one of his pieces for *The Nation*, is striking:

Westminster ceased to be the city towards which the Irish bowed and made pilgrimage. An organisation, centring in Dublin, connected the People; and oratory full of Gaelic passion and popular idiom galvanised them. Thus there has been, from 1842 – when the Repeal agitation became serious – an incessant progress in Literature and Nationality. A Press, Irish in subjects, style and purpose, has been formed – a National Poetry has grown up – the National Schools have prepared their students for the more earnest study of National politics and history. . .

Yet the power of British utilitarian literature continues. The wealthy classes are slowly getting an admirable and costly National Literature from Petrie, and O'Donovan, and Ferguson, and Lefanu, and the *University Magazine*. The poorer are left to the newspaper, and the meeting, and an occasional serial of very moderate merits. That class, now becoming the rulers of Ireland, who have taste for the higher studies, but whose means are small, have only a few scattered works within their reach, and some of them, not content to use these exclusively, are driven to foreign studies and exposed to alien influence.

To give to the country a National Library, exact enough for the wisest, high enough for the purest, and cheap enough for all readers, appears the object of 'The Library of Ireland'.[32]

This is a good example of what Yeats was later to call 'the schoolboy thought'[33] of Young Ireland. Davis had noble aims – in fact he gave the word 'noble' a currency in Irish writing that was to endure for over a century – but he imagined the conversion of Ireland to the principle of nationality as the consequence of a change in consciousness brought about by education. This new consciousness would, he believed, harmonize the conflicting interests of the peasantry and the Ascendancy. He was, in fact, inventing the symbolism of a complete 'spiritual' nationhood, finding its chief alternative in British utilitarianism. His natural inheritor in this respect was Matthew Arnold and, beyond him, Yeats. Even the Joyce of the Trieste lectures and articles of 1907 follows this line.[34] But the most complete refutation of his ideal came two years after his death in a series of letters to *The Nation*, written by James Fintan Lalor, in which he defined the new battleground of Irish politics after the Famine – the Land. The war of tenant against landlord, to be carried through by Davitt's Land League from 1879 onwards, was the real conflict of which Davis's writings were no more than a symbolic resolution. Astonishingly, this displacement of history into literature was to be continued into the twentieth century by Yeats in his search for 'Unity of Culture', a phrase which might stand as an appropriate epitaph for the desire embodied in the writings of Davis and Ferguson.

However, Davis had another legacy to bequeath. This was the political ballad.[35] Moore's theme of fidelity to a lost cause, often treated in a mildly sexual and sensual manner, was rendered by Davis in a militarist idiom. His first ballad, 'Lament of Eoghan Ruadh O'Neill', printed in the sixth number of *The Nation*, was followed by almost eighty others. These, in turn, were supplemented by ballads from other contributors. All of them were collected in two volumes of 'Political Songs and National Ballads', published in 1843 under the title *The Spirit of the Nation*. A single volume edition appeared in 1845, *The New Spirit of the Nation*. The fiftieth edition of the 1843 volumes appeared in 1870. This collection of 'Ballads and Songs/with/Original and Ancient Music,/ Arranged for the Voice and Piano-Forte' outshone even Moore's *Melodies* in popular affection. The first editions were badly printed, had no accompanying music, and cost sixpence. As their fame grew, their format became more elaborate. In 1882, the year of De Valera's and Joyce's birth, an elaborate new edition appeared in all the glory of the green and gold bindings with harp and shamrock motifs, a frontispiece containing Celtic harpists, a Celtic warrior, female representations of Mother Ireland and, in the centre, the eagle of freedom slaying the serpent of despotism. The first ballad in the collection was Gavan Duffy's *Fag An Bealach* (*Clear the Way*), a well known military cry in faction fights and in Irish continental regiments. An appended note reads:

To make the general tone, and some of the allusions in this song intelligible, we should, perhaps, mention that it was written in October, 1841, when the hope and the spirits of the people were low; and published in the third number of the *Nation*, as the Charter Song of the contributors.[36]

This accurately defines the tone and purpose of the whole enterprise. As with Moore's *Melodies*, these ballads need to be sung. Yeats admitted that he could never hear 'The West's Asleep' by Davis 'without great excitement'.[37] Although he wanted to resist this reaction, he was at one with the general public in acceding to it. The song is set to an air published in Bunting's 1840 volume *The Ancient Music of Ireland*:

When all beside a vigil keep,
The West's asleep, the West's asleep –
Alas! and well may Erin weep,
When Connaught lies in slumber deep.
There lake and plain smile fair and free,
'Mid rocks – their guardian chivalry –
Sing oh! let man learn liberty
From crashing wind and lashing sea.

Davis had a good heart but a cloth ear.

One of John O'Daly's collaborators in *The Poets and Poetry of Munster* (1849) was James Clarence Mangan. Mangan was also a contributor to *The Nation*. In addition he was employed at the Ordnance Survey office where, since 1833, the great project for the Ordnance Survey Map of Ireland had been carried on.[38] Although its original scope was reduced, it remained a nucleus of Irish scholarship, numbering John O'Donovan, Eugene O'Curry and George Petrie among its outstanding talents. Both O'Daly and O'Curry, and sometimes O'Donovan, supplied Mangan with prose translations of Irish poems, which he would then 'translate' into his own peculiar English. George Petrie directed those working on topographical material for the Ordnance Survey. His house was the office where this group, and Ferguson and W. F. Wakeman, would meet between 1838 and 1841, when the topographical activities were discontinued for financial and political reasons. Petrie was the editor of the *Dublin Penny Journal* from 1832 to 1836 and of *The Irish Penny Journal* (1840–1). William Carleton and Mangan were among his most famous contributors. Painter, archaeologist and musicologist, Petrie's contribution to Irish scholarship was immense. His essay of 1833, 'The Round Towers of Ireland' is still well known. More generally he is remembered for his version of the beautiful song, 'The Snowy-Breasted Pearl'; most of all he is remembered for the passage in the introduction to *The Petrie Collection of the Ancient Music of Ireland* (2 vols, 1855–82), in which he described the Great Silence which descended upon Ireland in the wake of the Great Famine:

The 'land of song' was no longer tuneful; or, if a human sound met the traveller's ear, it was only that of the feeble and despairing wail for the dead. This awful, unwonted silence, which, during the famine and subsequent years, almost everywhere prevailed, struck more fearfully upon their imaginations, as many Irish gentlemen informed me, and gave them a deeper feeling of the desolation with which the country had been visited, than any other circumstance which had forced itself upon their attention. . .[39]

Mangan was dead of cholera six years before that passage was published. It is an appropriate backdrop to his life and work. 'The land', wrote Engels to Marx in 1856, 'is an utter desert which nobody wants'. English liberty based on colonial oppression, the country seats of the landowners 'surrounded by enormous, wonderfully beautiful parks, but all around is waste land'[40] – these contradictions noted by Engels were most glaringly obvious in mid-century Ireland and were to be adverted to over and over again in later Irish writing, from Standish O'Grady to James Connolly. Engels thought the landowners ought to be shot. Mitchel, in 1860, after describing one of the many thousands of evictions, says simply, 'There were not half enough of them shot'.[41] The cultural unity, or the dream of it, which inspired Ferguson and Davis, was not even a remote possibility under such conditions. Mangan's writings are at home here in this homelessness.

In other circumstances he might have been a great writer. In the actual circumstances he became the exemplary ruin of one. Joyce considered him to be 'the most significant poet of the modern Celtic world',[42] the archetypal romantic entrapped by history.

Love of grief, despair, high-sounding threats – these are the great traditions of the race of James Clarence Mangan, and in that impoverished figure, thin and weakened, an hysterical nationalism receives its final justification.[43]

Yeats discovered in him a 'passionate self-abandonment',[44] which was excessive and impressive at the same time. The translations of J. J. Callanan and Edward Walsh, Thomas Furlong and Ferguson were more attractive to Yeats because they created something like a genuine Irish ballad tradition in English as opposed to the propagandist militancy of Davis and *The Spirit of the Nation*. But Mangan belonged to neither group. He wrote for *The Nation*, he translated, like Walsh and Callanan, for O'Daly. Unlike them, he knew little or no Irish; unlike Davis, he felt no commitment to and had no energy for a programme of national education. Poverty, drink, opium, a mysterious autobiography, a sad death and obscurity have given to him all the required characteristics of the doomed, romantic genius. He looked the part, he dressed the part and, in an astonishing way, he wrote in accord with it. Most of his work is translation or versions of poems which had appeared in other languages – German, French, Coptic, Irish – although even his own original work is described as translation too. Clearly, translation is an obsession with him, a way of displacing his own voice, a ventriloquism of the kind which Yeats was to raise to the dignity of an aesthetic. But it is not surprising that Mangan should make a fetish of it in a culture dominated by a linguistic and a cultural crisis, from which it sought escape through translation, through imaginative repossession of that which was once native and had become foreign (the Irish language) into that which had once been foreign and had become native (the English language). Mangan lived through the critical transition from one to the other in an atmosphere of gloom and disaster which it is hard to imagine. What made him attractive to later writers was his ability to internalize these crises, to see history as an expression of his own life, to recognize within himself the psychic stress of the country's political and social condition. Ireland's history usurped Mangan's imagination. His one defence of his negatived self, and his central expression of it, was the creation of the original world of which his poems were merely the reflection, version, or translation. His concentration, then, is on the nature, not on the function, of literature. His life, with all its romantic-tragic trappings, is the history of an imagination driven back upon its own resources and finding them insufficient. To call a poem a translation is to provide an excuse for its failure to be anything more than a secondary thing, a trace of an original which does not lie in German or in Irish but in the poet himself, in the poem that he did not, because he could not, write. In addition, the English of Mangan's poetry is itself a secondary language. All his originals are non-English. This, too, is a species of nationalism, but of a nationalism mobilized in the interests of a creative gift, which was achieving a reluctant eloquence in the oppressive language which had also become the symptom of Ireland's inarticulateness. One can see why Joyce brooded on this poet and made of his early essay of 1902 the basis for Stephen Daedalus's aesthetic theories. Mangan, the intensely Catholic, decadent poet of the 1830s and 1840s, became a symbolic figure for the Irish writers of the later part of the century – Joyce, Yeats, Lionel Johnson – because he was, to them, the one great artist destroyed by nineteenth-century Ireland.

Thus Mangan's poetry is full of waste places, lost patrons and leaders, visions and dreams that contrast with or embody a chilling reality. Although a number of nineteenth-century Irish poets had a considerable metrical skill, none had Mangan's rhythmic sense, his gift for counterpointing the movement of the voice against the fixed measure of the metre. This produces sudden and effective inflections and intensifications of feeling, as in the last line of this stanza from 'Siberia':

> And the exile there
> Is one with those;
> They are part, and he is part,
> For the sands are in his heart,
> And the killing snows.[45]

He also has command of more complex stanza forms, although he governs them too often by employing an incantatory rhythm and a series of refrains and repetitions, which can have a monotonous effect. 'A Lamentation For the Death of Sir Maurice Fitzgerald, Knight of Kerry' is characteristic in its adopted pose of the poet-retainer who has lost his Gaelic patron. It is based on the Irish of Pierce Ferriter:

> There was lifted up one voice of woe,
>   One lament of more than mortal grief,
> Through the wide South to and fro,
>   For a fallen Chief.
> In the dead of night that cry thrilled through me,
>   I looked out upon the midnight air!
> Mine own soul was all as gloomy,
>   And I knelt in prayer.[46]

Mangan's reputation as the Irish Poe is well earned in poems such as 'A Vision of Connaught in the Thirteenth Century', 'The Nameless One', 'And Then No More', 'Ichabod! Thy Glory Has Departed' and 'Song'. 'Twenty Golden Years Ago' gives some impression of the poet he might have been had he not been so given to the melodrama of historical catastrophe. Midway through the third stanza, the feeling concentrates:

> Doctors think I'll neither live nor thrive
>   If I mope at home so – I don't know –
> *Am* I living *now*? I *was* alive
>   Twenty golden years ago.
>
> Wifeless, friendless, flagonless, alone,
>   Not quite bookless, though, unless I chuse,
> Left with nought to do, except to groan,
>   Not a soul to woo, except the Muse –
> O! this, this is hard for *me* to bear,
>   Me, who whilome lived so much *en haut*,
> Me, who broke all hearts like chinaware
>   Twenty golden years ago![47]

His best-known poems, however, include O'Hussey's 'Ode to the Maguire', based on an Irish original, but made over by Mangan into a lament of his own declamatory kind:

Where is my Chief, my Master, this bleak night, *mavrone*!
O cold, cold, miserably cold is this bleak night for Hugh,
Its showery, arrowy, speary sleet pierceth one through and through,
Pierceth one to the very bone![48]

There the alexandrine is put to use in an attempt to allow for the interplay of sound in the Gaelic original. Best-known of all is 'Dark Rosaleen', a poem which Ferguson argued concerned a priest's love for a woman, but which was generally regarded as a parable of Irish loyalty to the motherland, the Dark Rosaleen of the title. Mangan took up this interpretation but with it we may see as well that the poem is also an address to his Muse. As is often the case in Mangan, and of course in Irish Jacobite poetry, aid comes from abroad. But the alien support is not always a political gesture in his verse. It is also an imaginative impulse, coming to give life to his stricken Muse:

O my Dark Rosaleen,
  Do not sigh, do not weep!
The priests are on the ocean green,
  They march along the Deep.
There's wine from the royal Pope
  Upon the ocean green;
And Spanish ale shall give you hope,
  My Dark Rosaleen!
  My own Rosaleen!
Shall glad your heart, shall give you hope,
Shall give you health, and help, and hope,
  My Dark Rosaleen.[49]

That poem was published in *The Nation* on 30 May 1846. By then, Davis was dead, the Famine had well begun, and Mangan had only three years to live. He lost his position in the library of Trinity College and seems to have lived in extreme penury thereafter, although 1846 was the year of his finest poems. He died as did many in the Famine years – 'his miserable body', Joyce reminds us, 'made the attendants shudder'.[50] There was a kind of perfection in the life, if not in the work. The battle between the exoticism of the foreign climate or of the distant time and the drabness of the native present was engaged by Mangan at a level other than, though still intimate with, the political. Joyce wanted to claim him as Ireland's national poet; in doing so he used the exact terminology, even the right tone of histrionic assertion:

Mangan will be accepted by the Irish as their national poet on the day when the conflict will be decided between my native land and the foreign powers – Anglo-Saxon and Roman Catholic, and a new civilization will arise, either indigenous or completely foreign.[51]

The dispute between Anglo-Saxon and Celtic, Protestant and Catholic, Irish and English became one of the dominant features of British politics when Gladstone decided, in 1868, to take it up. The year before, Matthew Arnold published his famous essay 'On the Study of Celtic Literature'. That was also the year of the Fenian uprising and of the Manchester Martyrs, not a good time, one would have thought, for an English Celtic overture. For more than twenty years afterwards, Arnold wrote extensively on Irish affairs – on Home Rule, the Universities Bill, the Land Acts, Coercion and, most of all, on the failure of the English, Protestant, utilitarian, middle-class sytem to absorb the fiery, Irish, Catholic, imaginative, imprac-tical, child-like and yet passionate Celt. It was Thomas Davis rewritten for the Murdstones. Arnold strengthened his arguments with appeals to Burke, the great Irish founder of the best of English political thought. It is strange to see Burke readapted, by Arnold, John Morley, Stephen and, with some characteristically severe modifications, Lord Acton,[52] in the hope that he might solve or throw light upon the so-called Irish problem of the 1880s and 1890s, when his advice in the same decades of the previous century had been so totally ignored. Burke's thought was, nevertheless, reincorporated into Irish culture, most particularly by Arnold, in such a manner that its chief bearing upon the question of revolution was altered to include the problem of Ireland in as prominent a position as America, France and India had occupied. The Irish eighteenth and the Irish nineteenth century were rejoined more effectively by Arnold than by the great Irish historian Lecky, whose *History of Ireland in the Eighteenth Century* (5 vols, 1892, with five editions by 1909) and *The Leaders of Public Opinion in Ireland* (1871) devoted so much attention to the period between 1780 and O'Connell without giving any important emphasis to Burke. How-ever, with the Celtic revival beginning again after the shock of the Famine, Burke gained a new visibility. A great deal of what Yeats has to say about the Irish eighteenth century and its connection with the Celtic element in Irish history derives from Davis and Arnold.

Arnold's essays of 1878–81, 'Irish Catholicism and British Liberalism', 'The Incompatibles' and 'An Unregarded Irish Grievance', along with his Oxford lecture of 1867 and the anthology of Burke he edited in 1881, *Edmund Burke on Irish Affairs*, constitute his chief contribution to the Irish Revival. Provoked by Fenianism, he lapsed into Celticism. But he reaffirmed, in doing so, a neo-Burkian version of cultural nationalism as a philosophy designed to act as an alternative to and even a safeguard against revolutionary republicanism. This view became a conviction with Yeats, as indeed it had been with the entire Ascendancy tradition since Ferguson. Arnold could hardly imagine Ireland as constitutionally separate from Britain. For him, Home Rule was altogether too risky. What he sought was a series of healing measures from Westminster, elicited from a middle-class civilization which had been leavened by 'culture' and thus enabled to achieve the generosity of spirit which would allow the Irish their especial 'Celtic' difference. It was in some ways a noble, in some ways a naive attempt to rescue a situation which had begun to pass out of British control. After the death of Parnell in 1890, literature took up the running and, led by Yeats, attempted to create a new Irish literature in the English language, the cultural version of Home Rule.

Arnold's Irish essays coincided chronologically, but not in any other substantial way, with a strange *History of Ireland: The Heroic Period* (1878) and, in hot pursuit, the second volume, *Cuchulain and His Contemporaries*, by Standish James O'Grady, often assigned the title of Father of the Irish Revival. O'Grady, unabashed by his ignorance of the Irish language, decided that the tales surrounding Cuchulainn had 'a general historical credibility'. Although no one else had quite this capacity for literal belief in legendary material, O'Grady may be said to have given to his generation, in the figure of Cuchulainn, an archetype of literary and political heroism, which was to endure in the writings of Pearse and Yeats and in the imagination of the general public. In his book of essays, *The Story of Ireland* (1894), his description of the sky 'bright with strange lights and flames'[53] as Parnell's remains were lowered to the grave, initiated the Parnell legend in literature. As if that were not enough, he also launched a savage attack upon the futility of the landlord class in conspiring to bring about their own destruction, and asserted, in overheated prose, the need for aristocratic discipline to control and gain obedience from the unruly democratic mass of the Irish peasantry. This thesis, spelt out in his pamphlet *Tory-ism and the Tory Democracy* (1886), had a profound effect upon the anti-democratic and aristocratic theories of Yeats, blended, for dignity's sake, with the opinions of Burke. In O'Grady's political writings we hear the beginning of the long and furious lamentation for the extinction of the Ascendancy. In his more literary and historical work, we hear a renewal of the old claim that the Irish, for all their strife, share a cultural unity, although he is more specific than most of the revivalists in claiming that this is also a Biblical unity, shared by the modern Protestant and the pre-Norman Irish Church. The essential ground-theme of all his writings is that of a lonely heroism betrayed. That, branching into the accompanying threnody for the loss of a sublime moment in civilization, and its replacement by a squalid, money-counting mass society, completes the background of Yeats's social thought. O'Grady taught Yeats not to take the destruction of his class lying down. He is the Ascendancy partner to the Fenian Mitchel, who gave the same lesson to the victims of the Famine. From the disestablishment of the Irish Church in 1869 to Wyndham's Land Act of 1903, the descendants of Anglo-Irish landowners and clergymen fought to come to terms with the collapse of their traditional authority. In doing so, they became recognizably modern writers – George Moore, Douglas Hyde, Lady Gregory, Yeats and Synge.

After O'Grady, there was the Revival. Or, more accurately, there were two revivals, one literary and one political. They managed to stay distinct, without ever ceasing to be intimate. One kept appearing in the guise of the other. George Moore's witticism about his portrait (in *Ave*) of Douglas Hyde may serve as a parable for the relationship. When AE (George Russell) told Moore that his portrait of Hyde was unfair,

he replied that it was a case of Jekyll and Hyde, he had painted Hyde and Jekyll was coming on.[54]

Notes

1   Gerald Bullett, *Sydney Smith: A biography and a selection* (London, 1951), p. 224. The matching passage in Burke is in *Tracts relative to the Laws Against Popery in Ireland*, *Works* VI, p. 45.

2 *The Autobiography of Theobald Wolfe Tone*, ed. R. B. O'Brien, 2 vols (London, 1893), I, pp. 50–1.

3 *The Autobiography of William Carleton* (London, 1896; revised ed. 1968), Preface by Patrick Kavanagh, p. 37.

4 *The Collected Works of Samuel Taylor Coleridge; Essays on His Times*, ed. D. V. Erdman, 3 vols (London and Princeton, 1978), II, pp. 411–13; Robert Southey, 'On the Catholic Question' (essays of 1809, 1812, 1828), in *Essays Moral and Political*, 2 vols (London, 1832), II, pp. 263–443. These include references to Thomas Moore's *Memoirs of Captain Rock* (II, pp. 35–55). John Wilson Croker (1780–1857), *A Sketch of the Present State of Ireland Past and Present* (Dublin, 1808); *Essays on The Early Period of the French Revolution* (London, 1857). Croker provided the model for the characters of Conway Townshend Crawley in Lady Morgan's *Florence Macartny* (1819), of Rigby in Disraeli's *Coningsby* and of Wenham in Thackeray's *Vanity Fair*. Myron F. Brightfield, *John Wilson Croker* (London, 1940); Patrick Rafroidi, *Irish Literature in English: The Romantic Period (1789–1850)*, 2 vols (London, 1980), I, pp. 21–3; K. G. Feiling, *Sketches in Nineteenth Century Biography* (London, 1930), pp. 55–67, where it is said 'And party . . . sinks in Croker to that congealed, time-restricted dogmatism characteristic of the Irish Protestantism whence he rose'.

5 E. D. Snyder, *The Celtic Revival in English Literature, 1760–1800* (Cambridge, Mass., 1923); Lois Whitney, *Primitivism and the Idea of Progress in English Popular Literature of the Eighteenth Century* (Baltimore, 1934); Samuel S. Monk, *The Sublime: A Study of Critical Theories in Eighteenth Century England* (New York, 1935), pp. 119–21, 124–9; Rene Wellek, *The Rise of English Literary History* (Chapel Hill, 1941); Derick S. Thompson, *The Gaelic Sources of Macpherson's 'Ossian'* (Edinburgh and London, 1952); K. F. Gantz, 'Charlotte Brooke's *Reliques of Irish Poetry* and the Ossianic Controversy', *Studies in English* XX (1940), 137–56.

6 Norman Vance, 'Celts, Carthaginians and Constitutions: Anglo-Irish Literary Relations, 1780–1820', *Irish Historical Studies* XXII (1980), 216–30.

7 Quoted in Rafroidi, I, p. 164.

8 *Autobiography*, I, p. 97.

9 *The Letters of Thomas Moore*, ed. W. S. Dowden, 2 vols (Oxford, 1964), I, p. 116.

10 *The Complete Works of William Hazlitt*, ed. P. P. Howe, 21 vols (London, 1930), VII, p. 234.

11 *Letters*, I, p. 117.

12 For Griffin, see Thomas Flanagan, *The Irish Novelists, 1800–1850* (New York, 1959), p. 206; for Kickham, R. V. Comerford, *Charles J. Kickham* (Dublin, 1979), p. 190.

13   For accounts of these poets, see Robert Welch, *Irish Poetry from Moore to Yeats* (London, 1980); Patrick C. Power, *The Story of Anglo-Irish Poetry, 1800–1922* (Cork, 1967); Terence Brown, *Northern Voices: Poets from Ulster* (Dublin, 1975). For Moore, see *Poetical Works* (London, 1853–4 and Oxford, 1910); the best biographies are Howard Mumford Jones, *The Harp that Once* (New York, 1937), Miriam Allen de Ford, *Thomas Moore* (New York, 1967); H. H. Jordan, *Bolt Upright* (Salzburg, 1975); Terence de Vere White, *Tom Moore, the Irish Poet* (London, 1977). On translations, see Cathal G. Ó'Háinle, 'Towards the Revival, Some Translations of Irish Poetry: 1789–1897', in *Literature and the Changing Ireland*, ed. Peter Connolly (London and New Jersey, 1982), pp. 37–57. The best anthologies are by Geoffrey Taylor, *Irish Poets of the Nineteenth Century* (London, 1951) and Brendan Kennelly, *The Penguin Book of Irish Verse* (Harmondsworth, 1979). For further bibliographical details, see Rafroidi, II.

14   James Hardiman, *Irish Minstrelsy; or, Bardic Remains of Ireland with English Poetical Translations*, 2 vols (London, 1831), I, p. v.

15   For listings, see Rafroidi, II, pp. 161–8.

16   M. C. Ferguson, *Sir Samuel Ferguson in the Ireland of his Day*, 2 vols (Edinburgh and London, 1896), I, p. 47; quoted in Frank O'Connor, *The Backward Look: A Survey of Irish Literature* (London, 1967), p. 150.

17   *Dublin University Magazine* 2 (1833), p. 588.

18   Taylor, *Irish Poets of the Nineteenth Century*, p. 124.

19   idem, p. 125.

20   Quoted by Welch, *Irish Poetry from Moore to Yeats*, p. 127.

21   Kerby A. Miller, with Bruce Boling and David N. Doyle, 'Emigrants and Exiles: Irish Cultures and Irish Emigration to North America, 1790–1822', *Irish Historical Studies* XXII (September, 1980), 97–125.

22   Preface to *Reliques of Irish Jacobite Poetry* (Dublin, 1844).

23   Gearóid Ó'Tuathaig, *Ireland Before the Famine, 1798–1848* (Dublin, 1972), especially pp. 226–7.

24   *Jail Journal* (Dublin, 1913), p. 357.

25   *The Last Conquest of Ireland (Perhaps)* (London, 1860), p. 220.

26   On this and related topics, see Vivian Mercier, 'Victorian Evangelicalism and the Anglo-Irish Literary Revival', in *Literature and the Changing Ireland*, pp. 59–102.

27   *History of Ireland in the Eighteenth Century*, 5 vols (London, 1909 ed.), III, p. 418.

28   Thomas Davis, *Prose Writings: Essays on Ireland, p. xiii.*

29   Malcolm Brown, *The Politics of Irish Literature from Thomas Davis to W. B. Yeats* (Seattle, 1972), p. 93.

30   *Prose Writings*, 'The Library of Ireland', p. 225.

31 *Reliques of Irish Poetry* (London, 1789), p. viii.
32 *Prose Writings*, pp. 225–6.
33 *Memoirs*, ed. D. Donoghue (London, 1972), p. 184.
34 *The Critical Writings*, ed. E. Mason and R. Ellmann (New York, 1965), pp. 154–74.
35 Georges-Denis Zimmermann, *Songs of Irish Rebellion: Political Street Ballads and Rebel Songs 1780–1900* (Geneva, 1966); Colin Meir, *The Ballads and Songs of W. B. Yeats: The Anglo-Irish Heritage in Subject and Style* (New York, 1974); Yeats, 'Popular Ballad Poetry in Ireland', in *Uncollected Prose*, ed. J. P. Frayne (New York, 1970), p. 147.
36 *The Spirit of the Nation* (Dublin, 1882), p. 2.
37 Quoted by Malcolm Brown, *The Politics of Irish Literature*, p. 64.
38 J. H. Andrews, *A Paper Landscape* (Oxford, 1979).
39 For a first-hand account, see W. Steuart Trench, *Realities of Irish Life* (2nd ed., London, 1869), especially Chs VII and VIII.
40 Marx Engels, *Selected Correspondence, 1846–95* (London, 1934), pp. 92–4.
41 *The Last Conquest of Ireland (Perhaps)*, p. 67.
42 *Critical Writings*, p. 179.
43 idem, p. 186.
44 Quoted in Mary Helen Thuente, *W. B. Yeats and Irish Folklore* (Dublin, 1980), p. 159; see also pp. 16–19.
45 Taylor, p. 248.
46 idem, p. 223.
47 idem, pp. 249–50.
48 idem, pp. 219–20.
49 idem, p. 217.
50 *Critical Writings*, p. 179.
51 idem, p. 179.
52 R. H. Super (ed.), *The Complete Prose Works of Matthew Arnold*, 10 vols (Ann Arbor, 1968–73), III, IV, IX; John Morley, *Burke* (London, 1879); Fitzjames Stephen, *Horae Sabbaticae*, 3 vols (London, 1892), III, pp. 114–15; my 'Lord Acton and Edmund Burke', *Journal of the History of Ideas* XXXIII, no. 2 (April–June, 1972), 325–35.
53 *The Story of Ireland*, pp. 211–12.
54 Susan Mitchell, *George Moore* (Dublin, 1916), p. 83.

4 Nineteenth-century fiction

Two women, Maria Edgeworth and Lady Morgan, dominate Irish fiction in the first two decades of the nineteenth century. Edgeworth's four Irish novels – *Castle Rackrent* (1800), *Ennui* (1809), *The Absentee* (1812) and *Ormond* (1817) – provide the first serious attempt in fiction to analyse and recommend improvements for Irish society as it was, after the Act of Union in 1800 had extinguished the bright hopes associated with the frail parliamentary independence of 1782 and the dark fears arising from the fierce rebellion of 1798. The price to be paid for the Union with Great Britain was to be Catholic Emancipation. Promised by the British Prime Minister Pitt, it was refused by George III and successive administrations, until it was won by Daniel O'Connell in 1829 after a long campaign of disciplined pressure, exercised through mass meetings and the increasingly organized power of the Catholic clergy. The measure, which would have been politically more effective had it been freely given, had the unforeseen consequence of bringing into being the powerful Catholic nation, which felt little gratitude for what it had been forced to win for itself. Between the Union and Emancipation, therefore, the Protestant Ascendancy lost its last chance to retain political leadership in Ireland. Maria Edgeworth attempted to show how that leadership could have been preserved; Lady Morgan unwittingly demonstrated in her novels why it could not have been. Both of them finally despaired of writing about the different Ireland that emerged after 1829. Yet each bore witness to the fact that the writing of Irish fiction, like the writing of Irish history in the same period, was inescapably bound up with the increasingly partisan debate about the condition of Ireland and the means of improving it. Lady Morgan's four Irish novels – *The Wild Irish Girl* (1806), *O'Donnel: A National Tale* (1814), *Florence Macarthy: An Irish Tale* (1819) and *The O'Briens and the O'Flahertys: A National Tale* (1827) – form a startling contrast to Edgeworth's. Her incorrigibly romantic Ireland of wild landscapes, harps, round towers and the like belongs to the world of the Celtic revival, while Edgeworth's Ireland is a dilapidated province desperately in need of the practical improvements of the Enlightenment. The contrast is real and is further reinforced by the fact that Edgeworth was by far the greater artist of the two. She was the first novelist to find an effective means of representing in fiction the subjugation of the individual to social forces. She achieved in the novel what Mme de Stael achieved in her essays and discursive writings, the absorption into literature of the ideas of the great Enlightenment thinkers on the nature of social formations – Montesquieu, Adam Smith, Adam Ferguson, John Miller and Thomas Reid.[1] As a novelist, however, Mme de Stael was closer in *Corinne* (1802) and *Delphine* (1807) to Lady Morgan. In both, the concentration upon the depiction of a romantic heroine (or hero) against a tempestuous background, precludes the possibility of their showing how the individual is incorporated into inherited social and economic systems. The romantic hero found his home in poetry, not in the novel. Sir Walter Scott, profoundly impressed by *The Absentee*, followed in Maria Edgeworth's footsteps by portraying a whole community, hitherto ignored or the object of cariacture and antipathy, in its historical reality as reflected through a relatively colourless central character. As a consequence, ancillary groups or characters are often more vividly represented, because they are the object of observation. The observer is always to some degree detached, a commentator as well as a participant.

Yet this is precisely what we do not find in *Castle Rackrent*, the first of Edgeworth's Irish tales. As a tale, it belongs to a specific genre, perfected in the eighteenth century by Voltaire, Dr Johnson and Marmontel – that of the philosophic fable, which is neither novel nor short story but more given than either to didactic illustration. The problem with *Rackrent* is that there has been much dispute about what is being illustrated. Therefore, as a tale, it is not effective. The narrator, Thady M'Quirk, recounts the story of the ruin of the Rackrent family over four generations. He is illiterate, so his story is dictated to the 'Editor', a device for the presentation of dialect speech which Edgeworth made popular. Thady is feudally loyal to his useless masters, whose only skill is in self-destruction – 'Sir Patrick by drink, Sir Murtagh by law, Sir Kit by gambling, and Sir Condy, in the amplest portrait of all, by the spendthrift life of politics'.[2] His final loyalty to Sir Condy, the most attractive of the quartet, forces him to choose his master over his son, Jason,

Attorney Quirk, who has assumed control of the Rackrent property with that silent rapacity characteristic of the land agent or middleman much used by absentee or feckless landlords in the administration of their Irish estates. The tale is set in the eighteenth century, in the years before the achievement of parliamentary independence in 1782. After that, not much else is certain, except that Thady's voice is a new one in fiction. He has more than a dialect, he has a style – insinuating, colourful and agreeable. But is it also ironic? Is Thady a pseudo-simpleton, taking a degree of pleasure in telling the tale of Ascendancy ruin and the rise of the Irish middle class, represented by his son Jason of whom he pretends to disapprove? If this reading is dismissed, it can quickly be replaced by the more sombre view of the tale as a requiem for the Ascendancy, to which Maria Edgeworth belonged and for which the Union was the final stroke of doom. It could even be a lament for the passing of that ramshackle but warm-hearted Ireland of the early century, replaced now by the more sober and duller society that was still in a state of shock after 1798 and the Union. Or, finally, and perhaps most persuasively, *Rackrent* is the aggressive prelude to Edgeworth's later novels on Ireland, a demonstration of the ruin which an irresponsible aristocracy brings upon itself and upon its dependents. This is a moral judgement not accessible to Thady, who is, bluntly, too stupid and blinded by his pathetic loyalty, to see the significance of the tale he tells. Certainly, Edgeworth's later work supports this last reading, although the other readings are important too in their readiness to see in this work a useful point of origin for the representation of modern Ireland in fiction. The meaning of the relationship between landlord and peasant may be a matter of dispute, but its centrality is not. In that respect, *Rackrent* does point towards the future, even though it is also concerned to dismiss an unfortunate past.[3]

Maria Edgeworth introduced the English public to the Irish problem even more effectively than Arthur Young's brilliant survey, *Tour in Ireland* (1780). Because she was writing fiction in an age which still thought of novels as faintly disreputable and unreliable, she went to some pains to affirm that she was relaying the truth, however improbable it might seem to a non-Irish audience:

. . . to those who are totally unacquainted with Ireland, the following Memoirs will perhaps be scarcely intelligible, or probably they may appear perfectly incredible.[4]

This note is to be heard time and again throughout the century in Irish fiction, even in those numerous forms of memoir, which were not, consciously at least, offered as fiction. In the preface to *The Black Prophet* (1847), William Carleton feels bound to assure his audience that his account of famine conditions is not exaggerated:

. . . the reader – especially if he is English or Scotch – may rest assured that the author has not at all coloured beyond the truth.[5]

W. S. Trench, a land agent anxious to give the English public some idea of the problems faced by an improving landlord and some hope that Ireland is 'not altogether unmanageable', prefaces his *Realities of Irish Life* (1868) with the comment that

. . . it has been my lot to live surrounded by a kind of poetic turbulence and almost romantic violence, which I believe could scarcely belong to real life in any other country in the world.[6]

The examples could be multiplied. But, along with this problem of the incredulous audience, went another – the presentation of the Irish, especially the Catholic Irish, as a people deserving sympathy and help. Maria Edgeworth, as part of her educational enterprise to both the Irish and English, wished to demonstrate that the Irish needed justice and responsible government so that they might become more recognizably 'civil', inhabitants of the modern world of industrial Britain rather than the eccentric remains of an out-moded past. She therefore tended to avail of the stereotyped view of the vivacious, endearingly child-like Irish, in order to arouse sym-pathy on their behalf. But in doing so, she allowed Celtic Ireland to intrude upon her fiction and was therefore never quite able to distance her work from that vast body of writing on the Irish national character, its habits, inclinations, tendencies, customs, rites and its peculiar essence, which casts its apologetic shadow over the literature of this century. Still, she should be rescued from the bondage of too close an association with Lady Morgan and the Catholic novelists of the 1820–50 period.

For Edgeworth is too pragmatic to be persuaded by the almost metaphysical appeal of the idea of national character, which seduced so many of her English and Irish compatriots. As a novelist, she had enough problems to go on with. She had to persuade a disbelieving audience of the truth of Irish conditions; she had to advocate a means to their improvement by allocating responsibility for their creation, among the Protestant Ascendancy, Orange bigots and the Government in London, as well as the Catholic peasantry themselves, though to a lesser degree, since they were the victims of the situation. The representation of daily life was a much more fraught issue for her than for someone like Jane Austen. English commentators, like Coleridge and Southey, and later, Carlyle and de Quincey, were ready to espouse the notion of an Irish national character which was degraded and at the same time, as de Quincey put it, full of 'a spirit of fiery misrepresentation'.[7] It was hard to believe what passed for reality in Ireland, especially if the reporter was Irish and therefore untrustworthy. The untrustworthiness was often confirmed for the English reader by any attempt to blame or even cast in a disobliging light the vagaries of English misrule or cruelty. National character was a perfect escape hatch for those who found the condition of Ireland intractable and would take no responsibility for it. At the same time, it was appealing for those who wanted to exploit Irish difference – as a romantic race – for an English audience. Yet it was also a serious idea, based on the conviction, which Burke had promoted more effectively than anyone else in recent history, that the character of a race was formed by the conditions in which it had developed, the customs to which it had adhered, the mentality which it had inherited. The transition from the analysis of a society to the stereotyping or exploitation of it was rapid in those 'national' novels, which became so popular in the early nineteenth century in Ireland and in Scotland (with Scott and John Galt). For the novelist who subscribed to this idea in any of its forms, the problem of representation was severe, largely because the possibility of misrepresentation was so easy. If the 'people' were to be represented by someone not of them for a foreign audience, and if their situation was an extreme one, the novelist, who was of and not of the people, was in a politically and aesthetically difficult, if not perilous, position. Perhaps only Walter Scott and Turgenev could be said to have mastered it, and both of them claimed to have learned much from Maria Edgeworth.

Yet the 'national' novel, so-called, retains its early intimacy with the didactic tale and Edgeworth set the precedent for this. From the 1820s, Ireland produced a sub-genre of memoirs, sketches, tales, legends, all of which were devoted to the recording of the hitherto occluded life of the Irish peasantry and many of which did so in an antiquarian spirit, setting down what they feared would soon be lost forever. These were sometimes almost indistinguishable from Irish fiction, both in purpose and quality. Among many examples, one could select Gerald Griffin's *Tales of the Munster Festivals* (1827), *Tales of the O'Hara Family* in the same year by the Banim brothers, Crofton Croker's *Fairy Legends and Traditions of the South of Ireland*, Eyre Evans Crowe's *Today In Ireland*, both of 1825, Cesar Otway's *Sketches in Ireland* (1827), Mrs A. M. Hall's *Sketches of Irish Character* (1829) and, later, Sir William Wilde's *Irish Popular Superstitions* (1852), in the preface to which he declared that, 'Nothing contributes more to uproot superstitious rites and forms than to print them'.[8] The recording of oral tradition certainly alters or ends it, but most of these works are impelled by the desire to give the audience a last glimpse of a dying Gaelic civilization which, in its new printed version, resumes a new species of existence as Celtic Ireland. As the didactic intent which Edgeworth had kept pre-eminent – both in her *Moral Tales for Young People* (1801) and even in her *Essay on Irish Bulls* (1802) – began to give way before the antiquarian or nostalgic spirit, the tale became less like the philosophic fable or *conte* of the eighteenth century, and more a part of the folklore record. However, in the hands of an artist, it could, so to speak, change direction and become more akin to its descendant, the modern short story. Carleton, in his *Traits and Stories of the Irish Peasantry* (1830–3), shows the short story emerging from the original shell of the tale. It may be that the popularity and success of the short story in modern Ireland has a foundation in the blending of the moral tale with the folklorish elements collected as evidence of the forever elusive national character of the forever vanishing Irish. Maria Edgeworth's role in this process is seminal.

But in *Ennui* and *The Absentee*, her will to educate may be felt to have turned potentially brilliant stories into treatises, which unreservedly recommend Irish landlords to return to their estates in Ireland and forgo the second-rate life of absenteeism in England. In *Ennui*, the Irish-born hero Lord Glenthorn does return to Ireland in a state of vacuous boredom and there undergoes an education in his responsibilities at the hands of his agent, a Scotsman, M'Leod, who is something of a cross between Adam Smith in his ideas and James Mill in his charm. Opposition to the new M'Leod scheme of improvement is provided by the local squire-bigot, Hardcastle. The year is 1798 and Glenthorn is improbably involved in the rebellion, gains a glorious reputation for capturing a band of rebels and then discovers that he is not the rightful heir to the property after all. His

Irish nurse turns out to be his real mother, but the newly discovered blood bond between them cannot overcome the cultural differences which their different ways of life have created. Glenthorn, having finally been educated into the problems of Irish life, having given up the useless life of the absentee gentleman for the useful life of a professional and expert improver, is at the end of all forced to retire to England, and the great ancestral house is burned down by its new Irish peasant owner. The reader is left to wonder if this tale is a treatise on the benefits of educated responsibility or a fable about their inapplicability to the Irish situation. *The Absentee*, less celebrated but possibly finer than *Castle Rackrent*, raises no such doubts. It tells the story of young Lord Colambre, the son of the absentee landlord Lord Clonbrony and his giddy wife, who returns incognito to his Irish estates to redeem them from the ramshackle mess, to which they have been reduced by grasping agents, and remodel them on the pattern laid down by Burke, who is that rare specimen, an honest and industrious agent. Colambre, ashamed of the spectacle presented by his mother in London, where she has repaired to forget her accent and her responsibilities together, is given a quick course in Irish history after the Union by a Dublin friend, Sir James Brooke.[9] This is to reassure him that Dublin and Ireland in general have recovered from the shock of the constitutional revolution. Thus, in these three works, Edgeworth is careful to associate the story with crucial moments in recent Irish history – the period before 1782, the rebellion of 1798, the Act of Union in 1800 – and to suggest that the recovery from these crises can be achieved through a programme of enlightened leadership on the part of the landed gentry, pursued for their own benefit and for that of the peasantry.

In her last Irish novel, *Ormond* (1817), the young hero of the title, orphaned and dispossessed of his property at birth, is faced with a choice between three modes of life, which represent Edgeworth's vision of the three kinds of leadership available to Ireland. Two of these are attractive but delinquent. Ormond's uncle Ulick O'Shane, a corrupt politician and a Rackrent type, belongs to the sophisticated urban world of the Anglo-Irish of the eighteenth century. His brother, Corny O'Shane, King of the Black Islands, (anticipated by the sketch of Count O'Halloran in *The Absentee*) is in some ways a noble and in other ways an absurd remnant of the old Gaelic order. Neither can offer Ormond or Ireland a future. The best hope for that lies with the Annaly family, the very epitome of

English steadiness and responsibility. Ormond marries the Annaly daughter, Florence, and inherits King Corny's position as ruler and owner of the Black Islands. The Anglo-Irish, the Gaelic and the English elements are thus reconciled in a dapper conclusion. As always, the Edgeworth hero receives an education which helps to extricate him from the past and prepare him for the future. Yet Ormond's growth as an individual is much less programmatic than that of Glenthorn or Colambre. He grows up to become a leader after serving his apprenticeship to the idea of being led.

Leadership is the preoccupation of these novels. The Protestant landlords in their shattered estates, the Catholic aristocrats in their Gaelic time-warp, represent to the peasantry an idea of leadership which has never been embodied in action. Thady M'Quirk in *Castle Rackrent* may be said to insist on the reality of the idea in order to find something worthy of his devotion. His peculiar attraction, though, is scarcely capable of surviving the repellent aspects of his personality. He is a character only a hairsbreadth removed from caricature. Indeed, most of Edgeworth's people are in this condition. Her utilitarians tend to be as prescribed as her peasants. She observes, although she does not respond very interestingly to the observation, that all classes and types behave in a highly histrionic fashion. They are real in so far as they are close to the fulfilling of a stereotype. In that respect, she not only differs from, say, Jane Austen, but points up a difference between the English and the Irish novel at that time (and later). In the Irish colonial situation there was an irresistible temptation to impersonate the idea of oneself which was entertained by others. Landlord or peasant, English improver or Gaelic remnant, played out roles ascribed to them by a situation which had robbed them of the central sense of responsibility, by effectively denying them basic executive power. Thus it was very Irish to be irresponsible and very English to be responsible and very typical of the English–Irish confrontation to find that neither one could learn from or teach the other. This was a paradigm for much of the century's voluminous writings on the issue. It was a stylized representation of a powerless condition.

The impersonation was not confined to novels. Sydney Owenson, later Lady Morgan (1776–1859), was the daughter of an actor-manager who had successfully portrayed the eighteenth-century stage-Irishman in the course of an undistinguished theatrical career. His daughter far outdid him, but in the new Romantic vein, after the success of her first novel, *The Wild Irish Girl* (1806), a work deficient in almost everything a novel should have, except success. She adopted the name, dress and musical inclinations of the heroine of her novel and became for a time the Glorvina of the blue cloak and pedal harp of the London drawing rooms. *The Wild Irish Girl* tells the story of the discovery by a young man, Mortimer, the son of an absentee landlord, of the Romantic Ireland of stormy landscapes, Gaelic chieftains, ruined castles and raging seas, the orchestral accompaniment to Glorvina's harp concerto. He vows to bring justice and reconciliation to the encounter between the Hibernian and the English civilizations, by restoring property and titles to the old dispensation by the simple expedient of marrying into it, thereby retaining for himself that which he was simultaneously restoring to others. This feat achieved, Ireland belongs again to dispossessor and dispossessed, a romantic kingdom united and part of the United Kingdom. The attraction of this misty resolution for an English audience is obvious but, more importantly, it worked its charm on the liberal Protestant Irish Whigs, who saw in Catholic Emancipation the completion of the programme of the Protestant parliament of 1782, the final act of conciliation of the Catholics, who would be thereby brought in from the penal cold to the warm glow of the constitutional fireside. This was Lady Morgan's central constituency and her novels were viewed as the most attractive version of its national aspirations. She was subtler than Maria Edgeworth in one respect; she knew, with intimacy, the various shades of Protestant Ireland's complex attitudes and was able to offer Emancipation as a reparation on the part of the Irish Protestant Whigs for the oppressions of the Irish Protestant Tories. Yet, in doing so, she had to insist on the loyalty of the Irish Catholics to the British Crown and, by extension, to the security of the existing land settlement. For her, a measure of constitutional justice was sufficient repayment. Anything more than that would mean rebellion or revolution. So *O'Donnel* (1814) transmutes the story of the sixteenth-century rebel against Elizabeth into a contemporary account of the unjust treatment of his descendant, Roderick O'Donnel, who has offered his services to the English King and been spurned. The fair-minded English Whig, Lord Glentworth, takes up his cause. Similarly in *Florence Macarthy*, the final, if improbable, marriage between Fitzwalter and Lady Clancare is an allegorical reconciliation of the Norman and the Gael, bonded together against the grasping and disreputable Crawleys. The Gaelic Macarthy family supplies the Catholic sanction to the Protestant leadership provided by Fitzwalter. The restless peasantry are assumed to acquiesce in this, their legendary devotion to effective mastery appeased. However, in *The O'Briens and the O'Flahertys* (1827), the possibility of reconciliation has gone. This remarkable novel reveals the hopeless plight of Murrough O'Brien, the son of a father in whom historical loyalties and historical betrayals have conspired to produce insanity and a plot for a Catholic holy war against everything English and Protestant in Ireland. Seeking for an alternative to this scheme, Murrough espouses the Protestant Whig cause of Grattan, but that is crushed; then he turns to the more radical cause of the United Irishmen, but 1798 puts an end to that; finally he departs for Napoleonic France and a military career apart from Ireland and its intractable despairs and dreams. Lady Morgan, like Maria Edgeworth before her, found it impossible to write about the new Ireland that had emerged under Daniel O'Connell, the King of the Beggars, the creator of a politicized Catholicism, for which Emancipation was only the beginning, not the end, of the Irish historical destiny. Only in her last novel did Lady Morgan show any awareness of the unreality of her Whig dream of reconciliation. All the trappings of her antiquarian nationalism were preserved for the rest of the century, but her inability to recognize until it was too late the anachronistic nature of her political convictions left her with no choice but the traditional one of exile and bitterness.

Those Irish Protestant Tory writers who attacked Lady Morgan in the English reviews lived lives of exile in London until the founding of the *Dublin University Magazine* in 1833 gave the Protestant intelligentsia a new focus and new heart. But men like John Wilson Croker, the notoriously venomous reviewer of the *Quarterly Review* and the greatest English-speaking expert on the French Revolution he abhorred, were inclined to pursue Lady Morgan's eccentric versions of Irish history and her even more eccentric ideas of what constituted a novel with an implacable contempt, because they recognized that she was unwittingly contributing to a nationalism which would exclude both her and them from the new Catholic Ireland and from the affections of the English public. However, the most remarkable form of exile was the internal version represented by Charles Robert Maturin (1780–1824), the first of the Irish Gothic novelists. He first came to attention with his deliberate imitations of Lady Morgan, *The Wild Irish Boy* (1808) and *The Milesian Chief* (1812), although it was his *Melmoth the Wanderer* (1820), which finally established his reputation. His vein of romantic rapture, modified by the occasional requirements of plot, allows him to display every possible feature of the Romantic criminal personality. All his heroes are figures of extraordinary powers, which are aborted by the effects of demonic crime. Orazio in his first novel *The Fatal Revenge* (1807), Deloraine in *The Wild Irish Boy*, Connal and Desmond, the brothers in *The Milesian Chief*, and Melmoth are all finally ruined, the latter in true Faustian fashion for the sale of his soul to the devil in return for a prolonged life. The ruins in Maturin's wild Irish landscapes are more menacing than anything in Lady Morgan. They are emblems of an alienation and a failure, which the destitution of the peasantry intensifies. Maturin was an ordained minister and his hatred of Catholicism helps to explain the sense of homelessness which pervades his writings. In 1824 he preached *Five Sermons on the Errors of the Roman Catholic Church*, in which he described the degradation of Catholic countries like Ireland, Italy, Spain and Portugal as the inevitable consequence of a religion which destroyed itself as surely as it destroyed civil life. 'She meant to be an assassin, but she becomes a suicide.'[10] Maturin's ruins are the evacuated houses of Protestant civilization blighted by an environing and enervating Catholicism; his Romantic heroes are Irish Protestants in an Irish Catholic world which they repudiate and by which they are repudiated. A less melodramatic but a more haunting sense of estrangement issues from the work of the greatest of Irish Gothic writers, Joseph Sheridan Le Fanu (1814–73). Le Fanu was also a man who felt increasingly excluded from Ireland by the triumphs of O'Connell, by Emancipation, the Tithe War of the early thirties, the Famine, the rise of Fenianism. His most important attempt at writing a novel of reconciliation between Protestant and Catholic is *The Cock and Anchor* (1845), but it is in *Uncle Silas* (1864) that the sense of a terrifying isolation within a faintly disguised English version of the Irish Big House is given its most memorable formulation. Irish Gothic establishes the abiding presence in the latter part of the century of the dilapidated Ascendancy house, in which the former masters are increasingly isolated from the surrounding tenantry and reduced, politically and economically, to a state of psychic exhaustion.[11] Charles Lever's *The Martins of Cro'Martin* (1856), George Moore's *A Drama in Muslin* (1886) and *The Real Charlotte* (1894) by Somerville and Ross mark stages in a decline of which Le Fanu's work is the most extreme and introverted representation. Thus the dream of Protestant leadership, initiated by Maria Edgeworth and

Lady Morgan, came to a tragic ending. Standish O'Grady was to write its bitter obituary (in *The Crisis in Ireland* (1882), *Toryism and the Tory Democracy* (1886) and in his editorials for his newspaper the *Kilkenny Moderator* (1898–1901)), while Yeats was to provide it with a new life in his poetry after 1913.

In the meantime, the Catholic middle class, released from the restrictions of the Penal Laws, was making its way into literature. Its contribution in fiction was at first determined by the assumptions of Edgeworth's and Lady Morgan's fiction. These included the need to provide Ireland with an effective leadership, to grant Catholics full civil rights under the constitution, to heal old wounds and reconcile the separated factions and to sponsor the idea that the Irish had a specific national character, which needed to be explained to an English audience. It is ironic that, for all the efforts of Irish fiction, Irish political writing and the appointment of '114 commissions and 60 select committees to investigate Irish affairs' by Parliament between 1810 and 1833,[12] the English public remained invincibly ignorant of the country's circumstances and history. Maria Edgeworth, at the beginning of the century, had reservations about the possibility of the Irish ever becoming Anglicized at all. By the end of the century it had been decided that, in order to rediscover their identity, about which they were alarmingly negligent, the Irish would have to become de-Anglicized. It might therefore be argued that the Irish had not been successful in advocating any of the causes or realizing any of the assumptions listed above, except for one. That exception was the idea of Irish national character, its integrity enhanced by a century of apologetic and exploitative writing.

One of the best known and most loved of the Catholic writers was Gerald Griffin (1803–40), whose most important novel, *The Collegians* (1829), is full of descriptions of 'national' characteristics. He uses the word quite regularly as an epithet. Mr Daly has 'a national predilection' for Irish history; Lowry Looby has 'the national talent for adroit flattery'; Doctor Leake has 'a national turn of character'; Mrs Cregan 'possessed all the national warmth of temperament and liveliness of feeling'.[13] In addition, there are long disquisitions on the manners of Irish gentlemen and the habits of the Irish peasantry, the qualities of mountainy men, middlemen and so on. Yet these folklorish traces and the display of documentary expertise find their justification in the frequent allusions to the 'English reader', to whom the novel is addressed and for whom it is presented as, at once, an apologia for Irish Catholics and Catholic Emancipation and a thrilling Romantic-Irish tale of violence and extreme passion. Griffin's heavily upholstered prose indicates his desire to achieve perfect respectability in the eyes of his English audience. He translates everything for that audience's benefit. He places his story in the past – again before 1782 – to draw the sting from the contemporaneity of the novel. He espouses the cause of the respectable and civilized Daly family against that of the hard-drinking, duelling, rapscallion Cregans and Connollys of the small gentry – the 'half-sirs' as they were called in Ireland. In fact, he presents what is always lacking in Maria Edgeworth – an alternative ruling class for post-Union Ireland, disguised with the help of references to Goldsmith and Sheridan, as an eighteenth-century formation long ignored by the English.

Such, in happier days than ours, was the life of a Munster farmer. Indeed, the word is ill adapted to convey to an English reader an idea of the class of persons whom it is intended to designate, for they were and are, in mind and education, far superior to persons who occupy that rank in other countries. Opprobrious as the term 'middle-man' has been rendered in our own time, it is certain that the original formation of the sept was both natural and beneficial. When the country was deserted by its gentry, a general promotion of one grade took place among those who remained at home. The farmers became gentlemen and the labourers became farmers, the former assuming, together with the station and influence, the quick and honourable spirit, the love of pleasure, and the feudal authority, which distinguished their aristocratic archetypes, while the humbler classes looked up to them for advice and assistance, with the same feeling of respect and of dependence which they had once entertained for the actual proprietors of the soil. The covetousness of landlords themselves, in selling leases to the highest bidder, without any inquiry into his character or fortune, first tended to throw imputations on this respectable and useful body of men, which in progress of time swelled into a popular outcry, and ended in an act of the legislature for their gradual extirpation. There are few now on that class as prosperous, or many as intelligent and high-principled, as Mr. Daly.[14]

Griffin is speaking here of the economic boom of the 1770s and 1780s, from which landlords and middlemen profited handsomely. Things were certainly different in the 1820s. But the pastoralism of this passage and of the whole novel had a powerful appeal for many readers. It implied a background of security and ease, against which the ominous present could be judged. In 1878, Charles Kickham's *Knocknagow*, a rewriting, in many respects, of *The Collegians*, became the most loved and read of all Irish novels by creating a similar Munster background of pastoral quiet and traditional activity, very much out of keeping with the political conditions of that year.[15]

At the centre of Griffin's novel lies a very conventional opposition. On the one hand, there is Kyrle Daly, a respectable young gentleman of regular habits, moderate disposition and equable temperament. On the other, there is Hardress Cregan, his friend, a passionate and romantic figure, beloved by the peasantry for his headlong generosity and flaring temper. He is the Natural man confronted by Civil man. The disreputable streak in his character, family and class – Cregan is a Protestant gentleman – exposes itself in his elopement with a beautiful young peasant girl, Eily O'Connor, his abandonment and eventually his murder of her, a process brought on by his increasing infatuation for Ann Chute, a young woman of his own standing in society. Kyrle loves Ann and is rejected; at first Hardress ignores her, and is loved. Although Hardress is eventually arrested for the crime and dies on his way to penal exile, and Kyrle marries Ann, the power of the story is sadly compromised by the ready-made conclusion. In a repetition of the problem which lay at the heart of Maria Edgeworth's fiction, we are presented with a social and political reading which favours Kyrle Daly and all that he represents and a sharply realized personal crisis which commits our sympathy and attention to Hardress Cregan. The tragedy of young Cregan, like that of the Rackrents, so attracts us that we cannot view those who replace him or them with much warmth. This goes against the grain of what Griffin insistently preaches. There are several set pieces, in which the two young men debate the pros and cons of the ordered against the natural life. Kyrle has the better of these interpolated discussions, but he has much the worse of the dramatic contest between his own patient and dull goodness and Hardess's violent paroxysms of guilt and winning social manners. The Natural man, we find, is the true aristocrat; Civil man is the true bourgeois. Despite the sermons, despite the political anxieties of the novel, the aristocrat – decayed and corrupt as he is – is much the more interesting. The memorable minor figures – the foolish but warm-hearted Lowry Looby, the proud and eloquent Myles of the Ponies, the Amazonian Poll Naughten and the sinister-pathetic hunchback, Danny Mann – belong more naturally to Cregan's disorderly, untamed world than to that of the self-consciously respectable Dalys. They have sent their son to Trinity College. This is a rare and deliberate decision for Irish Catholics of the time. Hardress goes there as of right. As Thomas Flanagan has pointed out, the very pictures on the walls of their living room are carefully chosen to enhance their claims to social respectability, even though this is so far removed from their natural political loyalties that the effect is incongruous and grotesque.[16] Griffin seems to indicate that the marriage of Kyrle Daly to Ann Chute can stand for the reconciliation of Ascendancy and Catholic traditions. With the brutality of the ruling class purged away and the violence of the peasantry properly chastened, the remaining best of both traditions can get on with managing the country. But it is an extremely pallid hope. With the old Ascendancy and the peasantry, which was so curiously allied to it in spirit, there goes everything that is vital. The Dalys are altogether too deferential and respectable to be imagined as leaders of anything. They are like Maria Edgeworth's absentee landlords returning to their estates – illusory figures who, because they have become separated from historical actuality, never can achieve the presence of individuals. The English reader, to whom Griffin so assiduously addressed himself, could easily be forgiven for not taking Kyrle Daly's Catholic Ireland too seriously. Instead, the melodramatic element in the novel took precedence over the political. *The Collegians* became famous all over again in Boucicault's stage adaptation, *The Colleen Bawn* (1860), and Benedict's famous opera, *The Lily of Killarney* (1862). With these transmutations, it became nothing more than the caricature of Romantic-Irish lore, which doomed so many Irish works to popularity in the nineteenth century.

Between 1825 and 1830, the Catholic middle classes of Ireland found their voices in fiction as well as in politics. *The Collegians*, however, rendered the violence and instability of life in Ireland in such a way that these features did not entirely destroy the enchanted, pastoral quality of the story. The best work of the Banim brothers, but most particularly that of John Banim, is guiltless of such idealization. Indeed, after the first two series of *Tales by the O'Hara Family* in 1825 and 1826, John's work, although still influenced by the intimate and circumstantial tone and detail contributed by his brother Michael, becomes increasingly unable to find any accommodation between the factions of the Irish society he portrays. Apart from some of the Tales themselves – *John Doe* and

The Nowlans – his most important works are *The Boyne Water* (1826) and *The Anglo-Irish of the Nineteenth Century* (1828). The malady of history is a deep-seated disease in his fiction. In *The Nowlans*, the true centre of the story is the plight of John Nowlan, a young man whose training, sensibility and beliefs are irredeemably wounded by his experiences in the ramshackle, sexually promiscuous, hard-drinking household of his doltish uncle Aby. There he meets his young cousin, Maggy Nowlan, an illegitimate child of his uncle's. Sexually attracted to her, he resists the temptation and returns to his studies for the priesthood. But he has been maimed by the experience. Banim surrounds it with an account of the various sectarian, economic and political pressures which encompassed a Catholic family of the time, all of them inflamed by the mounting campaigns for Catholic Emancipation and the counteracting Protestant evangelical 'New Reformation' movement of the 1820s. The plot becomes absurdly melodramatic. John runs away with Letty Adams, the daughter of a prosperous Protestant of pronounced anti-Catholic views. After a bleak stay in Protestant lodgings in Dublin, John loses his teaching post, Letty dies and their innocent marriage comes to an end in the harrowing poverty and misery so often witnessed at Irish roadsides. The matching plot, involving the forced marriage of John's sister Peggy to Letty's nefarious brother, Frank, is no more than a piece of machinery. Nowlan's terrible plight is surrendered in the end to the satisfaction of an English audience's demand for artificial stimulus. Having taken his final vows as a Catholic priest, he cannot in conscience consider himself truly married to Letty; she, being Protestant, cannot quite understand the anguish of her husband and his isolation from her. Nor could Banim find a way of centring upon this situation. Nowlan is psychologically disfigured by history. But, although we are aware of the historical forces which wreak the damage upon him, the nature of that damage remains obscure. The novel should have been the history of a lost soul. Instead, it remains little more than an explanation of the circumstances which could lead to that state of spiritual loneliness.

In *The Boyne Water* we have a similar theme and structure. A Protestant brother and sister, Robert and Esther Evelyn, from the north of Ireland, meet a Catholic brother and sister, Edmund and Eva O'Connell, from the south-west. The couples fall in love. But the year is 1685. James II has succeeded to the English throne. The consequences for Ireland are far-reaching. Within five years, at the

Battle of the Boyne, Protestant Ireland is established, Catholic Ireland is ruined. The European significance of this battle reminds us of the concentration of interests, which made the resulting Irish political situation so implacably insoluble. Ireland was for that period the arena in which Protestant England and Catholic France decided the balance of European power. After that, any change in Ireland could upset that precarious settlement. The Irish situation was thus frozen into a mould, which the French could never break and the English would never allow to be broken. It is, therefore, understandable that Banim, in giving us a series of vignettes of historical personages in this novel – William, James, Sarsfield, Governor Walker and the like – should find that history was pre-empting fiction. For in fiction, there is a sense of an ending, of some final conciliation between opposing forces. In Irish history, there was none. Banim, deeply influenced by Scott's great example, could never achieve any comparable adjustment between fiction and history. Ireland offered no instance of that possibility, Scotland did. Although *The Boyne Water* is one of the most important of all Irish historical novels, its essential failure as a novel is an ominous tribute to the supremacy in Irish experience of historical division. The structural symmetries of the plot, in which brothers and sisters, Catholics and Protestants, rapparees and Orangemen, victims and bigots of each persuasion, are balanced one against the other, provide the reader with nothing more than sets of representative types. History is the hero of the novel, but no one person embodies its force. All are subject to it.

The Anglo-Irish of the Nineteenth Century appeared anonymously in 1828. In its bare outlines, it is another story of the return of an absentee landlord – the Honourable Gerald Blount – to his estate in Ireland, somewhere about the close of the Napoleonic wars. Before he returns there, Gerald is indoctrinated, both by English and Irish Protestant friends, in a hatred and contempt for the savage and uncivilized Catholic Irish. Banim reveals here the irreconcilable nature of the feelings between the two races and creeds. Although the story closes with Blount settling in Ireland, having learned to sympathize with the cause of the Irish Catholic, the reader cannot take this as much more than a desperate plea by Banim for a degree of understanding, which a long history of prejudice and oppression has made improbable. Banim's fiction often reads like an essay on Irish history. His opposition to the New Reformation is explained for the English audience in a disquisition by the Protestant Mr

Long, in *The Nowlans*. But the speaker is no more than a mouth-piece, although his religion is obviously meant to be significant. But does this sound like something that would be said at a rowdy dinner?

Pardon me, Mr. Stokes; even the esteemed plan of supplying to the Irish translations of the Bible in their own language is one hundred and forty years old. In my Lord Spencer's rare and valuable library, I have seen, while in England, a quarto edition of the Holy Bible, translated under the care of Bedel, Bishop of Kilmore, 'for the public good of the Irish nation', in 1685; also a pocket edition of the reprint of the quarto, five years after, that is in 1690; so, Sir, I am at liberty to call upon the past as well as the future for an answer to my question, which still is – what good has been done?[17]

Expository essays, melodramatic plots, pictures of Irish peasant life and deep political pessimism were the chief ingredients of Banim's fiction. He could not educate the English audience in Irish history and, at the same time, write popular novels. The didactic intention needed a large audience for its fulfilment; but the large audience made the didactic element incongruous in its melodramatic setting. The Irish novelist was hopelessly compromised by the situation in which he was obliged to write.

Griffin gave up writing to join a religious teaching order. Banim was stricken by illness. Edgeworth found Ireland intractable by 1834. In 1863, William Carleton, almost blind and entirely broke, wrote to a friend in Belfast (from whom he wanted £30) that his proposed autobiography, which he never completed, would 'contain the general history of Irish literature', which it never did. He went on:

The only three names that Ireland can point out with pride are Griffin's, Banim's, and . . . my own. Banim and Griffin are gone, and I will soon follow them – *ultimus Romanorum*, and after that will come a lull, an obscurity of perhaps half a century.[18]

Of all the nineteenth-century Irish victims of Irish conditions – Mangan, Griffin, Banim – Carleton is the most famous or the most notorious. He never lost an opportunity to complain about his lot and was not over-scrupulous in his determination to improve it. Born among the Catholic peasantry of Country Tyrone, he first became famous as a writer for the rabidly anti-Catholic magazine,

The Christian Examiner, owned by Caesar Otway, one of the most fervent and fanatical leaders of the New Reformation, which Banim disliked so much. The bitterness of his attacks upon Catholicism made his early work memorable, for the wrong reasons, to some of the more unforgiving spirits on both sides. But the *Traits and Stories of the Irish Peasantry*, published in five volumes in Dublin, 1830–3, were truly memorable for the power with which they evoked the life of the Irish peasantry rather than for their polemical vigour. What distinguished his work from that of his predecessors was the degree of imaginative sympathy with which individual scenes and characters were conceived. The apologetic or polemical purposes of the stories and novels are so far forgotten at times that there is nothing left to obtrude between the reader and the intensity of the writing. Although Carleton's achievement is streaked and flawed in many ways, he succeeded, more than any other novelist, in going beyond the depiction of individuals as types of the national character. The pedantry, which often weighs so heavily on his writing, was in part the self-consciousness of a man who wanted to impress his audience with his command of 'educated' English, a language over which he had a very uncertain control. He knew Irish and, from his preparation for the priesthood, some Latin. The three languages combine together in his work to produce incongruous effects, although Carleton found a way of exploiting these in the comic figure of Denis O'Shaughnessy, whose pedantry is an aspect of his character. Imagining the pleasures of a priest at a 'station dinner' – that is, a dinner at a house chosen for his visitation to a part of the parish without a church of its own – Denis proclaims:

Then, then does the priest appropriate to himself his due share of enjoyment. Then does he, like Elias, throw his garment of inspiration upon his coadjutors. Then is the goose cut up, and the farmer's distilled Latin is found to be purer and more edifying than the distillation of Maynooth.

> 'Drink deep, or taste not the Pierian spring;
> A little learning is a dangerous thing.'

And so it is, as far as this inspiring language is concerned. A station dinner is the very pinnacle of a priest's happiness. There is the fun and frolic; then does the lemon-juice of mirth and humour come out of their reverences, like secret writing, as soon as they get properly warm. The song and the joke, the laugh and the leer, the shaking of hands, the making of matches, and the projection of weddings, the nipping on the ribs, and the pressing of the toes, the poking and the joking – och, I must conclude or my brisk fancy will dissolve in the deluding vision! Here's to my celebrity tomorrow, and may the Bishop catch a Tarthar in your son, my excellent and logical father! – as I tell you among ourselves he will do. Mark me, I say it – but its *inter nos*, it won't go further – but should he trouble me with profundity, I'll make a *ludibrium* of him.[19]

Unfortunately, most of Carleton's writings are miscellanies of prose styles, with stylistic breaks coming even in the midst of a single sentence. The linguistic instability and the wavering political and sectarian loyalties endemic to the Irish situation are themselves insufficient to account for the variations, which vex the pattern of his rhetoric. Carleton wrote for everybody – Protestant Evangelicals, Davis's *The Nation*, Mitchel's revolutionary paper *The Irish Tribune*, Richard Pigott's *The Shamrock*. In writing to Sir Robert Peel in 1842 to request that a Government pension, formerly granted to the late John Banim, be given to him, he claimed that he was poor because he 'published at home'.[20] This is, indeed, an important fact. It might help to explain Carleton's conversion to Protestantism, for his audience would have been, to an important degree, an Irish Protestant one. But it is also true that he found in Protestantism a discipline and order, which was lacking in the more vivacious but unruly Catholicism into which he had been born. The rational principle and the affective energy were separated in his culture. To find a way of reconciling them he attacked the excesses of each. Orangeism (attacked in *Valentine M'Clutchy*), and Ribbonism (attacked in the same year, 1845, in *Rody the Rover*) were obvious targets. So too were clericalism, in its O'Connellite Catholic form and the rancorous evangelicalism of Otway and his like. But in attacking these excesses, Carleton became a propagandist and reverted to the portrayal of types. The deepest needs of his nature as a writer lay in the desire to find a formal mode of articulating a dishevelled and rich cultural inheritance. But only the tale or the sketch allowed him to achieve a degree of intensity. In that form his wonderful sense of detail, his alertness to the rhythms of speech and for the minutiae of the social life, was nurtured. More sustained forms were beyond him. His novels are too melodramatic or too laconic. His short fiction is capable of sudden concentrations, which give it the economy and force of a short story. *Wildgoose Lodge* is the most famous example. But usually the oral tradition is predominant and the tale, despite the freshness and ease of the narration, lapses back into the silence of the culture from which it emerged. In Carleton, the evolution from the folk tale to the modern short story is enacted. The declining culture of Gaelic Ireland is painfully translated into a self-consciously literary English.

Thus Carleton, Griffin and Banim did not register a living culture in their tales. They recorded a vanishing one and, in doing so, helped to speed its disappearance and its replacement by another. The folk culture was to remain part of the hinterland to the nationalism they promoted but it could never be comfortably possessed. It had to be written into the programme by being written out of its natural state. Translation, whether in poetry or in prose, was always to remain an integral part of a literature for which it was both a necessary act of repossession and an acknowledgement of an inescapable loss. The living texture of the old society was disintegrating as schools, railways and the print-culture took over.

God help us! How many admirable and original characters are there in life of whom the world neither has nor knows anything – men whom to examine would present a profound and interesting study to him who wishes to become thoroughly acquainted with human nature. They pass away, however, like the phantoms of a dream, and leave no memory or impression behind.[21]

In place of this, Carleton could offer little more than a pious hope, designed to impress an English audience, that his people might be educated into an appreciation of the modern world where, along with their folk tales, they could leave their political disaffection behind. In the 1830 Preface to the First Series of his *Traits and Stories*, he said that his 'heart's desire and anxious wish' was

that his own dear, native mountain people may, through the influence of education, by the leadings of purer knowledge, and by the fosterings of a paternal government, become the pride, the strength and support of the British empire, instead of, as now, forming its weakness and reproach.[22]

This has an Edgeworthian ring to it, although the craven humility is Carleton's own. Yet Carleton's involvement in the Protestant evangelical revival, through Cesar Otway, and in the Protestant intellectual revival, which centred on the *Dublin University Magazine* in the 1830s and on the Young Ireland journal, *The Nation* in the 1840s, is in itself analogous to the convention of the 'racial marriage' so often found in the nineteenth-century novels (some of which were serialized in the *Dublin University Magazine*). That is to say, his native Catholicism and his adoptive Protestantism, his reconciliation of old Tyrone with contemporary Dublin, effected through his anti-clericalism, was an example of the felt need to unite in the life as well as in the work aspects of the Irish tradition which were in danger of becoming separated for good. Maria Edgeworth had been the first to write down the recipe; Lady Morgan had tried to live it and write it; Griffin had played with a variation of it in *The Collegians*. Carleton was perhaps the most oppressed and the most damaged writer of them all in his anxiety to follow the requirements his predecessors had laid down. Like Lady Morgan, he wrote for an Irish as well as an English audience and his Irish audience contained within it an important part of the Protestant liberal tradition, which she identified with Grattan and which, in Carleton's time, was revived in the work of Sir Samuel Ferguson and Thomas Davis. But in adhering to that audience and to that programme, he had to put some distance between himself and the new Catholic nation, from which he came and for which he was a leading voice.

In short, Carleton had to become a partisan of one group or another. He would have liked to be free of the need for his consistent adversarial status – itself bound up with his rejection of Catholicism – but there was in fact no alternative. For him there was a perhaps embarrassing resemblance between his own achievement and that of O'Connell. Both helped to give the Irish Catholic masses a sense of identity. Before O'Connell's agitation, 'the more respectable class of the peasantry', Carleton claimed, 'were simple, honest and sincere lovers of truth'.[23] Thereafter, they were corrupt. To preserve the integrity of the old way and attack the degeneracy of the new was part of his own curious plan of campaign. *The Emigrants of Ahadarra* (1848), with its protest against the policy of enforced emigration, especially painful to him after seeing the effect it had had on the valley of his childhood, demonstrates his anxiety to retain something of the old life. *The Tithe-Proctor*, on the other hand, is an outright and vengeful attack upon the O'Connellite Irish:

The Irishman of the present day – the creature of agitation – is neither honest, nor candid, nor manly, nor generous, but a poor skulking dupe, at once slavish and insolent, offensive and cowardly – who carries, as a

necessary consequence, the principles of political dishonesty into the
practices of private life and is consequently disingenuous and fraudulent.[24]

Yet Carleton himself transformed the Irish peasantry too, although
in doing so he had forsaken their religion and committed their
culture to print. If he was a betrayer, he nevertheless always spoke
of himself as betrayed. The beginnings of the Joycean complex are
discernible here – the renegade from his people who nevertheless is
their true interpreter, the writer sick of the politics he cannot
escape, the genius made miserable by Ireland. To Gavan Duffy,
Carleton wrote,

If . . . you ever utter an imprecation against your worst enemy – have
mercy – have mercy – and do not let the bitter malediction be that God
should make him a Man of Genius *in Ireland*.[25]

After the Famine and the collapse of the Rising of 1848, the
condition of Ireland was such that Carleton was for once not being
melodramatic when he spoke of the 'lull, an obscurity of perhaps
half a century', which would fall on Irish literature after his death. It
was, indeed, something of an exaggeration. But with Griffin and
Banim and Edgeworth, Carleton constitutes the culmination of an
attempt to create a new 'national' literature, in circumstances which
were hostile to the success of the enterprise. Yet that literature
emerged and, with it, a new national feeling, created by O'Connell,
Young Ireland, the antiquarian and scholarly movements which
produced the work of Ferguson, O'Donovan, Petrie and others, and
the Fenians. After *The Tithe-Proctor* (1849), Carleton produced
The Squanders of Castle Squander (1852) and the dreadfully popular *Willy Reilly and his Dear Colleen Bawn*, an early version in
1850–1, a later one in 1855. But his career ended, in all important
respects, at mid-century.

Carleton died in 1869, the year in which the Church of Ireland
was disestablished and in which James Connolly, the most important Irish socialist and one of the leaders of the 1916 rebellion, was
born. Both events indicated the rapidity of the changes which were
taking place in the structure of Irish politics. In the following year,
Anthony Trollope wrote one of his five 'Irish' novels, *An Eye for an
Eye*. Trollope had studied Carleton but seems to have learned little
from him. For, although he concentrates upon the illusions – fondly
Romantic and bitterly anti-Catholic – which can create ruin in Irish

conditions, he has no close feeling for the texture of Irish life. The whole novel is concerned primarily with the moral dilemmas confronted by Fred Neville and his aunt, the Countess of Scroope, dilemmas which arise from their mistreatment of the O'Hara family. The O'Haras themselves, particularly the daughter Kate, are no more than the occasion for this dilemma. Their moral life is almost nonexistent. In his last, unfinished novel, *The Landleaguers* (1882), also set in Ireland, the possibility of a happy ending seems to be almost beyond even Trollope's ingenuity, for here he had more courageously confronted the irreconcilable forces in Irish life. The English Captain Clayton tells the landlord Frank Jones that the Irish problem could be solved by adopting the traditional coercive measures. Hang ten rebels in a row, he says, and

to those who desire to have their country once more human, once more fit for an honest man to live in, these ten men hanging in a row will be a goodly sight.[26]

Such coercion had been tried before and would be tried again. Connolly was to be a victim of it in 1916. Carleton had seen an example in 1818 in County Louth, the greater part of which he found 'studded with gibbets'. Twenty-four bodies of Ribbonmen, slung in tar sacks, were suspended from these gibbets which had been set up near their homes.

During that autumn, fruit in the county of Louth was avoided, as something which could not be eaten. . . . There were in all twenty-four dead bodies swinging from gibbets in different directions throughout the county of Louth. The autumn was an unusually hot one; the flesh of the suspended felons became putrid, and fell down in decomposed masses to the bottom of the sacks; the pitch which covered the sacks was melted by the strong heat of the sun, and the morbid mass which fell to the bottom of the sacks oozed out, and fell, . . . in slimy ropes, at the sight of which, I was told, many women fainted. Every sack was literally covered with flies, which having enjoyed their feast, passed away in millions upon millions throughout the country.[27]

This is the well known passage in Carleton's *Autobiography*, which brings to a close the story of Paddy Devaun and is the seed of *Wildgoose Lodge*, the most fearsome of his tales. Carleton is considerably closer to atrocity than is Trollope's Captain Clayton. But it is that closeness which made the English audience wince in the face of much Irish fiction of that century and led it to demand, from Trollope as from the Irish writers themselves, a more winsome view of the Irish as an entertaining people rather than a people horribly mutilated and demoralized by English misrule.

The demand was met, of course, and the Ireland of the 'humourist's Arcadia', as Yeats called it, came into being. It began in the 1820s among the Irish expatriate writers who had gone to London after the Union. The outstanding personality in the group was William Maginn (1794–1842), a journalist and a promoter of Irish talent, Griffin and John Banim being among his discoveries. Maginn's *The O'Dogherty Papers* and Father Prout's *The Reliques of Father Prout* (1859), a whimsical collection of essays by Sylvester Mahony (1804–66), are the best-known examples of that humorous pedantry and designedly overblown eloquence which gave literary respectability to the revamped figure of the stage-Irishman. (It was Mahony who invented the fame of the Blarney Stone.) But the novelists went beyond their drollery in the creation of such figures as Andy Rooney in Samuel Lover's *Handy Andy* (1842), a classic version of the Irish servant man, whose language and antics are designed to amuse an English audience and permit it to infuse its condescension with a generous hilarity. Charles Lever's *The Confessions of Harry Lorrequer* (1839) and *Some Experiences of an Irish R.M.* (1899) by Somerville and Ross (Edith Somerville, 1858–1949, and Violet Martin 1862–1915) were the best examples of this genre. The tale and the sketch of Irish manners and eccentricities were susceptible to all kinds of variation. This particular brand of humour emphasizes the importance of the idea of national character and the pressure of the English audience, two of the features which were part of every Irish writer's consciousness in this century. The determination to be endlessly entertaining can be extremely wearisome, but Somerville and Ross were particularly gifted observers whose work, taken in all, is a lament for as well as a celebration of an almost feudal relationship between landlord and tenant. As with the bulk of Irish fiction, it centres on the related issues of leadership and authority exercised in a context of anarchy, farce or violence. The serious point, which these humorous sketches ultimately dwelt upon, was the incompatability between the English idea of rational authority and the native Irish idea of irrational or non-rational obedience. It was, finally, a way of saying that the Irish were scamps, not rebels. It was their national character which made them behave so endearingly, not the perfectly sensible political and economic structure in which they lived.

In 1882, the year Joyce and de Valera were born, Alexander M. Sullivan looked back on the changes which had taken place in the representation of Irish peasant life since the days of the Famine:

> The Irish peasant of forty years ago – his home, his habits, manners, dress; his wit and humour, his tender feeling, his angry passions, his inveterate prejudices – all these have been portrayed with more or less of exaggeration a hundred times. Caricature has done its worst with the subject; but justice has sometimes touched the theme. One of the changes most pleasing in our time is the fact that in England the clumsy 'stage Irishman' of former days is no longer rapturously declared to be the very acme of truthful delineation. The Irish are keenly sensitive to ridicule or derision; and to see the national character travestied in miserable novel or brutal farce – the Irish peasant as a compound of idiot and buffoon – for the merriment of the master race, was an exasperation more fruitful of hatred between the peoples than the fiercest invective of those 'agitators' whom it has been the fashion to credit with the exclusive manufacture of Irish sedition.
>
> Banim and Griffin, Mrs. Hall and Carleton, have left pictures of Irish life and character which on the whole cannot be surpassed for fidelity and effectiveness.[28]

This was the voice of the ascending Catholic middle classes. But the infinite capacity for deviousness and for sentimental kitsch, which Sullivan manifested in his career and in his writings, was still not allied to any considerable political achievement that could be said to have any chance of enduring. The strict heroics of the 1916 rebellion were to supply that steely element which the nineteenth-century Catholic nation lacked. As for the other novels of that period, their various recipes for a successful conclusion to the Irish saga were all failures. All the novelists were entranced by the idea of a new leadership based on a renovated alliance between separated factions, most especially between an idea of an aristocratic caste and a peasant mass. By the close of the century the weight of the indictment for failure in achieving this had begun to move from the dying Ascendancy and towards the middle classes. Ireland was weary of failure. Literature now began to look for a language and for forms predicated on the idea of success:

> One thing alone seems clear to me. It is well past time for Ireland to have

done once and for all with failure. If she is truly capable of reviving, let her awake, or let her cover up her head and lie down decently in her grave forever. 'We Irishmen', said Oscar Wilde one day to a friend of mine, 'have done nothing, but we are the greatest talkers since the time of the Greeks.' But though the Irish are eloquent, a revolution is not made of human breath and compromises. Ireland has already had enough equivocations and misunderstandings. If she wants to put on the play that we have waited for so long, this time let it be whole, and complete, and definitive.[29]

The date of that passage is 1907, the author is James Joyce, and the friend Oscar Wilde spoke to was W. B. Yeats.

Notes

1   See especially her *Der la littérature considerée dans ses rapports avec les institutions sociales* (Paris, 1800).
2   Maria Edgeworth, *Castle Rackrent*, ed. with introduction by George Watson, (London, 1964), pp. xx.
3   On Maria Edgeworth in general and on *Castle Rackrent* in particular, see Marilyn Butler, *Maria Edgeworth: A Literary Biography* (Oxford, 1972); J. M. S. Tompkins, *The Popular Novel in England, 1770–1800* (London, 1932), p. 187; Harrison R. Steeves, *Before Jane Austen* (London, 1966), pp. 315–31; Thomas Flanagan, *The Irish Novelists, 1800–1850* (New York, 1960), pp. 54–106; John Cronin, *The Anglo-Irish Novel* I (Belfast, 1980); 'The Nineteenth Century: A Retrospect', in *The Genius of Irish Prose*, ed. A. Martin (Dublin and Cork, 1985), pp. 10–21; James Cahalan, *The Irish Historical Novel* (New York, 1984), pp. 10–25.
4   *Castle Rackrent*, Preface, p. 4.
5   *The Black Prophet*, introduction by Timothy Webb (Shannon, 1972), Author's Preface, pp. vii–viii.
6   *Realities of Irish Life* (2nd ed., 1869), p. vii.
7   De Quincey, 'Autobiographic Sketches', in *De Quincey's Works*, 15 vols (Edinburgh, 1863), XIV, p. 285n; Coleridge, *Essays on His Own Times*, 3 vols, ed. D. V. Erdman (London and New Jersey, 1978), I, pp. 106, 120–1; III, pp. 11–12, pp. 238–46; Carlyle, 'Chartism' and 'Downing Street', in *The Works of Thomas Carlyle*, 30 vols (London, 1898–9), XX and XXIX; Southey, 'On The Catholic Question', in *Essays, Moral and Political* (London, 1832), 2 vols, II, pp. 263–433.
8   *Irish Popular Superstitions* (Shannon, 1972), p. 17.
9   W. J. McCormack, 'The Absentee', and Maria Edgeworth's 'Notion of Didactic Fiction', *Atlantis*, no. 5 (April, 1973), pp. 123–35.

10 Claude Fiérobe, *Charles Robert Maturin (1780–1824); L'Homme et L'Oeuvre* (Lille, 1974), p. 447.
11 W. J. McCormack, *Sheridan Le Fanu and Victorian Ireland* (Oxford, 1980).
12 Nicholas Mansergh, *The Irish Question, 1840–1921* (new and revised ed. London, 1965), p. 49.
13 *The Collegians* (Dublin and London, 1942), p. 20, p. 31, p. 81, p. 173.
14 ibid., ch. IV, pp. 40–1. On Griffin, see John Cronin, *The Anglo-Irish Novel* I, pp. 64–81; *Gerald Griffin, 1803–1840: A Critical Biography* (Cambridge, 1978); David Daiches, *The Heyday of Sir Walter Scott* (London, 1961), ch. IV; Thomas Flanagan, *The Irish Novelists, 1800–1850*, pp. 219–31.
15 R. V. Comerford, *Charles J. Kickham: A Biography* (Dublin, 1979), pp. 197–203; Cronin, *The Anglo-Irish Novel*, pp. 101–13.
16 Flanagan, p. 223.
17 *Tales by the O'Hara Family*, Second Series, 3 vols (New York and London, 1978), pp. 289–90. See also the valuable introduction to this reprint series by Robert Lee Wolff, 'The Fiction of the O'Hara Family', pp. v–lii, and Mark D. Hawthorne, *John and Michael Banim (The 'O'Hara Brothers'): A Study in The Early Development of the Anglo-Irish Novel* (Salzburg, 1975), as well as the relevant chapters in Flanagan and Cronin.
18 D. J. O'Donoghue, *The Life of William Carleton*, 2 vols (London, 1896), II, p. 293. See also Benedict Kiely, *Poor Scholar: a study of the works and days of William Carleton* (London, 1947); Andre Boué, *William Carleton, romancier irlandais (1794–1869)* (Paris, 1978); Barbara Hayley, *Carleton's Traits and Stories and the 19th century Anglo-Irish Tradition* (Gerrard's Cross, 1983).
19 *Traits and Stories of the Irish Peasantry*, introduction by M. Harmon, 8 vols (Cork and Dublin, 1973), II, pp. 68–9.
20 Quoted in *Boué*, p. 348.
21 *The Autobiography of William Carleton* (London, 1968), p. 141.
22 Quoted in *Hayley*, p. 34.
23 Quoted in *Boué*, p. 257.
24 *The Tithe-Proctor: A Novel* (London and Belfast, 1849), p. 362.
25 *Autobiography*, p. 151.
26 *The Landleaguers* (Oxford, 1965), pp. 259–60. See R. Tracy, *Trollope's Later Novels* (Berkeley, 1978), pp. 322–8.
27 *Autobiography*, p. 157.
28 *New Ireland: Political Sketches and Personal Reminiscences of Thirty Years of Irish Public Life* (Glasgow, 1884), p. 3.
29 'Ireland, Island of Saints and Sages', in *The Critical Writings*, eds E. Mason and R. Ellman (New York, 1965), p. 174.

5 The drama: Farquhar to Shaw

According to Frank O'Connor, Swift's *A Modest Proposal* (1729) is the 'first great masterpiece of literature written in English in this country'.[1] The political note which it strikes is, for him, characteristic of all Anglo-Irish literature. Yet, when we come to the drama of the Anglo-Irish playwrights – Farquhar, Steele, Macklin, Murphy, Goldsmith and Sheridan, as well as lesser figures like John O'Keeffe, William Philips, Hugh Kelly and Isaac Bickerstaffe – the political coloration is very slight indeed. Although the Smock Alley Theatre in Dublin was totally wrecked in 1754 by an enraged mob which had seized upon a speech from Voltaire's *Mahomet* to express its resentment at the temporary suspension of the Irish parliament, the Irish theatre scarcely engaged with the dominant political issues of the day.[2] This was, in part, because it was heavily dependent on Vice-regal favour. It was also little more than a reflection of the London theatres, Drury Lane and Covent Garden, governed by what was fashionable and successful there, especially in the field of light entertainment. Although there was a good deal of coming and going between the London and the Dublin theatres, London had the best of the bargain both in performers – Peg Woffington, Spranger Barry, Dorothy Jordan – and in authors – Farquhar, Goldsmith and Sheridan. In return, Dublin received Charles Shadwell, son of Thomas, the undistinguished English poet laureate. Shadwell presented his first and last tragedy in the 1719–20 season to a Dublin public already stirred to political consciousness by the Declaratory Act of that year. *Rotherick O'Connor* is a dreadful play, but it has a certain historical importance in that it makes two clear propositions to the Irish theatre-going public. The first is that the benefits of an orderly civilization are the chief fruits of English rule and that the Ascendancy is the class or group bearing these gifts to the 'wild, ungovernable Crew' of the native Irish. The second, not entirely compatible proposition is that the Irish are different from the English because, as the heroine Eva declares:

Here we are govern'd by Nature's Dictates,
Not by dissembling Art, which teaches Men
To act quite opposite to what they think:
Wisdom makes Hypocrites, Nature makes none.[3]

This distinction between the 'natural' Irish and the polished, 'dissembling' English was to be rewritten throughout the eighteenth and the nineteenth centuries in the course of the various debates between the Natural and the Artificial, which played such a central role in the burgeoning sentimental and romantic movements. In Ireland, it retained a specific political importance, but it never entirely freed itself from the prior commitment to the idea of English civilization which was so crucial to the ideology of the Ascendancy. Culturally speaking, the virtues of Irish warmth, enthusiasm and spontaneity could be sponsored up to a certain point; when that was passed, those virtues became political vices, characteristic of an ungovernable and unruly race. There was no easy reconciliation between the two, nor was there any escape from their contradictory attractions.

Taking this distinction as a cue, it would be possible to proceed with the well known claim that Anglo-Irish drama has a recognizable and unresolvable tension at its heart. This takes the form of an opposition between the provincial and the cosmopolitan, between the natural and the artificially polished, between, one might say, the 'Irish' and the 'English' virtues. Although this opposition is cast in the conventional forms of Restoration and Georgian comedy, its presence within them adds a pungency and force which has the tonic effect of enlivening the stereotypes of the aristocratic and philandering aristocrats, the awkward and 'natural' country cousins, the last-minute recognitions and resolutions. George Farquhar, born in Derry in 1678, educated at Trinity College Dublin, began his stage career as an actor in Dublin, but left for London where he became popular with his first play, *Love and a Bottle* (1699). His work is often taken to exemplify the distinction between the natural and artificial comedies of the Restoration period. His rakish hero of this first play, Sir George Roebuck, and Sir Harry Wildair in the next, *The Constant Couple* (1699), undergo the standard frustrations and temporary alienations of comedy before being restored to marriage and happiness simultaneously. Although there is nothing remarkable in this plot-scheme, it can be argued that both of these men regard the conventions of English society from a distance which lends a degree of disenchantment to the view. As in much eighteenth-century satire, the chief commentator on the corruptions and oddities of society is a foreigner or outsider. Roebuck, because he is Irish, is an outsider; but, because he is British, and therefore a member of a civilization common to both islands, he is also an insider. In conversation with the heroine, Lucinda, his nationality is disclosed:

Luc. Oh horrible! an Irish-man: a mere Wolf-Dog, I protest.

Roeb. Ben't surpris'd Child; the Wolf-Dog is as well natur'd an Animal as any of your Country Bull-Dogs, and a much more fawning Creature, let me tell you. (*Lays hold on her*)

Luc. Pray good *Caesar*, keep off your Paws; no scraping acquaintance, for Heaven's sake. Tell us some more news of your Country; I have heard the strangest Stories, that the people wear Horns and Hoofs.

Roeb. Yes, faith, a great many wear Horns: but we had that among other laudable fashions, from *London*. I think it came over with your mode of wearing high Topknots; for ever since, the Men and Wives bear their heads exalted alike. They were both fashions that took wonderfully.[4]

In this kind of exchange, the cosmopolitan is rebuked by the provincial and the political question of nationality is absorbed into the social question of fashionability. The Irishman, in such a situation, redeems with his wit a position in which inferiority is ascribed to him by rote. But part of the humour of this scene relies on the assumption that Lucinda's view of the Irish is shared by the audience and that Roebuck's rejoinders are themselves characteristic of the Irish gift of witty inversion of accepted views. This assumption condemns the Irishman to permanent displacement. Dublin is not London, but only an Irishman can make it appear to be so.

In Farquhar's best play, *The Beaux' Stratagem* (1707), another Irishman appears. Much more disreputable than Roebuck, he is a papish priest, pretending to be French but betrayed by his comic accent to the chief dissemblers Aimwell and Archer. His name is Foigard:

Aim. Foigard! a very good name for a clergyman. Pray, Doctor Foigard, were you ever in Ireland?

Foi. Ireland! no, joy. Fat sort of place is dat saam Ireland? Dey say de people are catched dere when dey are young.

Aim. And some of 'em when they are old: – as for example – (*Takes FOIGARD by the shoulder.*) Sir, I arrest you as a traitor against the government; you're a subject of England, and this morning showed me a commission, by which you served as chaplain in the French army. This is death by our law, and your reverence must hang for it.

Foi. Upon my shoul, noble friend, dis is strange news you tell me! Fader Foigard a subject of England! de son of a burgomaster of Brussels, a subject of England! ubooboo

Aim. The son of a bog-trotter in Ireland! Sir, your tongue will condemn you before any bench in the kingdom.

Foi. And is my tongue all your evidensh, joy?

Aim. That's enough.[5]

The political and religious divide between English and Irish is more pronounced here than in the scene from *Love and a Bottle*. But its importance recedes when we consider that the episode is of minor importance in the play as a whole and when we further consider that it is presented, not as a serious, but as a laughing matter. Dialect, or the mispronunciation of words, or the imperfect mastery of English by those to whom it is a foreign language, is an especially powerful source of comedy in drama which is self-consciously urban and urbane. The connection between correctness in speech and correctness in political, religious and moral attitudes is reinforced by such comic episodes. Foigard is shown to be a fraud, immoral, a papist, and worse than a foreigner:

Aim. (*aside*) A foreigner! A downright Teague, by this light!

By the early eighteenth century, Teague was already a stock figure in English drama. Since the last decade of the sixteenth century, he had been making regular appearances on the stage, well supplied with a barbarous accent, a witty but often treacherous disposition, as prone to violence as to sentimentality. This was the early version of the stage-Irishman. Shakespeare (in *Henry V*), Ben Jonson, Thomas Dekker, Susanna Centlivre, Thomas Sheridan, the father of Richard Brinsley, and Farquhar again, in *The Twin Rivals* (1702), all availed of him, turning to jest a tragic conflict.[6]

Yet, after the Whig Revolution of 1688, up to the twentieth century, the stage-Irishman was exploited as a figure of fun by Irish

more than by English dramatists. He was a popular figure on the
Smock Alley stage, arousing spontaneous cheers and applause from
the audience on his first appearance. As a figure of fun he was
clearly more valuable to the Irish Ascendancy than to the English
theatre, even though some of his most memorable embodiments are
to be found in English plays, like Richard Cumberland's *The West
Indian* (1771), with the amiable and helpful Major O'Flaherty in an
important, if ancillary, role. Farquhar and his compatriot Richard
Steele were prominent in modulating the aristocratic tone of
Restoration comedy and making it more amenable to the tastes of
the middle classes. In doing this, they were also identifying themselves with the new dispensation in England, using the estranged
status of the provincial Irishman as an image of authenticity, in
contrast to the metropolitan frivolity of the earlier, Stuart drama.
Although Farquhar manages to do this without losing the savour of
Congreve's or Vanbrugh's prose, Steele effects the transposition
much less successfully, turning even Molière into stage homilies –
particularly in *The Lying Lover* (1704) and *The Tender Husband*
(1705), although the traditional dolt in this latter play, Humphry
Gubbin, is also derived in part from the stage-Irish figure in Thomas
Shadwell's *The Lancashire Witches and Tegue O'Divelly the Irish
Priest* (1682). After the attacks on the immorality of the stage,
initiated by Jeremy Collier in his notorious and savage *Short View of
the Immorality and Profaneness of the English Stage* (1698), Steele
took it upon himself

> To Chasten Wit, and Moralize the Stage.[7]

In doing so, he introduced to the theatre a species of lachrymose
sentimentality which was both an antidote to lascivious wit and an
alternative form of sexual morality. Domestic bliss is now constituted by a harmonious relationship between Passion, Property and
Providence. The music that emanates from their proper arrangement brings tears to the eyes. In Steele's last play, *The Conscious
Lovers* (1722), one of the models for the sentimental comedy of the
century, Mr Sealand, the merchant, discovers his long-lost daughter
Indiana. In this scene, we have a duet between the idioms of trade
and of love:

> *Indiana.* Have I then at last a Father's Sanction on my Love! His bounteous
> Hand to give, and make my Heart a Present worthy of *Bevil's*
> Generosity?

Mr Sealand. O my Child! how are our Sorrows past o'erpaid by such a Meeting! Though I have lost so many Years of soft paternal Dalliance with thee, Yet, in one Day, to find thee thus, and thus bestow thee, in such perfect Happiness! is ample! ample Reparation! And yet again the Merit of thy Lover.

Indiana. O! had I Spirits left to tell you of his Actions! how strongly Filial Duty has suppressed his Love; and how Concealment still has doubled all his Obligations; the Pride, the Joy of his Alliance, Sir, would warm your Heart, as he has conquer'd mine.

Mr Sealand. How laudable is Love, when born of Virtue! I burn to embrace him . . .[8]

Feeling has replaced wit and has, in the process, become the ground of morality. Although the terrain opened by Steele was to be more thoroughly explored in the novel than in the drama thereafter, his greatest theatrical successor, Goldsmith, was to give a new turn to the didactic solemnities of *The Conscious Lovers*, allowing virtue its reward but not so entirely at the expense of humour. The appropriation of sentiment in alliance with morality by the English middle classes is, at this early period of the eighteenth century, no more than vaguely reflected in the association of honest feeling with provincial straightforwardness. But this weak association between the two strengthened gradually to such a degree that genuine feeling became, in the end, the preserve, not of a class, but of a race. Sometimes the race was British, sometimes Irish. The process is part of the history of national feeling in both countries. It is strange to witness, in the late nineteenth century, a reaction against the self-regarding nationalism of this kind of drama led by two other Irish writers, Wilde and Shaw, both of whom reintroduced wit as a tonic alternative to its sentimental pieties. They finally turned the tide against the sentimental drama, which their compatriots Farquhar and Steele had helped to initiate and which Goldsmith, above all, had brought to perfection.

Sentimentalism, as it emerged from the works of Steele, was an expression of middle-class values in which sexual morality and patriotism were intimately fused. The figure of John Bull – plain-living and hearty Briton that he was – is given a final delineation in the pages of Steele's *Tatler* and Addison's *Spectator*. The repudiation of a frivolous sophistication – itself closely bound up with the English hostility to the French as well as with middle-class hostility to the Restoration wits – led to the apotheosis of the provincial, both as Man of Feeling and as Patriot. On the other hand, by the end of the century, sentimentalism, renamed sincerity, had entered into an alliance with radical political theories. In the drama, Thomas Holcroft was the best-known exponent of the new radicalism which reassembled the materials of the old distinction between the natural and the artificial life. Plays like *Love's Frailties* (1794) and *The Deserted Daughter* (1795) propagate, in their absurd way, the political lessons of the unspoiled affections of those who live the natural life. The local patriotism of one mode of sentimentalism and the radical universalism of the other became increasingly incompatible until, with the onset of the French Revolution, the breach between them was complete. In the interval, Goldsmith and Sheridan found an alternative to these profoundly solemn modes, although it might be said that they did so only by avoiding commitment to the political implications of each. The integrity of each individual people and civilization and the concept of a universal human (and humane) civilization are contradictory notions which grew out of the opposition between the provincial and cosmopolitan figures, which dominated early eighteenth-century drama. The Anglo-Irish dramatists, from Goldsmith to Shaw, looked for a way to modify and deflect the political choice implicit in this opposition. After all, they were in the painful position of provincials who wanted to assert what Burke called the principle of 'common naturalisation'[9] between the inhabitants of Ireland and Great Britain. By asserting that, they could enter into the heritage of the European Enlightenment, advocates of a humanism which was not limited by loyalties to provincial origins. On the other hand, sentimentalism nurtured these loyalties and associated them with all that was 'natural'. The final combination of sentimental patriotism with revolutionary doctrines of natural rights in the closing decade of the century contributed to the formation of Irish Republicanism and the movement of the United Irishmen under Wolfe Tone. Burke's political thought was bedevilled by the insoluble problem of attaching the affections of local Irish patriotism to the English political system. He could not reconcile these incompatibilities, partly because English misrule in Ireland rendered it impossible. Sentimentalism, then, posed a threat to Anglo-Irish writers. It drove them towards a species of proto-nationalism, or it drove them towards revolutionary internationalism. The achievement of an intervening position depended, then, on the writer's power to diminish the force of sentimentalism without ignoring its importance. This Goldsmith did.

Irish fiction before *The Vicar of Wakefield* (1766) had tended to vacillate between preoccupations with specific Irish issues and more general human concerns, although all of it remained faithful to the code of the sentimental traveller which is central to Goldsmith's poetry. The traveller who surveys a variety of cultures may finally come to rest in the bosom of his own; or he may settle for a moral sententiousness about the human condition which is, ostensibly, less restricted in its scope. William Chaigneau's *The History of Jack Connor* (1752) is the most notable example of the first type; the second is best represented by the jumbled picaresque fiction of Thomas Amory, especially *The Life of John Buncle, Esq.* (1756–66), and of Henry Brooke, in his famous *The Fool of Quality, or the History of Henry, Earl of Moreland* (1766–70). Brooke's novel had a curious fate when it was reprinted in 1781 in an edition edited by John Wesley. Its five volumes became two and its chief public became Wesleyans. These novels, however interesting historically, had a limited impact. In the theatre, material which had a particularly Irish appeal was even less successful. The comic but true-hearted Captain O'Blunder of Thomas Sheridan's *The Brave Irishman* (possibly 1737) was a great favourite of Dublin audiences, but had no comparable success in London; Charles Macklin's *Love à la Mode* (1759) contained, in Callaghan O'Brallaghan, a very Shavian version of the stage-Irishman, cool and rational and detached. But this play never competed with his much more traditionally 'English' *The Man of the World*, produced in 1781. Only Sheridan's stage-Irishman, Sir Lucius O'Trigger, in *The Rivals*, produced in 1775, seemed to gain in London a recognition comparable to that which it received in Dublin. The variant forms of the stage-Irishman – the comic perpetrator of malapropisms and stupidities – and the intelligent observer of the foibles of the fashionable English world – are symptomatic of the general vacillation in all this literature between the ideals of local particularity, however stereotyped, and those of universal rationality and humanism. This same variation is presented to us again in the contrast between Goldsmith the writer and Goldsmith the man. His tendency to blunder socially, or the failure of his English friends to observe his irony, forms a startling contrast with what Henry James called the 'amenity' of his style.[10]

The man whom Thackeray called 'the most beloved of English

writers'[11] carries, within his life and work, a suppressed ambiguity which owes its origin to his Anglo-Irish inheritance. De Quincey extends the Victorian misreading of Goldsmith by remarking that

In our days, if the *Vicar of Wakefield* had been published as a Christmas tale, it would have produced a fortune to the writer.[12]

To read the novel thus, as a counterpart to the saccharine Christmas fare of the mid-nineteenth century audience, is to miss the irony which is consistently undermining the theme of the Vicar's inexhaustible benevolence. All of Goldsmith's versions of pastoral, but particularly this novel and *The Deserted Village*, are ambivalent. The desolation of the village and the contrast with the former contentment are explained for us by a most unconvincing attack upon 'Luxury'.[13] This is Goldsmith's half-hearted way of dealing with the ever-renewable dispute between metropolitan and provincial life, between, say, the Lissoy of his youth and the Vauxhall he patronized in his maturity. In Ireland, the contrast between the world of fashionable Dublin and the rest of the country was especially painful. If Luxury were the cause of it, then Luxury was only another name for colonialism of the most rapacious kind. But, like the rest of his Irish friends, Goldsmith could not quite see Ireland as a colony of England. It had to be, in some fashion, incorporated into English civilization, an integral part of it. Burke and Sheridan had similar views. They could inveigh against the depredations of Warren Hastings in India, against confiscation of native lands, the destruction of native culture, the slaughter of innocent civilians, the breaking of solemn treaties – but every one of these things had happened in Ireland too. The chief difference was that these men were, however uneasily, the beneficiaries of such events. Their unexceptionably patriotic Britishness helped them to recognize in America and in India the risks involved in unlimited exploitation. In his 1762 essay, *The Revolution of Low Life*, Goldsmith deplores the effects of foreign trade in the separation of the population into 'the very rich and very poor',[14] but all the cautionary examples from history which he adduces there – Venice, Genoa and Holland – are either inaccurate or irrelevant. Ireland, after all, would have prospered a great deal more had the restrictions on its trade been lifted. In effect, Goldsmith's account of the passage from provincial pastoralism to urban frivolity and materialism is futile, because it amounts to little more than an amateur attempt to explain away the

Irish-English tension which was at the heart of his experience.
However, in *The Good Natur'd Man* (1768) and *She Stoops to Conquer* (1773), Goldsmith, according to his friend Samuel Foote, 'was the first to attack this illegitimate species of writing', by which he meant sentimentalism, and helped to lay 'the ghost of *sentimental comedy*'.[15] Honeywood, the 'good natur'd man' of the title, is hopelessly benevolent. His fashionable pose of goodness is finally shown to be a barrier to self-knowledge and, in particular, a hindrance to genuine feeling. For young Honeywood is taught in the end that his love for Miss Richland must take the priority over general diffused sentiment. Although much more genially embraced within the comic frame, this is identical to Burke's later attack on Rousseauism; on, that is, the system of universal philanthropy which ignored the immediate and the local duties of personal life. Although Burke's *Letters on a Regicide Peace* are far removed in tone from Goldsmith's comedies, the difference between them consists solely in this – Burke has drawn out the political implications of the sentimental movement, and has defined the confrontation which lay within it: he feared the loss

. . . of that narrow scheme of relations called our country, with all its pride, its prejudices, and its partial affections. All the quiet little rivulets, that watered an humble, a contracted, but not an unfruitful field, are to be lost in the waste expanses and boundless, barren ocean of the homicide philanthropy of France.[16]

Burke's nostalgia and Goldsmith's pastoralism are identical. Each imagines the loss of authentic virtue and its replacement by a spurious benevolence. Each regards the past in terms of a provincial integrity sacrificed to the cosmopolitan superficialities of the present. In this light, *The Good Natur'd Man* is more than an attack on sentimentalism. It is part of the Anglo-Irish lament for the vanished possibility of reconciling the native dignity of the little world of natural with the large world of artificial feeling.

Just as *The Good Natur'd Man* will always be associated with the play by Goldsmith's Irish rival, Hugh Kelly, whose *False Delicacy* was preferred both by Garrick and by the public when it was put on a week before at Drury Lane, so too *She Stoops to Conquer* will always be associated with Goldsmith's Irish friend, Isaac Bickerstaffe, who supplied a model for it in his *Love in A Village*, first performed in 1762. By common consent, Goldsmith's greatest play, perhaps his greatest work, *She Stoops to Conquer* exploits the ambivalences by which Goldsmith himself had been up to then exploited. The private house which is misrepresented as an inn, the lady who is taken as a barmaid, the gentleman who is almost pathologically shy in the presence of ladies and equally aggressive towards those women he regards as his social inferiors and the spoilt dolt, Tony Lumpkin, who is the intelligence behind all these masquerades and whose idea of freedom consists in liberation from women, either as mother or as wife – all of these are brilliant improvisations on the obsessive theme of the relationship between rusticity and sophistication, the natural and the artificial. The elegance of the play does not depend on wit, for there is little in the way of the kind of verbal polish that we associate with Congreve or with Sheridan. Instead, there is a recognition of a sane alternative to the stereotypes of sexual behaviour, which young Marlow represented before the disclosure of Kate's true identity. Neither a preachy figure out of Steele nor a rake out of Vanbrugh, he is forced to undergo the humiliation of becoming himself:

Miss Hardcastle. Yes, Sir, that very identical tall squinting lady you were pleased to take me for (*curtseying*). She that you addressed as the mild, modest sentimental man of gravity, and the bold forward agreeable Rattle of the ladies club; ha, ha, ha.

Marlow. Zounds, there's no bearing this; it's worse than death.

Miss Hardcastle. In which of your characters, Sir, will you give us leave to address you. As the faultering gentleman, with looks on the ground, that speaks just to be heard, and hates hypocrisy; or the loud confident creature, that keeps it up with Mrs Mantrap, and old Miss Biddy Buckskin, till three in the morning; ha, ha, ha.[17]

Before this, Marlow himself has begun to glimpse the truth about Kate's identity. He too expresses his perception of it in the customary antitheses:

What at first seem'd rustic plainness, now appears refin'd simplicity. What seem'd forward assurance, now strikes me as the result of courageous innocence, and conscious virtue.[18]

The last word, however, remains with the loutish Tony Lumpkin, in whose character the Epilogue is spoken:

Zounds, we shall make these London gentry say,
We know what's damn'd genteel, as well as they.[19]

He and his beloved 'big Bett Bouncer' propose to take the town by
storm. This is an act of revenge on gentility by rusticity; but it is also
an acknowledgement that the refinement of the one and the crudity
of the other are not in collision but in collusion. The connection
between them is as close as money can make it. Goldsmith finally
leaves us with the conviction that the gentleman and the lout are
comically intimate. Swift had seen this intimacy in a tragic or savage
spirit in his confrontation of Houyhnhnm and Yahoo; Burke saw it
in fright and fury in the association between the Voltairian rational
man and the Rousseauistic Man of Nature. It was a relationship
which had profound meaning for all European civilization, but
these Irish writers felt its ambivalence with an especial sensitivity.
For its bearing upon their own deeply divided country, and upon
their own lives in English society, was inescapable.

Sheridan had two careers. One, as a dramatist and the manager of
Drury Lane as successor to Garrick, had been prefaced by an
elopement with a renowned beauty and two notorious duels; the
other, as a member of the Whig party and a brilliant Parliamentary
orator, was succeeded by financial ruin and a squalid and pathetic
death. More than Burke or Goldsmith or any of that large colony of
expatriate Irishmen who were to be found in the Inns of Court, in
the theatrical coffee houses, in the East India Company's specula-
tions and in the House of Commons, Sheridan was the Irish adven-
turer. Self-possessed, worldly, witty, he was in almost every respect
the antithesis of Goldsmith. But, like Goldsmith, he suffered from a
sense of displacement. As a player and a dramatist, he was, like his
father before him, only grudgingly accorded the status of a gentleman. As a friend of the Prince of Wales and of Fox, he imagined that
he might one day inherit the leadership of the Whig party, a notion
that would not have found much favour among the Whigs themselves. To them, Sheridan, however great a luminary, was still an
outsider, not an English gentleman, but an Irish performer. His
plays, especially *The Rivals* (1775) and *The School for Scandal*
(1777), his most enduring works, are centred on the glittering and
fashionable world of Bath, insulated in its insolent sophistication
and yet, as in Steele or Goldsmith, enacting the old battle between
genuine feeling and worldly heartlessness. Sheridan's linguistic virtuosity derives from his gift of caricature. His figures both command

and are commanded by the language they speak. Everybody has a strain of Mrs Malaprop:

> There, Sir! an attack upon my language! what do you think of that? – an aspersion upon my parts of speech! was ever such a brute! Sure if I reprehend any thing in this world, it is the use of my oracular tongue, and a nice derangement of epitaphs![20]

In similar vein, Sir Anthony Absolute, the apostle of coolness, flies into a rage to defend this virtue to his son, Captain Absolute, who himself embodies it:

> So you will fly out! can't you be coll, like me? What the devil good can *Passion* do – *Passion* is of no service, you impudent, insolent, over-bearing Reprobate! – There you sneer again – don't provoke me! – but you rely upon the mildness of my temper – you do, you Dog! you play upon the meekness of my disposition! Yet take care – the patience of a saint may be overcome at last! – but mark! I give you six hours and a half to consider of this: if you then agree, without any condition, to do every thing on earth that I choose, why – confound you! I may in time forgive you – If not, z—ds! don't enter the same hemisphere with me! don't dare to breathe the same air, or use the same light with me; but get an atmosphere and sun of your own! I'll strip you of your commission; I'll lodge five-and-threepence in the hands of the trustrees, and you shall live on the interest. – I'll disown you, I'll disinherit you, I'll unget you! and – d—n me, if I ever call you Jack again![21]

This is not simple contradiction or hypocrisy. Such characters are liberated by the thoroughness of their self-deceit. They do not play a role; what they are is itself a role. Like Snake, in *The School for Scandal*, they can declare:

> Ah! Sir – consider I live by the Badness of my Character! – I have nothing but my Infamy to depend on! and if it were once known that I had been betray'd into an honest Action I should lose every Friend I have in the world.[22]

The gap between moral conduct and social behaviour is narrow in Sheridan. At times we have a premonition of Oscar Wilde's comment:

> It is only shallow people who do not judge by appearances.[23]

But the tradition of sentimental comedy, reinforced by the eighteenth-century novel, is still sufficiently strong to sustain the division between Head and Heart, naturalness and artificiality. Although Sheridan was credited by many contemporaries with having subdued 'the Dragon of mere sentimental drama',[24] the praise was excessive. The regenerative power of his comedy was sufficient to establish the world of fashionable society as the proper arena for the drama. Lacking the naturalism of Goldsmith, he concentrated his attention on the manipulation of a code of manners and of language, which, paradoxically, took its power from the asphyxiatingly narrow sphere in which it operated. A notion of society so strictly quarantined from the complex world beyond found its ideal of excellence in an aristocratic intelligence rather than in any form of middle-class morality. Virtue and Vice still exist but the difference between them consists of the superior ability of the first to survive without the deceptions and delusions so necessary to the latter. The heroes and heroines of comedy, after Sheridan, became markedly more intelligent than the villains. Villainy, indeed, becomes identified with conventionality; virtue with a radical independence from convention. The way lay open to Wilde and Shaw. Much of what we have seen of eighteenth-century comedy did, after all, stress the 'vital Importance of Being Earnest'. It was characteristic of the Irish contribution to this literature to express a profound ambivalence by converting its basic moral prescription into a pun.

After the Act of Union in 1800, Ireland became an integral part of the political system of the United Kingdom. At the same time, it began to distinguish itself as a culturally separate civilization, one of the many buried cultures brought to life by the Romantic movement. The articulation of this new identity was achieved in the English language, for the most part; but what had to be recovered was almost entirely in the Irish language. From the outset there was, therefore, at the heart of Irish writing, a linguistic crisis which first expressed itself in translations, adaptations, reductions into English terms of Gaelic materials. Thomas Moore was the first Irish author to deal with the pressures of this transformed situation. He succeeded Sheridan as the Irish darling of the Whigs and, by the time Sheridan died in 1816, had replaced him in the affections of those who belonged to the Holland House Circle. Moore's *Irish Melodies*, published in ten numbers between 1807 and 1834, are limp enough as poetry; but they come to life when they are taken together with his *National Airs*, that is, when they are recognized as songs in which the lyrics are written to enhance and revivify the melodies of former times or of other civilizations. Moore was an exponent of the virtues of 'local patriotism'. He confirmed the association between vivid feeling, provincial integrity and racial destiny, which had been implicit in much eighteenth-century literature. In relation to the immediate past in Ireland. Moore touched on two figures who represented two very different aspects of Ireland's connection with England. He wrote the biographies of Lord Edward Fitzgerald, the rebel leader executed for his part in preparing the rebellion of 1798, and of Sheridan. Neither of these works is particularly inspired, but both are records of the alternatives presented by contemporary conditions to Irish leaders – separation from England or integration with her. Moore tried to have it both ways, as Whig pamphleteer and as Ireland's national poet. Irish literature after him tended to follow the national line, pursuing the ideal of an essential Irishness, which had to be recovered from the chaotic interfusion of cultures and the desolate history which had made Ireland what it was. Of those writers who fled from the risks of obscurity and provincialism which were involved in this choice, the most remarkable were Wilde and Shaw, although George Moore, for most of his writing life, is among them too. The work of these two insists on the liberation of intelligence through language from all that is provincial, conventional, consensual. Yet, both of them played a role for the English audience – that of the stage-Irishman, transposed into the intelligent outsider who is remarkable for his linguistic gifts – by which they were themselves ultimately defined. While remaining within the tradition of English writing, they created for themselves a detachment from English society, which they flaunted as style but which was also an aspect of the importance of being Irish. Wilde acknowledged what Richard Ellman has called 'the two turning-points in his life' which occurred 'when my father sent me to Oxford, and when society sent me to prison'.[25] Ruskin and Pater provided him with the religion of style, as Henry George and Karl Marx provided Shaw with a style of religion. In the 1921 Preface to his early novel *Immaturity*, written in 1879, Shaw explained his reasons for going to London and his 'abandonment of Dublin':

Every Irishman who felt that his business in life was on the higher planes of the cultural professions felt that he must have a metropolitan domicile and an international culture: that is, he felt that his first business was to get out

of Ireland. I had the same feeling. For London as London, or England as
England, I cared nothing . . . But as the English language was my
weapon, there was nothing for it but London.[26]

Thereafter, he played an endless game of confusing the stereotypes
of the English and the Irish, fully aware that his paradoxes and
iconoclasm made him irresistibly 'Irish' to an English audience
which, in so accepting him, revealed its hopelessly English block-
headedness. By 1904, he is able to say, in the Preface to *John Bull's
Other Island*, 'that Ireland is the only spot on earth which produces
the ideal Englishman of history'.[27] Shaw, therefore, found a means
of exploiting the stage-Irish tradition, which a dramatist like Dion
Boucicault had made so popular in mid-century, in order to affirm
his commitment to the metropolitan rather than to the provincial
culture. Although he has no kind word to say of Sheridan, the wit
which Shaw associates with 'faithlessness',[28] with, that is, an
incapacity to be committed to any foolish idealism, links them
together as the inhabitants of a peculiarly cosmopolitan culture, the
Anglo-Irishman's alternative to the restricted fate of being either
wholly Irish or wholly English. Shaw's contempt for the Ireland of
nineteenth-century romance, so effectively invented by Moore and
Boucicault – whom he called 'a coaxing, blandandhering sort of
liar'[29] – was such that he declared himself 'quite ready to help the
saving work of reducing the sham Ireland of romance to a heap of
unsightly ruins'.[30] But this was to save the British Empire, which he
conceived to be so dependent on Irish talent and character for its
survival. Even more than his eighteenth-century predecessors,
Shaw interrogated, over and over again, the attractions of international humanism and the seductions of a rooted nationalism. This
was to remain a central issue in Irish writing for the next century.

In *The Critic as Artist* (1890), Wilde declared,

It is Criticism that makes us cosmopolitan.

and went on to explain:

It is only by the cultivation of the habit of intellectual criticism that we
shall be able to rise superior to race prejudices. . . Criticism will annihilate
race-prejudices, by insisting upon the unity of the human mind in the
variety of its forms. If we are tempted to make war upon another nation, we
shall remember that we are seeking to destroy an element of our own

culture, and possibly its most important element. As long as war is regarded as wicked, it will always have its fascination. When it is looked upon as vulgar, it will cease to be popular.[31]

Wilde's 'new Hellenism', in which what he called in *The Soul of Man Under Socialism* (1890) 'individualism' would be in perfect harmony with all of human thought, is closely allied to Shaw's 'metropolitan domicile and an international culture'. Both of them regarded the great English public as the inveterate enemy. Its vulgarity made the triumph of reason and of refinement difficult. Morality, dictated by the popular press and by the Churches, was the form of that vulgarity. Just as Wilde read this collision in aesthetic, and Shaw in political and moral terms, Yeats was to read it in a conflation of both, restoring to it the division between Irish and English civilization and thereby bringing together the cosmopolitan and the national impulses of his country's tradition in literature. The relentlessness of Shaw's and of Wilde's attacks on the English middle classes provided Yeats with the opportunity to convert their cosmopolitanism into his own peculiar brand of literary nationalism. Wilde's languid dandyism was converted by Yeats into images of historical catastrophe. *The Second Coming*, for instance, is amusingly anticipated in the following passage from *The Decay of Lying* (1889):

The solid, stolid British intellect lies in the desert sands like the Sphinx in Flaubert's marvellous tale, and fantasy, La Chimere, dances round it, and calls to it with her false, flute-toned voice. It may not hear her now, but surely some day, when we are all bored to death with the commonplace character of modern fiction, it will hearken to her and try to borrow her wings.[32]

Yet it is Joyce, rather than Yeats, who sensed the symbolic value of Wilde's career in the Irish tradition. In his essay of 1909 on Wilde, he looks first at the meaning of Oscar's success:

. . . and only with the presentation of his brilliant comedies did he enter the short last phase of his life – luxury and wealth. In the tradition of the Irish writers of comedy that runs from the days of Sheridan and Goldsmith to Bernard Shaw, Wilde became, like them, court jester to the English. He became the standard of elegance in the metropolis. . .[33]

Then he looks at Wilde's failure:

Here we touch the pulse of Wilde's art – sin. He deceived himself into believing that he was the bearer of good news of neo-paganism to an enslaved people. His own distinctive qualities, the qualities, perhaps, of his race – keenness, generosity, and a sexless intellect – he placed at the service of a theory of beauty which . . . was to bring back the Golden Age and the joy of the world's youth. But if some truth adheres . . . to his restless thought . . . its very base is the truth inherent in the soul of Catholicism: that man cannot reach the divine heart except through that sense of separation and loss called sin.[34]

Between them Yeats and Joyce recognize in Wilde the first Irish writer in whom the tragic plight of the modern artist is fully represented. More effectively than Shaw, he embodied in his life and in his art contradictions by which he was victimized and, at the same time, stimulated. The light and bright and sparkling element, which is most pronounced in his comedies, coexisted with a darker and more sinister force, most pronounced in his fiction. Success and disgrace, the morality of art and the immorality of sin, beauty and vulgarity, elitism and the popular audience, wit and Gothic terror, were all combined in his career, illuminated throughout by a series of essays which had the sententiousness of a collection of *obiter dicta* on general issues and was also a commentary upon his own work. Yeats learned from and emulated him in this respect.

The dark side of Wilde, which appealed to his Irish successors and contemporaries, is discovered most fully in *The Picture of Dorian Gray*, first published in *Lippincott's Magazine* in 1890. In March of the same year, *The Fortnightly Review* published the Preface which contained the famous remarks that were to be re-echoed in the first chapter of Joyce's *Ulysses*:

The nineteenth century dislike of Realism is the rage of Caliban seeing his own face in a glass.
The nineteenth century dislike of Romanticism is the rage of Caliban not seeing his own face in a glass.[35]

The novel is a parable about the retention of identity in art and its loss in experience. Dorian, in exploring the sub-world of London, keeps his youth and beauty in the midst of unspecified but searing experience. His portrait registers the horror of it, his self remains unimpaired until, in old age, the positions are reversed and Dorian becomes grotesque while the picture remains as the eternal portrait of him 'in all the wonder of his exquisite youth and beauty'.[36] It is the triumph of Art over Life but, as Joyce noticed, a triumph gained only through the experience of sin. Dorian's identity is separate from his personality, as is art from experience. It is appropriate that the germ of this novel is to be found in an incident in one of the most famous of all Irish Gothic fictions, *Melmoth the Wanderer* (1820), by Charles Robert Maturin, an uncle of Wilde's mother and a favourite author of his own mentors, Baudelaire and Balzac. The melodramatic connection between the Gothic villain and the dandy, lengthily expounded in this novel, lends to the Wildean conception of the artist the sinister glamour of a mysterious destiny. Yeats caught this in his account of the influence of pre-Raphaelite painting on literature:

. . and Wilde – a provincial like myself – found in that influence something of the mystery, something of the excitement, of a religious cult that promised an impossible distinction. It was precisely because he was not of it by birth and by early association that he caught up phrases and adjectives for their own sake and not because they were a natural part of his design, and spoke them to others as though it were his duty to pass on some pass-word, sign or countersign.[37]

In such comments we see how Yeats learned to transform Wilde's idea of the cosmopolitan spirit into his own conception of the world-soul, with all its occult trappings – a form of spiritual dandyism.

Wilde's four social comedies, *Lady Windermere's Fan* (1892), *A Woman of No Importance* (1893), *An Ideal Husband* (1894) and *The Importance of Being Earnest* (1895), are based on the well worn comic device of the revealed secret upon which social pretensions and much moralizing are based. The denouement in *An Ideal Husband* is closely modelled on the famous screen scene from *The School for Scandal*, although Wilde's conclusion is a good deal more sentimental. In the other plays, with the exception of *Earnest*, the subversive element is almost entirely confined to the dialogue. The plots are highly conventional in the eighteenth-century mode of sentimental comedy. But in *Earnest*, plot and dialogue are in perfect accord. Instead of a sentimental comedy, we are provided with a philosophy of the mask, of the reality of the social role rather than the role of reality in social pretence. This is the bright side of *Dorian Gray*. Wilde solves the problem of the displaced person in a social world, to which he does not wholly belong, by making a social virtue of displacement. Moral identity becomes a fiction; truth becomes the role adopted by the individual. The power of that truth depends upon the style with which the role is played. Subtitled 'A Trivial Comedy for Serious People', it assumes an enclosed social world, the Victorian drawing room, as readily as Sheridan's comedy assumed the enclosed world of Georgian Bath. Within this frame, the serious can become trivial without becoming trivialized. Subversion is all the choicer for being enacted within the restrictions of a closed society:

Lady Bracknell. Good afternoon, dear Algernon, I hope you are behaving very well.

Algernon. I'm feeling very well, Aunt Augusta.

Lady Bracknell. That's not quite the same thing. In fact the two things rarely go together.[38]

Similarly, in the frosty meeting of Cecily and Gwendolen,

Cecily. . . . This is not the time for wearing the shallow mask of manners. When I see a spade I call it a spade.

Gwendolen. I am glad to say I have never seen a spade. It is obvious that our social spheres have been widely different.[39]

The verbal discriminations made here are in the form of rebukes to Algernon and to Cecily who have momentarily failed to abide by the logic of the fiction, called society, in which they live. This is the two-dimensional world of style; any attempt to move into another dimension, like that of feeling or of truth is quickly checked. The idea of society has now become the frame for the achievement of art.

John Bull's Other Island was written in 1904 at Yeats's request 'as a patriotic contribution to the repertory of the Irish Literary Theatre'.[40] As so often in Shaw, there is a double text. One is concerned with the inversion of English/Irish stereotypes. It is to this that he adverts, at his customary length, in his Preface. The other is concerned with his philosophy of Will and of the Life Force. Both attack the assumptions of an industrial world devoted to the ethic of Efficiency. As in Wilde, much of the humour depends on the assumption that society, however strange a fiction it may be, is a fact of Nature. Only Peter Keegan, the 'mad' priest, does not share this assumption. The basic inversion of the English/Irish text is that it is the 'practical' English, like Broadbent, who are the dreamers, and the 'impractical' Irish who are the hard-headed realists. The basic inversion of the second text is that it is through the dreamers, the irrational people (i.e. the English) that the Life Force works its spell, while the rational race (the Irish) are too clear headed to be subject to its blind instinctual drive. Thus the English muddle through and the Irish remain brilliant failures. In its paradoxical transformation of the stage-Irishman and of the stage-Englishman, in its exploitation of the comedy of manners for the development of the theatre of ideas, it is a culmination of two centuries of Anglo-Irish comic drama. In the Shavian character, Peter Keegan, it has provided a disguised position for the figure caught between two cultures, complementary to each other by nature but divided by history. Instead of the small-scale miniaturist society of the traditional, enclosed comedy of manners, Shaw takes as his natural territory the clash of two cultures – one which had been implicit in earlier dramas but is now explicit in his. Yet even Keegan, like Captain Shotover in *Heartbreak House*, reveals his displaced status within the drama by being, at crucial moments, little more than a voice-over, a man of opinions, which remain inoperable within the society which he addresses. More than Wilde, Shaw became the court jester to the English and to the Irish. His philosophy with its clear chain-of-command – the Reason in the grip of the Will, the Will in the grip of the Life Force – campaigned against the great army of prejudice, misplaced idealism, conventional posturings, which constituted society. But although he won every battle by the superior disposition of his rhetorical forces, he could not win the war. In his anxiety to become GBS, he became professionally quixotic and found himself to be, in the most ironic way possible, a victim of the tradition of the stage-Irishman, which he had done so much to subvert and exploit. Shaw was finally used by the conventions he abused. But the most recalcitrant of these, that of his Irishness, was not, at bottom, a convention at all. It was based on the plight of the Anglo-Irish class, well on the way to extinction by 1904, after two centuries of vacillation on the vexed question of its place within the political-cultural scheme of things in the two islands. The dream of Peter Keegan is an epilogue to that history;

but it is incomplete without the accompanying commentary of Broadbent, the English idiot of the practical life, and of Larry Doyle, the Irish cynic who has become Broadbent's executive:

Keegan. In my dreams it is a country where the State is the Church and the Church the people: three in one and one in three. It is a commonwealth in which work is play and play is life: three in one and one in three. It is a temple in which the priest is the worshipper and the worshipper the worshipped; three in one and one in three. It is a godhead in which all life is human and all humanity divine: three in one and one in three. It is, in short, the dream of a madman. (*He goes away across the hill.*)

Broadbent. (*looking after him affectionately*) What a regular old Church and State Tory he is! He's a character: he'll be an attraction here. Really almost equal to Ruskin and Carlyle.

Larry. Yes; and much good they did with all their talk!

Broadbent. Oh tut, tut, Larry! They improved my mind: they raised my tone enormously. I feel sincerely obliged to Keegan: he has made me feel a better man: distinctly better. (*with sincere elevation*) I feel now as I never did before that I am right in devoting my life to the cause of Ireland. Come along and help me choose the site for the hotel.[41]

Notes

1 *The Backward Look; A Survey of Irish Literature* (London, 1967), p. 121.
2 Madeleine Bingham, *Sheridan, The Track of a Comet* (London, 1972), pp. 29–41.
3 William S. Clark, *The Early Irish Stage; The Beginnings to 1720* (Oxford, 1955), p. 173.
4 *The Dramatic Works of George Farquhar*, 2 vols (London, 1825), I, pp. 14–15.
5 ibid., II, pp. 25–6.
6 Alan Bliss, *Spoken English in Ireland 1600–1740* (Dublin, 1979).
7 *The Plays of Richard Steele*, ed. S. S. Kenny (Oxford, 1971), Prologue to *The Conscious Lovers*, p. 304.
8 ibid., p. 377.
9 *The Works of the Right Honourable Edmund Burke*, 8 vols (London, 1877), V, p. 440 (from the Letter to Sir Charles Bingham, 1773).
10 *Goldsmith, The Critical Heritage*, ed. G. S. Rousseau (London, 1974), p. 69.

11 ibid., p. 338.
12 ibid., p. 345.
13 John Ginger, *The Notable Man; the Life and Times of Oliver Goldsmith* (London, 1977), pp. 254–7, 259–60, 270–3.
14 *Collected Works of Oliver Goldsmith*, ed. Arthur Friedman, 5 vols (Oxford, 1966), III, p. 198.
15 *Goldsmith, The Critical Heritage*, p. 180.
16 Burke, *Works* V, p. 268 (from *Letters on a Regicide Peace*, Letter III).
17 *Collected Works* V, pp. 212–13.
18 ibid., V, p. 210.
19 ibid., V, p. 217.
20 *The Dramatic Works of Richard Brinsley Sheridan*, ed. Cecil Price, 2 vols (Oxford, 1973), p. 110 (Act II, sc. iii).
21 Act II, sc. i, p. 99.
22 Act V, sc. ii, p. 440.
23 *The Letters of Oscar Wilde*, ed. R. Hart-Davis (London, 1962), p. 324.
24 Quoted from *The London Evening Post*, May, 1777, in *Dramatic Works* I, p. 315.
25 Richard Ellmann, *Golden Codgers* (Oxford, 1973), p. 42.
26 *Prefaces by Bernard Shaw* (London, 1938), p. 674.
27 ibid., p. 443.
28 ibid., p. 445.
29 *Our Theatre In the Nineties*, 3 vols (London, 1934), II, p. 32.
30 ibid., II, p. 31.
31 *Complete Works of Oscar Wilde* (London, 1971), pp. 1056–7.
32 ibid., pp. 990–1.
33 James Joyce, *The Critical Writings*, ed. E. Mason and R. Ellmann (New York, 1965), p. 202.
34 ibid., pp. 204–5.
35 *Complete Works*, p. 17.
36 ibid., p. 167.
37 W. B. Yeats. *Explorations*.
38 *Complete Works*, pp. 327–8 (Act I, sc. i).
39 ibid., p. 364 (Act III, sc. i).
40 *Prefaces*, p. 441.
41 *John Bull's Other Island*, Act IV, closing lines.

6 Irish modernism: poetry and drama

The literature of early modern Ireland is, in essence, a heroic literature, in which pride of place goes to the new idea of Ireland itself as a force variously embodied by outstanding individuals. The most important of these, from a political as well as a literary point of view, was Charles Stuart Parnell, the great leader of the Irish Parliamentary Party in the House of Commons, the 'uncrowned king of Ireland', the reserved aristocrat who briefly forged a powerful alliance of constitutional and physical force elements in his campaign for Home Rule. Cited as co-respondent in a divorce case in 1890, Parnell was abandoned by Gladstone and the Liberals, attacked by the Catholic Church in Ireland and finally undermined by division within his own party and defeat at the hands of the Irish electorate. He died in Brighton in 1891. When the ship carrying his remains arrived at Kingstown, Yeats was there to meet it, not because it bore the corpse of Parnell but because it brought back to Ireland Maud Gonne, the beautiful woman who had elicited from him an unrequited but unappeasable love. Parnell's funeral was the biggest ever seen in Dublin, a notable claim in a city which could boast of considerable expertise in this ritual. Portents were seen as the coffin was lowered into the grave. A meteor crossed the heavens, claimed one; another saw a star fall. The legend of a tragic hero was quickly established and it is perfectly appropriate that Yeats, however unwittingly, should, with his beloved, be in attendance at one of the solemn moments of its consolidation.[1]

The defeat of Parnell had many far-reaching consequences. It led to a weakening of constitutional nationalism and a proportionate strengthening of the appeal of the physical force movement among Irish nationalists. It distanced the Irish Catholic clergy from the new centres of Irish political activity. For Yeats, it meant that the young generation in Ireland turned in disgust from politics and gave their energies to cultural revival. He helped found the Irish Literary Society of London in 1891, the National Literary Society in Dublin

in 1892, the Irish Literary Theatre in 1897, the Irish National
Theatre Society in 1902 and the Abbey Theatre in 1904. Little
wonder he was called 'The Great Founder'. The same decade also
saw the foundation of The Gaelic League (1893), devoted to the
revival of the Irish language and initially sponsored by Douglas
Hyde and Eoin MacNeill, both of whom were to play important
roles in the emergence of the new Ireland. An Irish Race Convention was held in Dublin in 1896 and in 1898, the centenary year of
the Rising of 1798, James Connolly, Ireland's first Marxist thinker
and, later, a leader of the Easter Rebellion in 1916, produced his
newspaper *The Worker's Republic*. All of these organized groups
had a common aim – the redefinition of the idea of Ireland and of
the Irish community and its history.[2]

For the young Yeats, folklore was one of the sources for that
redefinition. The researches of the century before him, especially
those of Crofton Croker in 1825, were absorbed into his four
anthologies *Fairy and Folk Tales of the Irish Peasantry* (1888),
Stories from Carleton (1889), *Representative Irish Tales* (1891) and
Irish Fairy Tales (1892). In the three years 1889–92, he reviewed
numerous folklore collections and became something of an expert
in this field. Out of these grew the more personal essays of *The Celtic
Twilight* (1893, 2nd ed. 1902). At one time he intended to produce
'a big book about the commonwealth of faery' but abandoned the
enterprise and left as its only testimony his footnotes to Lady
Gregory's *Visions and Beliefs in the West of Ireland* (1920).[3] He
repudiated the stage-Irish, tourist Ireland of some of the
nineteenth-century collectors and emphasized in its stead the
importance of folklore for the realization of both nationality and
literature. 'There is no great literature without nationality, no great
nationality without literature'.[4] From the beginning, therefore,
there was an intimate connection between his political vision of
Ireland and occultism. The 'kingdom of Faery' was, in his view, a
natural part of the old civilization which English Puritanism and its
Irish middle-class Catholic descendant had destroyed. The solitary
and proud Parnell had appeared to offer to Ireland an image of her
old self, which was in remarkable contrast to 'the bragging rhetoric
and gregarious humour of O'Connell's generation and school',[5] and
the bond between him and the Irish people seemed to Yeats
analogous to the bond which linked the Anglo-Irish Ascendancy
and the Irish peasantry in a symbiotic imaginative relationship. The
fact that Parnell had been destroyed by the English and Irish middle

classes enhanced the hero's status as the true representative of nationality and nobility. In addition, Irish folk-tales and legends were local examples of the great world memory, in which the writings of Blake (which Yeats co-edited in 1893), Boehme and Swedenborg were prominent manifestations. Yeats founded the Dublin Hermetic Society in 1885. He became a member of Madam Blavatsky's Theosophical Society in 1887 and a member of the magical society known as the Order of the Golden Dawn in 1902. Yeats studied the key works of late nineteenth-century occultism with the same passion as he brought to Irish folklore. The two preoccupations were as one to him, despite the vast difference in literary quality between the respective bodies of material. Yet the figure of Parnell and the idea or ideal of Ireland which he represented remained a constant presence, modified in later years into other incarnations – Lady Gregory, Hugh Lane, Synge, Maud Gonne, Mussolini. At all times, Yeats was entranced by the possibility of history becoming legend before his eyes. The particularities of Irish history, intensely apprehended, could become the symbols of world history as they passed through the medium of art. In such a conception, Yeats would transcend the provincialism of mere nationalism and attain to the universality of art and legend.

Three great Irish writers had achieved, or were on their way to achieving, dominant reputations in the London of the early 1890s. Yeats described them as being 'too conscious of intellectual power to belong to party, George Bernard Shaw, Oscar Wilde, George Moore, the most complete individualists in the history of literature, abstract, isolated minds, without a memory or a landscape'.[6] Wilde and Shaw had missed out on the Irish revival. Moore was to be recruited for it as he turned away from the jingoism of England at the outbreak of the Boer War and rediscovered Ireland and an aspect of his artistic growth in the brilliant decade of 1901–10. Yeats's description of these three is ambiguous. To call them 'abstract' was, in his terminology, no compliment; but to praise their independence of party was a tribute to their artistic integrity in the bitter factionalism of the decade after Parnell's death. Wilde, the successful playwright and the outrageous dandy, had become a tragic figure after his conviction in 1895 for homosexual offences. As in the case of Parnell, Wilde became for Yeats the exemplary figure of the artist destroyed by middle-class moralism. He was also, of course, another Irish victim of English rancour. As a martyr, as a dethroned king, and as an enemy of all that was common and stereotyped in the English mind, Wilde attracted Yeats as a characteristic Celtic figure in an Anglo-Saxon world, an inheritor of the Anglo-Irish dramatic tradition in the line of Goldsmith and Sheridan. Although, in the end, he was to lower his opinion of Wilde's art, he never forgot the brilliant image of his life. Nor did he ignore what Wilde taught in his critical essay *Intentions* (1891) and in *The Soul of Man Under Socialism* (1895) – the necessity for the liberation of the personality, the complex theory of the Mask and the notion that 'there is no essential incongruity between crime and culture'.[7] Wilde challenged but did not entirely extricate himself from convention. Yeats resituated Wilde's career in his own version of the Irish community, the crucial grouping from which Wilde, despite his unimpeachably nationalist origins, had separated himself. Once he had entered the magnetic field of Yeats's myth-making energies, Wilde became, with Parnell, a harbinger and a type of the Irish hero, whose life had within it the potential for legend.

The same could not be said of Shaw. As Wilde was recruited, so Shaw was rejected. He too was iconoclastic and a dramatist in the rhetorical tradition of the eighteenth-century dramatists. In the preface to his play *Mrs. Warren's Profession* (1894, although the Lord Chamberlain refused to give it a licence for public performance), Shaw announced his 'determination to accept problem as the normal material of drama'.[8] This was anathema to Yeats, who preferred mystery to problem and ritual to energetic discussion. But this 'perfect modern Socialist and Creative Evolutionist' had more in common with Yeats than either of them supposed. He believed, like Yeats, that 'power and culture were in separate compartments';[9] he too devised a theory of historical destiny which yet gave room for the exercise of the heroic individual will; he too attacked British policy in Ireland on the ground that it failed to recognize the cultural differences between the two islands. Like Wilde, he played the Irishman in England, pleasing his audience by saying outrageous things about its most cherished convictions. But Shaw's mentors were Ibsen in drama and Marx and Darwin in political and social thought. He was far removed from the symbolists, pre-Raphaelites, aesthetes and folk-collectors, who provided Yeats with his intellectual background. Yeats, therefore, came to see him as a characteristic specimen of the modern rationalist mind, which sought in stage realism its appropriate form and in opinionated argument its appropriate rhetorical mode. Although the careers of the two men intertwined on occasion – Yeats's first play to be produced, *The Land of Heart's Desire*, was a curtain-raiser to Shaw's *Arms and the Man* in London in 1894; *John Bull's Other Island* (1904) was written for the Abbey, although not staged there until 1916; and Yeats defied British censorship by putting on Shaw's *The Shewing Up of Blanco Posnet* at the Abbey in 1909 – Yeats, in effect, expelled Shaw from his heroic pantheon and, in doing so, partly distorted Shaw's achievement in the eyes of the Irish audience. Both men fought against the propaganda, hypocrisy and lies which issued from the English press on Irish affairs, most notably in the case of the executed Roger Casement. But these alliances were less important than the differences which drove them apart. Shaw's liberal humanism was very far removed from the heroic nationalism and the magic-fed obscurantism of Yeats. Although both men finally admired authoritarian leadership as a rescue from the mass idiocies of early twentieth-century democracy, this ominous convergence enhances rather than blurs the essential differences between them.

George Moore, the last of this trio, was a different matter altogether. He had anticipated Yeats in his devotion to the ideal of making his own personality part of the subject matter of his writing and could be said to have outdone Yeats by making him the central character of Moore's own autobiographical masterpiece *Hail and Farewell*, published in 3 volumes, *Ave* (1911), *Salve* (1912), *Vale* (1913). As a novelist, Moore was a disciple of Zola, when he was at his best (in *A Modern Lover* (1883), *A Mummer's Wife* (1884, 1885), *A Drama in Muslin* (1886) and, above all, in *Esther Waters* (1894)); at his weakest, he was influenced by the decadent school (*A Mere Accident* (1887), *Spring Days* (1888) and *Mike Fletcher* (1889)). Moore had various missions in his writing life. At first, he saw himself as the man who would establish 'the aesthetic novel' in England, by introducing to George Eliot's London the Paris of Zola and the French symbolists and impressionists. Next he saw himself as a crusader against English moral and literary censorship, represented by the circulating libraries (which banned several of his novels) and the despotism of the three-volume novel. As he came increasingly under the influence of his Irish origins, he saw himself as the liberator of his native land from the thrall of priestcraft and Catholicism. Most of all, he was dedicated to charting the history of his 'soul', as he frequently called it. To that end, he produced a number of works of reminiscence and autobiography, which, taken together, form a remarkable account of the development of a modern consciousness. From *Confessions of a Young Man* (1888, revised editions in 1889, 1904, 1917, 1918), *Memoirs of My Dead Life* (1906), *Avowals* (1919, although first printed in 1904), *Hail and Farewell*, *A Story-Teller's Holiday* (1918), *Conversations in Ebury Street* (1924) and the unfinished *A Communication to my Friends*, which he was writing at the time of his death in 1933, Moore created in literature or as literature the history of the man who had been born at Moore Hall in County Mayo in 1852 and lived through the days of the Land League in Ireland, of the decadence in Paris and London and of the Irish revival in Dublin. Yeats never entirely recruited Moore but Moore certainly recruited Yeats and many others as contributors to the crystallization of his own personality. In him, as in Yeats, we see how history, refracted through literature, reappears as legendary fiction.

Although Moore did help to introduce the thought and art of France to the England of the 1890s, the critic Arthur Symons, most especially with his chief work *The Symbolist Movement in Literature* (1899), can take the credit for introducing Yeats to the literature of the continent, including that of Villiers de l'Isle-Adam, Mallarmé and Maeterlinck. It was Symons and Yeats and the landowner and playwright Edward Martyn (1859–1923) who invited Moore to join with them in founding a new Irish theatre. They met at Martyn's home, Tulira Castle in County Galway in 1896, visited the Aran Islands, and Yeats and Symons were invited to afternoon tea by Martyn's neighbour, Lady Gregory, who lived about four miles away at Coole Park. Thus was formed the nucleus of the Irish dramatic movement. Lady Gregory thenceforth became the most important of Yeats's mentors and collaborators. An Irish nationalist, a collector of folk-tales, a supporter of the movement to revive Irish and, eventually, a playwright (she wrote forty plays) and managing director of the Abbey Theatre, she became yet another of Yeats's heroic figures, although her practical aid and advice made her contribution a deal more specific than that of some of the other heroic shades to which Yeats paid his obeisance. A year later, Yeats met John Millington Synge in Paris and is alleged to have advised him to forsake the glittering city of the artistic decadence and to go instead to the Aran Islands to 'express a life that has never found expression'. Synge visited Aran in 1898. There the first phase of Yeats's dream came true. The Big House and the peasant folk of the

West of Ireland had been conjoined, in art, to produce the new Ireland, even though the representation of this strange land of the imagination would have to be made first to the predominantly middle-class Dubliners in the capital's theatres.

Yeats's second play *The Countess Cathleen*, performed in Dublin in 1899, inaugurated the modern Irish theatre's development with a premonitory row. The countess of the title sells her soul to the devil to save the Irish peasantry from famine. The Dublin public, including those members of it who had not seen or read the play, was outraged and condemned it as being irreligious and anti-national. The dispute which followed in the newspapers and journals, later published in a volume *Ideals in Ireland* (1901), revealed how readily the theatre could become a focus for national debate in Ireland, rather than a place of casual entertainment. Yeats exploited this situation to such a degree that his next play, *Cathleen Ni Houlihan*, became a central political text for those determined to overthrow English rule in Ireland. The setting of the play is 1798 in County Mayo, at the moment of the arrival of a French revolutionary army to support the rebels. An old woman persuades a young man to forgo marriage and realize a greater destiny by fighting for his country. On leaving the house, she is reported to have been transformed from old hag to young queen, thereby revealing her identity as the spirit of Ireland rejuvenated by heroic sacrifice. Maud Gonne played the title role and the audience was deeply moved. In these two plays Yeats had scandalized the religious convictions and inflamed the political ambitions of the Irish nationalists. He had begun the creation of his theatrical audience. Although the Abbey Theatre, as such, would not have its first production until 1904, the audience for it had begun to emerge by 1902.[10]

By that date, Yeats was already a well known poet. *The Wanderings of Oisin* (1889) and *The Countess Cathleen and Various Legends* (1892), followed in 1899 by *The Wind Among the Reeds*, had already established the fact that a knowledge of Irish folklore and legend would be an aid to understanding these beautiful blurred poems. But the Irish materials were also bound up with occult references. Yeats had proposed founding an Order of Celtic mysteries, partly in the hope of forging an understanding between himself and Maud Gonne. We see the combination of Celtic and occult references in a poem like 'The Secret Rose', where the Rosicrucian four-leaved rose enfolds Christian, pagan Celtic and William Morris figures:

Far-off, most secret, and inviolate Rose,
Enfold me in my hour of hours; where those
Who sought thee in the Holy Sepulchre,
Or in the wine-vat, dwell beyond the stir
And tumult of defeated dreams; and deep
Among pale eyelids, heavy with the sleep
Men have named beauty. Thy great leaves enfold
The ancient beards, the helms of ruby and gold
Of the crowned Magi; and the king whose eyes
Saw the Pierced Hands and Rood of elder rise
In Druid vapour and make the torches dim;
Till vain frenzy awoke and he died; and him
Who met Fand walking among the flaming dew
By a grey shore where the wind never blew,
And lost the world and Emer for a kiss; . . .

Yeats's knowledge of the legends of Cuchulain, Caoilte, Fand and
Emer came from the translations of Sir Samuel Ferguson and Standish O'Grady. He knew no Irish and was thereby denied access to
much that was vital in the Gaelic world. But his vision of that world
was determined by his belief that the specifically Irish national
energies had been occluded by the dominant discourses of Christianity and Science. Therefore they had a natural affinity with the
occult philosophy since both of them retained their faith in the deep
truths of the world's ancient wisdom. The combination of the two is
strange but increasingly powerful as Yeats labours to detach them
from their sectarian eccentricities and claim for them the prestige of
belonging to the universal world of the Great Memory. His fondness for organizing cultural and magical groups grew out of his
desire to belong to a privileged company of men and women who
would become the priesthood of a new spiritual revival:

Know, that I would accounted be
True brother of a company
That sang, to sweeten Ireland's wrong,
Ballad and story, rann and song;
Nor be I any less of them,
Because the red-rose bordered hem
Of her, whose history began
Before God made the angelic clan,
Trails all about the written page.

Maud Gonne, however, refused to become part of this special company. She repeatedly refused to marry him and, by so doing, compelled him to develop his belief in love as a discipline which demanded a wisdom denied to her and bequeathed to him. Her beauty was in one sense natural. In another sense it was the product of high culture. She took it as being the first only. He saw it as both. The labour of culture to produce a beauty which appeared completely natural became one of his favourite and most important analogies for the production of poetry, first defined in the famous poem of 1902, 'Adam's Curse':

> I said, 'A line will take us hours maybe;
> Yet if it does not seem a moment's thought,
> Our stitching and unstitching has been naught.

In a further extension of this thought, Yeats imagined Maud Gonne's beauty as a symbol of an heroic age, which she, its possessor, misread and vulgarized by surrendering it to the passionate but petty squabbles of a dilapidated present. Her marriage, in 1903, to Major John MacBride, confirmed this opinion. His Helen had, in effect, eloped with a guerilla fighter from the squalid Boer War, not with a Paris and not into the world-drama of the Trojan War. All that had been potentially noble was debased in modern conditions. His fight for Ireland was a battle against that debasement and for the realization of that nobility.

In turning to the theatre, he met the forces of debasement head-on. The Irish Literary Theatre ended in débâcle in 1901 with the production of *Diarmuid and Grainne*, a collaboration between Yeats and George Moore which merely demonstrated the impossibility of fusing the Celticism of the one with the literary Wagnerism of the other. But the same bill also contained Douglas Hyde's *Casadh an tSugáin* (*The Twisting of the Rope*), the first play in the Irish language to be staged in a proper theatre. The director was W. G. Fay who, with his brother Frank Fay, was to bring a particular style of acting and a specific idea of a national theatre to the Abbey stage. Hyde's play in Irish indicated the future contribution the Abbey would make to world drama. It was to be a folk theatre. When Fay's company merged with the Irish Literary Theatre to form the Irish National Theatre Society, it produced the first of the great folk plays associated with the Irish revival – John Millington Synge's *In the Shadow of the Glen*. In the next year, an Englishwoman,

Miss A. F. Horniman, presented the Theatre Society with the building known as the Abbey. Synge provided it with its first tragedy, *Riders to the Sea*. In 1907, with *The Playboy of the Western World*, Synge gave the Abbey his masterpiece and its most memorable row. The audience, which had begun to emerge in reaction to Yeats's *The Countess Cathleen* and *Cathleen Ni Houlihan*, now appeared in full force. The Abbey had become a national focus, not just another commercial theatre. Synge realized Yeats's idea of a theatre and Synge's audience made him alter it. The conflict between author and audience was construed (accurately enough) as yet another instance of the noble artist hounded by the motley crowd. Synge's death in 1909 confirmed the Parnellite theme. Thereafter, Synge was one of Yeats's heroic figures and his reaction to the poor response given Synge's last play, *Deirdre of the Sorrows* (1910), provoked him to write his great essay *The Tragic Theatre* (1910), in which Yeats distances himself from the theatre and audience he had done so much to create. The climax of Synge's play brings us, he claims, to that point 'where passion . . . becomes wisdom'. Theatre usually admires individual character. But now he sees

that tragedy must always be a drowning and breaking of the dykes that separate man from man, and that it is upon these dykes comedy keeps house.[11]

Yeats's conception of the tragic theatre, moulded by the work of Synge and the reception accorded to it, was never entirely at ease thereafter in the Abbey, where comedy and character predominated. Yet the theatre did remain a focus of the national life, even after the departure of the Fays in 1908, through the controversial American visit of 1911, and up to the next great row over Sean O'Casey's *The Plough and the Stars* in 1926, by which time it was subsidized by the new Irish state. Yeats's theatre and the Abbey Theatre were never quite the same thing but neither could have come into existence without the other.

It is difficult to extricate Synge from the subtle Yeatsian dialectic of heroism. He grew up in County Wicklow in a strict Protestant atmosphere and broke away from it slowly, though not entirely, by associating himself with the decadent movement in Paris and with the Irish *emigrés* there, most of whom belonged to Maude Gonne's militant Irish League organization. But Synge retained, throughout his short life, the integrity of a solitude which no group or organiza-tion ever breached. He dedicated himself to Ireland in an almost religious spirit and pursued his destiny through scholarship, at Trinity College and at the Sorbonne, where he studied Irish, and finally through the immersion of himself in the civilization of the Aran Islands, off the west coast, where he found a way of life that was as stark, lonely and vital as his own sensibility. Although he was attracted to and influenced by many of the leading figures of the literary scene – Yeats, Lady Gregory, George Russell and Stephen McKenna – and although he suffered a great deal in his passionate attachments to his mother and the two women whom he loved at different stages of his life, he remained implacably apart, a man who fed on loneliness. It is no surprise to find that words like 'lonesome' and 'lonely' dominate his plays. In the highly orchestrated speech which he derived from the talk of the Irish peasantry, he blended the melancholy of the *fin de siècle* Paris he knew so well with the imaginative vitality of the peasantry whom he would have liked to know better. The measured antiphonal patterns of the speeches in his plays confer upon them a stateliness, which is almost but never quite overborne by the lyrical intensities and excitement of their idiom. No one before him had ever incorporated the Irish language into English with such intimate thoroughness. In him, the nineteenth-century attempts to translate Gaelic into English reach an unexpected apotheosis. English had never been so effectively de-Anglicized.

Despite the melancholy atmosphere of his plays, they are all (with the exception of *Riders to the Sea*) subversively comic, because they manifest the triumph of the solitary imagination over the harsh actualities of social convention. His most typical hero is a sweet-tongued vagrant who talks himself and, sometimes, his female partner out of all sympathy with the world of common minds and into an acceptance of the supremacy of the adventure of self-discovery. In *The Shadow of the Glen* the tramp who entices the young wife Norah from her old husband makes his appeal from a world of nature and eternity against the world of the house, mar-riage and the slow monotony of age:

> Come along with me now, lady of the house, and it's not my blather you'll be hearing only, but you'll be hearing the herons crying out over the black lakes, and you'll be hearing the grouse and the owls with them, and the larks and the big thrushes when the days are warm, and

it's not from the like of them you'll be hearing a talk of getting old like
Peggy Cavanagh, and losing the hair off you, and the light of your eyes,
but it's fine songs you'll be hearing when the sun goes up, and there'll be
no old fellow wheezing, the like of a sick sheep, close to your ear.

Such speeches and such stories – taken by Synge from the folk
tradition – were bound to cause upset. *The Playboy* brought feelings
to a head. In the story of Christy Mahon's transformation from a
stuttering lout into the playboy poet who is finally master of his da
and of himself, Synge managed to cast a slur on the fair name of Irish
womanhood by having the young girls of the district appear in their
petticoats. In Old Mahon, Christy's father, he seemed to reintroduce the despised figure of the stage-Irishman. In making an
Irish community glamorize a man who was reputed to have killed
his father, he attacked that community's renowned capacity for
moral scruple. In fact, after eight riotous nights at the Abbey, during
which the theatre was lined with members of the Dublin Metropolitan Police, the DMP, whom Yeats led in on one occasion, the play
had become 'an event in the history of the Irish stage', as Synge
himself put it. The nationalists were enraged and rewrote Yeats's
own lines for him:

> Know that I would accounted be
> True brother of the DMP . . .[12]

Like Ibsen, Chekhov and Shaw – who caused a sensation in London
in 1913 by his use of the word 'bloody' in *Pygmalion* – Synge had
roused the ire of the middle classes. But in Ireland in 1907 the state
of national feeling was such that all things Irish were idealized to
such an absurd and sentimental degree that any breath of criticism
and any outspokenness on the famous 'national character' seemed
treacherous. Synge's plays, although part of the revival, are in fact
analyses of a dying culture, both in its Gaelic and in its Anglo-Irish
forms. The richness of speech contrasts with the poverty of action.
The gestures of freedom are made at the expense of the community,
because they are not possible in and through it. Pegeen Mike loses
the Playboy of the Western World, because he has achieved a
fullness the society can neither contain nor any longer find entertaining. In *The Well of the Saints* (1905), the blind couple, who have
their sight miraculously restored, prefer the blindness to which they
succumb again, so squalid was the sight of the actuality of the village

life they had glimpsed. Synge's comedies are able to establish the authority of the imagination with confidence only because no other form of authority – political, social or religious – is deemed worthy of respect.

In more sombre plays, *Riders to the Sea* and *Deirdre of the Sorrows*, the final authority belongs to death. *Riders* is a study in fatalism. The old mother, Maurya, sees her six sons taken from her by the sea and at first confronts this tragic condition with all the resources of ritual, both pagan and Christian, characteristic of the island culture to which she belongs. But with the death of her last son, Bartley, she resigns her motherhood and accepts the emptiness death brings:

> They're all gone now, and there isn't anything more the sea can do to me . . . I'll have no call now to be up crying and praying when the wind breaks from the south, and you can hear the surf is in the east, and the surf is in the west, making a great stir with the two noises, and they hitting one on the other. I'll have no call now to be going down and getting Holy Water in the dark nights after Samhain, and I won't care what way the sea is when the other women will be keening.

In *Deirdre*, death is seized by the young queen as an opportunity to escape a loveless marriage with Conchbor, the old king who has betrayed her and slaughtered her lover Naisi and his brothers. In escaping this, she also escapes 'grey hairs and the loosening of the teeth', the humiliations of age which come so severely after the consuming brightness of love and youth. Deirdre is Synge's last Romantic. His vagrant men lack her final courage, because their encounter is with the society that stifles consciousness rather than with the death that extinguishes it. Synge's acrid comic vision of the fading Irish culture is closer to that of Joyce in *Dubliners* and in *Portrait of the Artist* than it is to Yeats. But even so, Yeats had the last memorializing word in his poem 'On Those That Hated "The Playboy of the Western Word" ':

> Once, when midnight smote the air,
> Eunuchs ran through Hell and met
> On every crowded street to stare
> Upon great Juan riding by;
> Even like these to rail and sweat
> Staring upon his sinewy thigh.

Synge had imitators but no true follower. His exploitation of the literary resources of the Hiberno-English dialect was magnificent but also rather freakish. Ireland's linguistic instability and internal political and social divisions made Yeats's notion of 'Unity of Culture' seem a desperate hope rather than a realizable idea. Like so many of the modern Irish writers, Synge created a language, which for all its power never quite escaped a tendency towards self-caricature. This is true also of Joyce, Flann O'Brien, O'Casey and Beckett. It is only slightly less true of Yeats's prose and George Moore's reminiscences. The wish to establish a high literature which would articulate the national consciousness was undermined, in part, by the recognition that there was, socially speaking, no standard language which was the official voice of the nation at large. Irish, Anglo-Irish, Hiberno-English, West Briton, Celtic, Gaelic, English, British were all epithets that could be variously applied to social, political and linguistic groupings, which had been culturally Balkanized in the nineteenth century and were now being asked to become unified in the twentieth. After all, a regional dialect of English or Irish owed its vitality to the particular circumstances – usually circumstances of isolation – in which it lived. The odd thing about Synge's plays is the penury of their circumstantial detail. They are dateless, dislodged from history. This increases their appeal in one respect, but it also demonstrates their pronouncedly literary character in another. These are 'poetic', not 'realistic', plays. Their stories are parables that sometimes move rather uneasily in their folk costume. In his effort to create a national drama, Synge revealed the difficulty of avoiding the unease in relation to native culture, which is a feature of all colonial literature. This is equally evident in the reaction of the audience to his plays. The belief in that which was authentically Irish and therefore acceptable was the ground of the dispute between the author and the denizens of the pit. The assertiveness about authenticity was a symptom of the insecurity which surrounded the issue.

At its best, Synge's language is not open to the charge of mere eccentricity or of provincialism. It achieves 'a style that remembers many masters that it may escape contemporary suggestion'.[13] Yeats, however, felt that the controversy over Synge and, soon afterwards, the fresh controversy over the failure of the Dublin Corporation to build a gallery for the gift of Hugh Lane's great collection of paintings, had finally measured the distance between the 'schoolboy thought' of uneducated Ireland and his own conception of art. He therefore turned, in his plays, to a more esoteric audience and 'an unpopular theatre'. Yet at the same time his poetry moved in the opposite direction, becoming more hospitable to the actualities of daily life and speech. The publication of his *Collected Works* in 1908 (containing an almost valedictory essay on 'The Irish Dramatic Movement') marked the close of the first, long phase of his career. He was already the senior poet of the English speaking world and yet his greatest work still lay before him. The changes in style which mark *The Green Helmet and Other Poems* (1910) and *Responsibilities* (1914) leave the reader with a strong sense of the bitterness and anger Yeats felt at the spectacle of his private and public life in middle age. He was now very much 'the unfinished man', 'among his enemies'. In his bitter poem 'To A Shade' he advises Parnell to forsake the Dublin that has forsaken him:

> You had enough of sorrow before death –
> Away, away! You are safer in the tomb.

But his renewal of acquaintance with Ezra Pound in 1912 led to his discovery of the Japanese Nō drama and, with that, a definitive turn towards an experimental form of drama, which was to become the Irish theatre's next contribution to the European stage. Yeats combined what he learned of the Nō with what he already knew of symbolist drama and of the work of the great stage-designer Gordon Craig, to produce plays in which light, music, dance and words would combine on a stage redesigned to upset the expectations of realism fostered by the picture-frame setting of conventional theatre, to allure the audience 'almost to the intensity of trance'. Between 1915 and 1920 he wrote the *Four Plays for Dancers (At The Hawks Well, The Only Jealousy of Emer, The Dreaming of the Bones and Calvary)*, the first two of which reintroduce the key figure of the Irish saga hero, Cuchulainn, the tragic maimed hero, in whom Yeats's changing conception of Ireland was embodied, both in these and in three other plays – the earlier *On Baile's Strand* (1901–6), *The Green Helmet* (1910) and the final *The Death of Cuchulain* (1939). During these years Ireland was 'changed utterly'. The Easter Rising of 1916 and the subsequent executions, the electoral triumph of Sinn Fein over the Irish Parliamentary Party, the bitter War of Independence against the British, were the chief public events against which Yeats's private life sought comprehension and consolation. He married in 1917, bought a Norman tower in County Galway, close to Lady Gregory's estate, became father to two children, and began the construction of his systematic philosophy, which was to be published in 1925, and in revised form in 1937, as *A Vision*. By that time, the Irish Civil War had been fought, the Irish Free State established, the island partitioned and the local versions of European Fascism had been briefly consolidated. To Yeats, Ireland seemed to be enacting in microcosm the tragedy of Europe during and after the First World War. His training in occult theory had taught him to expect apocalypse and modern history certainly justified the sense of crisis which dominated his work from 1910 onwards. Yet again, as his poetry entered more and more into a series of outspoken meditations on history and violence, civilization and its discontents, his plays, preoccupied by the same themes, refused the dramatic confrontation between personality and event which vivified the poems and sought instead to render the themes in symbolic terms, seeking the appropriate emblems of adversity in arcane, mysteriously resonant, forms.

Yeats made the distinction himself, although he was speaking of the difference between graphic art and poetry. It nevertheless applies also to the difference between his poetry and his plays. It is 'poetry which sings the crisis itself' but at times it seems as if his theatre 'were the celebration of waiting'[14] – a remark which has obvious relevance to Beckett's plays also. The waiting is done in that strange 'architectonic'[15] space of Gordon Craig's stage, by masked figures or legendary emblems, which represent the opposed principles. In the reconciliation of such an opposition they will achieve fullness of being, forgiveness, the paradise of perfect beauty. They never do. But in a closing dance the spectacle of such fullness is revealed while they fade back into their stylized immobility and suffering. To describe the plays thus is, of course, to make them much more abstract and geometric than they actually are in performance. But the geometry is there, as it is in Yeats's figure of the Great Wheel of Time in *A Vision* and his obscure interpenetrating gyres or cones representing the dialectical nature of the historical process in the constant unravelling of the oppositions which characterize it. These oppositions have many names; we have primary as against antithetical, subjective and objective, darkness and radiance, violence and elegance, chaos and form. Yeats lived in an age given to apocalyptic philosophies of history. From Coleridge to Nietzsche to Spengler and, later, Toynbee, the interpretation of history was bound up with the conviction that the present was a moment of crisis in which the unfolding pattern of past, present and future became visible. Yeats's system is one among these and, although we may see through a glass darkly in reading *A Vision* and some of the plays, we can discern, in the figure of Cuchulain, the tragic emblem of Ireland's political strife and her dream of cultural unity. For Ireland, caught by the dream of integration, had enacted the process of disintegration. The country had found in actuality the perfect opposite to what it had conceived in its imagination. In Yeats's terms, it had found its Mask, or anti-self, something which he believed the individual, especially the artist, must also do, so that, in the tension thus generated, he can live in the energy of both. Of Bishop Berkeley, Ireland's foremost philosopher of the eighteenth century, he said, 'He that cannot live must dream'.[16] Equally, he that cannot dream must live. Yeats wanted the living and the dreaming, no matter what the strain. For he would neither be any longer a Romantic nor an Empiricist:

And why should I, whose ancestors never accepted the anarchic subjectivity of the nineteenth century, accept its recoil; why should men's heads ache that never drank?[17]

Nevertheless, if history were a matter of such ravelling and unravelling of opposed energies, where was peace to be found? The answer, unsurprisingly, was that it was to be found in art.

Still, the artist would remain time-bound. His creations would not. Hamlet belongs to the world's imagination, Shakespeare to its history. The tragedy of Ireland and of Cuchulainn was its failure to escape from history into that realm of the imagination:

Cuchulainn should (and could) earn deliverance from the wheel of becoming by participation in the higher self, after which he should offer his spiritual history to the world; instead he condemns himself to a career of violent and meaningless action, and this is responsible for the developing tragedy of his life.[18]

In these words and in this figure, Yeats identifies the central problem of his nation's literature. To offer its spiritual history to the world it must transcend the limitations of its origins. In failing to do so, it becomes a maimed and tragic literature. The terms of his argument are difficult here, as in the poems and plays, but that does not at all reduce the intensity of the feeling which informs them. 'Deep feeling', said Coleridge, 'has a tendency to combine with obscure ideas in preference to distinct and clear notions.'

The Easter Rebellion of 1916 provoked Yeats to write to Lady Gregory:

I had no idea that any public event could so deeply move me – and I am very despondent about the future. At the moment I feel that all the work of years has been overturned, all the bringing together of classes, all the freeing of Irish literature and criticism from politics.[19]

But the destructive consequences of the rebellion found their inevitable countering in the heroic impulse from which it arose and by which the mean society of the poem 'September 1913' had been transfigured. In 'Easter 1916' itself, a further opposition is introduced in the imagery of stream and stone, the first indicative of the flood of natural life, the other of fanaticism:

> Hearts with one purpose alone
> Through summer and winter seem
> Enchanted to a stone
> To trouble the living stream.

The 'terrible beauty' born in Easter week is, thus, transforming and disfiguring. Ireland has set an example to the world and, at the same time, thrown herself back into the factionalism of the bitter post-Parnellite days. So in all the great poems of the 1920s, we meet time and again magnificent rhetorical structures based upon antinomies – Ireland and Byzantium, youth and age, fecund life and stylized art, action and contemplation, love and war, violent energy and decadent civilization – which gain definition from one another without ever reaching, or seriously seeking, reconciliation. Dream and reverie (two of Yeats's favourite terms) were intensified by the discordant power of the surrounding violence. Yeats in his tower with its winding stair was a man living in a symbol. Itself the monument of a violent civilization, it surveyed another spasm of violence in which a new civilization was being born. By 1922, many Anglo-Irish Big Houses had been burnt by the anti-Treaty side, government executions and guerilla assassinations had brought six years of disturbance to a bloody climax and all that was humane and cultured seemed under threat. The modern apocalypse had come.

In his great volume of poems, *The Tower* (1928), Yeats sees European and Irish violence in the light of myth. Poems like 'Leda and the Swan' and 'The Second Coming' specify, in their opposed images of bird and beast, the ominous sense of subjectivity quenched, the dream of civilization translated into a formless nightmare. The First World War, the Russian Revolution and the Irish 'Troubles' all contribute to this charged vision, but the myth of the critical historical moment at which the bestial and the divine intersect is capacious enough to receive these without being filled by them.

In the 1930s, Yeats became involved with the Irish Fascist movement, the Blueshirts, led by one General O'Duffy. By this time he was laden with honours. The Nobel Prize for Literature in 1923, preceded the year before by his appointment to the Senate of the Irish Free State, honorary degrees and an awed reception for *The Tower* had all made him a figure of the most convincing respectability. Yet he again found his anti-self in poems and plays which displayed a renewed and bawdy preoccupation with sexual energies and in marching songs for his new-found political allies, which are as bumptious as they are bad. Yet again, in his last years, and most especially in *The Death of Cuchulain*, *Cuchulain Comforted* and *The Statues*, he seems finally to renew his faith in the idea of Ireland as the place of regeneration, the country which, having brought its great hero (Parnell/Cuchulain) down, reincarnates him once more:

> When Pearse summoned Cuchulainn to his side
> What stalked through the Post Office? What intellect,
> What calculation, number, measurement, replied?
> We Irish, born into that ancient sect
> But thrown upon this filthy modern tide
> And by its formless spawning fury wrecked,
> Climb to our proper dark, that we may trace
> The lineaments of a plummet-measured face.

Momentarily, the hero and the race are in accord with one another. In the poems on his own life and his great friends, Yeats had rewritten his account of modern Ireland as a place haunted by heroes. At the end of his life, he called for that heroism again, both from Irish writers and from the Irish people at large. Although he also saw that heroism was at a discount, that was merely in the oppositional nature of things. The murderers of Cuchulainn, the convicted cowards, the representatives of the common mob, find their opposites too:

> They had changed their throats and had the throats of birds.

Despite Yeats's reservations, the Abbey Theatre continued through all these years to produce (besides Yeats's own plays) its own peculiar blend of folk drama and basic Ibsen. Among the more memorable plays were those by Lady Gregory, written in the local dialect of her area, Kiltartan, between 1904 and 1910, including *Spreading The News*, *The Rising of the Moon* and *The Workhouse Ward*; Padraic Colum's *Thomas Muskerry* (1910); T. C. Murray's *Maurice Harte* (1912); George Fitzmaurice's *The Country Dressmaker* (1907), a play which Yeats believed at the time would lead to an even greater uproar than Synge's *Playboy*. Edward Martyn, after giving the theatre his own best play *The Heather Field*, broke away to found a new venture, the Irish Theatre, which survived from 1914 to 1920. Its first production, Martyn's *The Dream Physician* (1914), was a satire on Yeats and Moore and an act of kindly condescension to Lady Gregory. Otherwise, once that score had been paid, the theatre devoted itself to the production of contemporary continental drama, particularly Maeterlinck, Chekhov and Strindberg. Three of its chief personalities – Thomas MacDonagh, Joseph Plunkett and William Pearse – were executed after Easter 1916. This, along with various financial troubles, led to its closure a few years later. Its commitment to continental drama and its resistance to the commercially successful Abbey folk-farce was renewed later by the Gate Theatre, founded in 1928. Nevertheless, the Abbey, for all its faults, remained the national theatre, under Lady Gregory's shrewd and determined management. In 1926, the Abbey had another famous uproar, comparable to that which had greeted Synge's *Playboy* nineteen years before. The occasion was the first production of Sean O'Casey's *The Plough and the Stars*. 'I felt at the end of it', wrote Lady Gregory, 'as if I should never care to look at another; all others seemed so shadowy to the mind after this'. The third great Abbey dramatist had arrived. In a famous moment, Yeats faced the outraged audience:

> . . . you have disgraced yourselves again. Is this going to be a recurring celebration of Irish genius; Synge first, then O'Casey! . . . Dublin has again rocked the cradle of a reputation. From such a theatre as this went

forth the fame of Synge. Equally, the fame of O'Casey is born here tonight. This is his apotheosis.

O'Casey, listening in the wings, must have been pleased, if a little puzzled, for he had to wait until he got home and looked up 'apotheosis' in the dictionary before he quite knew what Yeats had meant.[20]

O'Casey's plays highlight one of the characteristics and one of the problematic features of Irish drama in particular and of Irish writing in general. They are linguistically self-conscious works, which display an uneasy relationship between their chosen form and their verbal vitality. Both Synge and Yeats had faced this issue. Synge had solved it in his way by giving primacy to a language which was simultaneously vital in its idiom and liturgically formal in its cadences and repetitive patternings. Yeats, still struggling with it in the 1920s, attempted various strategies – the Nō drama, the realist drama exploded from within as in *Words Upon the Window Pane*, in which the ghost of Swift erupts as an orphic voice in the middle of a dreary seance, the drama of mask, music and dance in which the movements of the body were allowed their opportunity for eloquence in competition with the speaking or chanting voice. From the outset of his career, O'Casey faced this problem too. It is customary to say that he resolved it less satisfactorily than the others, most especially after he had completed the three famous 'Dublin plays' about recent Irish history – *The Shadow of a Gunman* (1923) set against the background of the War of Independence against the British, *Juno and the Paycock* (1924) against the backdrop of the Irish Civil War and *The Plough and the Stars* (1926), which took the Easter Rising of ten years before as its setting. It is true that O'Casey owed a good deal to the Victorian Irish-American melodramatist, Dion Boucicault, in whose work the stage-Irishman had come into his fulsome own. The debt, greater than that O'Casey owed even to Shaw, makes it startlingly clear that there was no other dramatic tradition to which O'Casey or any other Irish dramatist of that time could comfortably belong. Wilde and Shaw had learned from the eighteenth century how to make a parade of their verbal eloquence. By the 1920s, that particular option was gone. When we hear in O'Casey's plays a strange mixture of music-hall voices, hell-fire preachers, phrases from Bunyan and the Authorised Version of the Bible, often deeply and naturally assimilated into colloquial speech, scraps of Shakespeare and

Shelley, which remain unassimilated, and Shavian soliloquies masquerading as dialogue, we can appreciate just how dishevelled O'Casey's literary and cultural inheritance was.[21]

Nor was this so because he was a member of the working class and an autodidact. Wilde, Shaw, Yeats, Synge and Moore were all writers of an anxiously eclectic spirit, who fashioned the most unlikely and anomalous materials into styles, poses and beliefs which are always more clear-cut at first sight than on closer examination. The idea of Ireland was a moulding element in the reading and writing of the Revival writers; it helped to bring their thoughts to the point where they could be hammered into unity, the unity of stylistic assurance. O'Casey, however, was disillusioned with the idea of Ireland so early and so traumatically that it became, for most of his career, a negative factor in his work, potent but embittering. As a Protestant member of the Dublin working class, he could hardly have been better placed to experience isolation and hardship. At the same time, he had a very different sense of who and what the Irish people, the possessors of the great communal voice, about which Yeats talked so much, really were. He sees history from their point of view. For the inhabitants of the Dublin tenement slums, the worst in Europe and among the worst in the world at that time, history is not part of an heroic destiny or a phase in an unfolding mythic drama. It is, above all things, chaotic, meaningless. But it is also a pageant which provides opportunities for posturing and talk. Clearly there are tragic and comic possibilities here and O'Casey realizes them to the full. But he seems unsure of what he finally wants to say. It is hardly enough to say that this revolutionary socialist who became a communist and stuck to his communist faith throughout the worst excesses of the Stalinist period in the 1930s was, at bottom, a pacifist. Yet such is the claim of many who have produced and commented upon the Dublin trilogy.

There is a strict division in these early plays between irresponsible and comic men and responsible, tragic women. The men drink and talk too much, work too little and indulge in heroic posturings. The women remain sober, worn down by poverty and authoritatively practical. They have all the famous set speeches, like Juno's, after the death of her own and Mrs Tancred's:

Take away our hearts o' stone, an' give us hearts o'flesh!
Take away this murdherin' hate, an' give us Thine own eternal love!

Yet the parasite Joxer and the useless husband and father Boyle have the last, winning malapropism:

The whole worl's in a terrible state o' chassis.

The humour and the morality never quite correspond with one another. O'Casey's condemnation of the male illusions which drive Dubliners to go to fight for an abstraction called Kathleen Ni Houlihan, while they are incapable of looking after the people in their own families and neighbourhoods, is so fierce that it betrays him into a condemnation of all political and ideological positions. The ignorance of the women would appear to be a safeguard against unfeelingness. These are highly stereotyped roles, taken straight from nineteenth-century melodrama and they are defeatingly strict for O'Casey's purposes. In *Drums Under the Windows* (1945), the third of his six volumes of *Autobiographies*, he tells of his reaction on reading Shaw's *John Bull's Other Island*:

Two elements fought each other here, back to back: a dream without efficiency, and efficiency without a dream; but with this tense difference: that from the dream efficiency could grow, but from the efficiency no dream could ever come. And now . . . The dreadful dreaming was being hitched to a power and a will to face the facts.[22]

O'Casey wanted the dream and the efficiency – a visionary social-ism. But the Irish Revolution of 1916–22 seemed to him to have given the dream only. The opportunity for a truly revolutionary outburst had been lost when James Connolly, the leader of the working-class and socialist Irish Citizen Army, had thrown in his lot with Padraig Pearse and the Irish Volunteers on that fatal Easter of 1916. O'Casey broke with the Citizen Army in 1914 because of the increasing rapprochement with the Volunteers and looked back on the Great Lockout of Dublin workers by the employers in 1913 as the truly significant moment in modern Irish history. His hero was James Larkin, the man who, in effect, organized Irish Labour against the employers. Once more, we see a writer fascinated by the spectacle of a hero betrayed, a noble cause sold, a glittering possi-bility denied. O'Casey's *The Story of the Irish Citizen Army* (1919) is the first of his threnodies on that theme. His *Autobiographies* (1939–54) is the last. The plays are a constant and anxious explora-tion of its complexities. O'Casey wanted to make it clear that abstraction, fanaticism and joylessness are especially dangerous when they make a sentimental appeal to the egoism and innocence of the individual. Politics, whether of the right or of the left, appears in his plays as nothing more than systematic oppression under the guise of some seductive illusion – one usually provided by religion. But this leads him, time and again, to identify joy, comic spirit and wit with an utterly amoral and apolitical stance of the sort we find in Captain Boyle and Joxer Daly in *Juno*. The uneasiness of this play is almost overcome in the great *The Plough and the Stars* (the title referring to the flag of the Citizen Army), but even there, when we see the final violation of the private, domestic world of the tenement by the British armed forces, we are left to wonder if violence as such has been condemned or whether only this kind of violence which does not lead to liberation for the mass of the people. In other words, the so-called pacifism of O'Casey's plays is bogus. He is opposed to useless violence but sees no escape from the futile illusions which promote it and the bibulous eloquence which seems to be its natural counterpart. The best talkers in O'Casey's early plays are the most useless people because talk has taken over entirely from action in a situation where no remedial action seems possible. The contrast with Synge is striking. Synge's people talk themselves out of inertia into action. O'Casey's people talk themselves into inertia for fear of action. In each case, talking is the central activity. The subject of the talk is the death of a community. The mode of talking is full of vitality. The vitality intensifies as the community degenerates. As a result, we finally witness the emergence of a wonderful individual performance, a virtuoso display in the midst of dilapidation. That is one of the appropriate images for Irish writing between Wilde and Beckett.

O'Casey recognized that the realism of the trilogy was insufficient for his purposes. When he turned from that towards a variety of expressionism, in *The Silver Tassie*, the Abbey (or, more precisely, Yeats) rejected it and O'Casey broke both with it and Ireland. He went to live in England and thereby, it is claimed, cut himself off from the roots which sustained him. After the *Tassie*, his plays become much more schematic. Colour symbolism abounds. Sexuality confronts Religion, Youth outfaces Age and, time and again, language runs out of control into false poeticism and absurd extravagance of a sort that would have made Boucicault blench. O'Casey seemed to be seeking for the form which would allow him to write a morality play about the liberation of humanity from institutional oppressions. But he could not find it. There was nothing in the eloquent Irish tradition which could supply him with the example or stimulus he needed. His degeneration as a writer had to do with the poverty of his inherited tradition quite as much as it had to do with his departure from Ireland. He was right to tell Yeats, in an angry response to Yeats's rejection of the *Tassie*, that

because of, or in spite of, the lack of a dominating character, [it] is a greater work than *The Plough and the Stars*.[23]

O'Casey, like Yeats himself, had learned to abandon realism and naturalism and the strong affection of these forms for outstanding characters. Instead he sought a drama of a new kind, in which music, light and dance – the Yeatsian ingredients – would be interfused within an expressionist frame with all the vigour and *brio* of the popular music hall. But O'Casey's plays were poorly staged in England, with the exception of *The Silver Tassie. Within The Gates* (1934), *Red Roses for Me* (produced in Dublin in 1943), *Purple Dust* (1943), *Cock-a-Doodle Dandy* (1949), *The Drums of Father Ned* (1959) are the most important of his later works. They are all abortive attempts on O'Casey's part to find a theatrical form that would not be literary, that would give the body as well as the voice the chance to proclaim its liberation. His emblems – the Rose, the Cock, the Lily, the Flood – are trite rather than simple. O'Casey, we may say, when he had the language, in his early plays, had yet to find the form; when he came close to finding the form, he lost control of the language. The rejection of *The Silver Tassie* by the Abbey may have had a great deal to do with this. But it would appear that O'Casey, the most hostile of all Irish writers to the literary and pretentious, was most prone to the attractions of a language which deserved both those epithets. As in his struggle between the demands of moral obligation and the delights of irresponsibility, between political ideology and a contempt for politics, he remained irresolute, a victim of a situation too complex for his gifts.

By mid-century, Ireland had passed through a series of political crises which had transformed it into a partitioned island containing an independent republic and a part of the United Kingdom. From the late 1920s to the mid-1950s, there was an increasingly strong reaction against the heroic vision which had helped to bring about the new state and the new literature. Sometimes this was expressed as hostility towards the Anglo-Irish Protestants, who had dominated the cultural revival. Sometimes it emerged as hostility to the grandiose ideals and militant fervour of the nationalism which had created the notion of an 'Irish Ireland' – one which would give pride of place to Catholicism and to the Irish language.[24] Despite these long decades of repudiation, the achievement of Yeats and his friends remains as one of the last flowerings of European romanticism and one of the first essays in what has been called International Modernism. Yeats's poetry clearly embraces both these elements. But they are also evident in his plays and in those of Synge and O'Casey. All of their work has to be seen in the light of that of their great contemporary James Joyce and of the young man for whom Joyce became a model of the modern artist, Samuel Beckett. His allegiance to Irish drama was spelt out in characteristic style when he was asked for a contribution to a centenary programme on Shaw. He replied:

I wouldn't suggest that G.B.S. is not a great playwright, whatever that is when it's at home. What I would do is give the whole unupsettable apple-cart for a sup of the Hawk's Well, or the Saints', or a whiff of Juno, to go no further.[25]

Although the community of the Irish nation and the community of the Irish artists were not at all identical, the relationship between them was carried on into the later part of the century – tense, disrespectful and inescapable.

Notes

1   Herbert Howarth, *The Irish Writers, 1880–1940: Literature Under Parnell's Star* (London, 1958), pp. 5–20.

2   R. Dudley Edwards, *A New History of Ireland* (Toronto and Dublin, 1972), pp. 256–60.

3   Edward Hirsch ' "Contention is better than loneliness": The Poet as Folklorist', in *The Genres of the Irish Literary Revival*, ed. R. Schleifer (Norman, Oklahoma and Dublin, 1980), pp. 11–25; Mary H. Thuente, *W. B. Yeats and Irish Folklore* (Dublin, 1980).

4   *Uncollected Prose* I, ed. J. Frayne (New York, 1970), p. 104.

5   *Autobiographies* (London, 1955), p. 195.

6   Commentary on the poem 'Parnell's Funeral', in *The King of the Great Clock Tower* (London, 1934). See also Michael Steinman, *Yeats's Heroic Figures: Wilde, Parnell, Swift, Casement* (London, 1983).

7   Quoted in Richard Ellmann, *Golden Codgers* (London, 1973), p. 73.
8   *Prefaces by Bernard Shaw* (London, 1938), p. 228.
9   ibid., Preface to *Heartbreak House*, p. 379.
10 Ian Jack, *The Poet and His Audience* (Cambridge, 1984), pp. 144–68.
11 *Essays and Introductions*, p. 241.
12 Hilary Berrow, 'Eight Nights in the Abbey', in *J. M. Synge Centenary Papers 1971*, ed. M. Harmon (Dublin, 1972), pp. 75–87.
13 *Essays and Introductions*, p. 243.
14 ibid., p. 244.
15 Quoted in Katharine Worth, *The Irish Drama of Europe from Yeats to Beckett* (New Jersey, 1978), p. 51.
16 *Essays and Introductions*, p. 399.
17 ibid., p. 407.
18 *A Vision* (London, 1937), p. 86.
19 *Letters of W. B. Yeats*, ed. Allan Wade (London, 1954), p. 613.
20 Ulick O'Connor, *Celtic Dawn: A Portrait of the Irish Literary Renaissance* (London, 1984), pp. 262–3.
21 John Arden, 'Ecce Hobo Sapiens: O'Casey's Theatre', in *Sean O'Casey: A Collection of Critical Essays*, ed. Thomas Kilroy (New Jersey, 1975), pp. 61–76; see also Introduction by Thomas Kilroy, pp. 1–16.
22 *Autobiographies*, 2 vols (London, 1981), I, p. 560.
23 Quoted in Kilroy, p. 116.
24 See Terence Brown, *Ireland, A Social and Cultural History, 1922–79* (Fontanta Paperbacks, 1981).
25 Quoted by Katharine Worth, op. cit., p. 242.

7 Irish modernism: fiction

In his last work, *A Communication to my Friends* (1933), George Moore gave his own peculiar account of his involvement with the Irish revival:

After a year and a half's residence in Ireland I began to see Ireland as a portrait, and the form in which to choose to draw her portrait was the scene of a dozen short stories . . . if I succeeded in doing this, I would supply the Irish writers not yet in being with models on which they might make their stories more authentic than mine. The title of the book should have been *A Portrait of Ireland*, but that seemed too flagrant and I chose another title *The Untilled Field*, which seemed to me sufficiently suggestive of the intention of the book, but I found no storyteller in Ireland who wished to take light from another; they all deemed that they possessed the light, and that when Ireland obtained her freedom she would rise higher than she had ever risen before; that the new Ireland would rival the Greece of Pericles. [1]

The Untilled Field first appeared in Gaelic in 1902. The first English edition of the following year is substantially different and, characteristically, Moore included further revisions in the editions of 1914, 1926 and 1931. The half-dozen stories in Irish and the thirteen in English expressed a dualism in Moore and in the Irish revival, which was to endure for some decades afterwards. They are stories about the necessity for exile by an exile who found it necessary to return. They depict an Ireland which is spiritually stifling but in such a manner that the ideal of liberation gains strength only in virtue of the forces which would deny it. They identify the oppressive element in Irish society as Catholicism at the moment when Irish Catholicism was assuming to itself the role of liberator from the thrall of British rule and Protestant Ascendancy. In other words. Moore asserts the primacy of individual freedom and is sceptical, to say the least, about the capacity or willingness of the national cultural and political revival to allow for it. His Ireland is a vacuum in which the free soul withers and dies. It is difficult to avoid seeing here the first modern crystallization of the declarations of spiritual independence, which form such an important part of the tradition of Irish fiction in Joyce, Beckett and others throughout the century. Despite the soft malice of his words in *A Communication to My Friends*, others did take their light from him although, in them too, the light cast ambiguous shadows in their fictions. Moore amalgamated so much of Irish literary and social experience in his life and writings that he is a perfectly appropriate stepfather to the dishevelled and quarrelsome brood of novelists who were to succeed and, in some instances, outshine him.

He was a Catholic landlord from County Mayo, who witnessed the slow death of the semi-feudal relationship between landowners and tenantry from the Land League disturbances of the 1880s to the burning of the Big Houses in the 1920s. Moore Hall was burned down during the Irish Civil War in 1923. In 1880, George's sojourn in Paris had been ruined by a letter informing him that the tenants would pay no more rent until a reduction was granted. This presage of financial disaster impelled him to go to London to earn his living as a writer. His first aim, though, was to be a writer; as for earning a living, his tenants could do that for him, at a lower level and with more reluctance than he found agreeable. But to be a writer, Moore found he had to assemble a mass of new and sometimes ready-made materials provided by a number of miscellaneous sources – Zola, Flaubert, the Goncourt brothers, Turgenev, Tolstoy, Wagner, the French symbolists, led by Mallarmé, the French impressionists, led for him by Manet and Dégas, Walter Pater and, finally, W. B. Yeats and Edward Martyn. The various artistic movements represented by these names all gained his adherence for a time and all were repudiated in time. In the course of his various enthusiasms, Moore produced a series of books, which bore the imprint of his discipleship and, occasionally, demonstrated a temporary mastery over the competing influences which he courted so assiduously. He was a scholar of gossip, conversation and anecdote, not of books, so he wears his light learning lightly. But his ability to absorb French and English cultural models into his own Irish experience is almost as inexhaustible as that of Yeats. Like Yeats, he was thereby furnishing an example to the modern Irish tradition of writing by demonstrating the advantages to be gained from indulging an eclectic fury in the service of a single domineering ambition – to become an artist. In his search for an ultimate style – what he was later to call the 'melodic line'[2] – he anticipates one of the anxieties of a literature which felt sharply the lack of a secure tradition and a consequent fascination with the twin problems of language and form.

Specifically, *The Untilled Field* is important because it demonstrated the art of composing a number of stories into a unified pattern, thereby making the total design of the collection more effective than the design of any individual story. This was a practice to be repeated, more famously, by Joyce in *Dubliners* and by Samuel Beckett in *More Pricks than Kicks*. The interwoven themes of exile and freedom, clerical despotism and the power of folk belief, repudiation of Ireland and attraction for it, sexual repression and sexual longing, were all to be taken up again and again in later years. But Moore's Ireland remains firmly lodged in the nineteenth century. It bears the marks of famine, emigration and dispossession. The people have almost melted into the lonely landscape:

They were scanty fields, drifting from thin grass into bog into thin grass again, and in the distance there was a rim of melancholy mountains, and the peasants I saw along the road seemed a counterpart of the landscape. 'The land has made them', I said, 'according to its own image and likeness', and I tried to find words to define the yearning that I read in their eyes as we drove past. But I could find no words that satisfied me.[3]

The limp syntax and the consequent limpidity of tone are characteristic features of Moore's style. The yearning in the peasants' eyes and the yearning of the artist to find the right words for it become as one, so that the reader is alerted to the intractability of the Irish experience for the Irish writer as much as for any agent of social improvement. (In fact the narrator in this instance is an agent for the Irish Industrial Society.) Socially, those who prohibit improvement are the priests. This is most painfully exposed in the volume's most famous story, 'Home Sickness', in which an exile, James Bryden, returns home to regain his health after thirteen years in the noisome atmosphere of a Bowery slum in New York. But, although he wants to marry a local girl, Margaret Dirken, and settle down in the beautiful landscape of his youth, the authoritarian interference of the local priest so discourages him that he finally returns to New York and abandons all that he loves. Yet, years later, the owner of the bar-room where he had served, married and with grown-up children, his memory lingers on Ireland and Margaret:

There is an unchanging, silent life within every man that none knows but himself, and his unchanging, silent life was his memory of Margaret Dirken. The bar-room was forgotten and all that concerned it and the things he saw most clearly were the green hill-side, and the bog lake and the rushes about it, and the greater lake in the distance, and behind it the blue line of wandering hills.[4]

The tender note of regret had not always been prominent in Moore's reaction to his native land. In 1887, a book of essays, *Parnell and his Island*, appeared in London, having previously been published in a series in a French newspaper. It is difficult to describe the tone of this book. Regret lingers there, evoked for the most part by the spectacle of the decline of Irish landlordism. But there is also a note of hatred so savage that it borders on the pathological. This is evinced by the Irish peasantry and by the ruinous, squalid conditions of their life. Moore recognizes that the landlord system deserves to die, but he cannot bear the thought that the peasantry will, in turn, take over. His ambivalence on this point is matched by that of Standish O'Grady and Yeats. All the imagery of aristocratic elegance and civility, which survives to this day in Irish fiction and even in Irish poetry, is darkened by the recognition that it arose out of plunder and oppression. Violence is its natural companion:

In Ireland every chicken eaten, every glass of champagne drunk, every silk dress trailed in the street, every rose worn at a ball, comes straight out of the peasant's cabin.[5]

A writer who had trained himself in the French school of naturalism could hardly fail to emphasize the filth and degradation of the peasant's living conditions. He had already shown his gifts in that line with the account of the degradation of Kate Ede in *A Mummer's Wife* (1885), a study of the collapse of a personality under the stress of a total change in environment. In his 'Dublin novel', *A Drama in Muslin* (1886), the peremptory influence of environment is tempered by the force of the inner life of the heroine, Alice Barton. But the environment is, nevertheless, powerful; Dublin and Ireland in decay, presided over by the Dublin Castle, which has lost its political function and is reduced to a grim imitation of the London season to bolster its self-image as the nerve-centre of the nation:

On the right murder has ended for the night; on the left, towards Merrion Square, the violins have ceased to sing in the ballrooms; and in their white beds the girls sleep their white sleep of celibacy. Passion and grief have ceased to trouble the aching heart, if not for ever, at least for a while; the murderer's and the virgin's reality are sunk beneath a swift-rolling tide of dreams – a tide deeper than the river that flows beneath the tears of the lonely lover. All but he are at rest; and now the city sleeps; wharves, walls, and bridges are veiled and have disappeared in the fog that has crept up from the sea; the shameless squalor of the outlying streets is enwrapped in the grey mist, but over them and dark against the sky the Castle still stretches out its arms as if for some monstrous embrace.[6]

A Drama in Muslin (re-titled *Muslin* in the revised edition of 1915), tells the story of a group of Galway convent girls who enter into the marriage market of Anglo-Irish society on their presentation at the Viceregal Court in Dublin. Their different responses to the commercial-sexual world of the Castle and to the divided world of the rich and the poor provide us with a social commentary on the society of late Victorian Dublin. The central figure, Alice Barton, reacts against a system which produces such poverty for the mass of the people and such humiliation for women. In the end, she marries and leaves Ireland, having learned something of the shallowness and deception of the muslin world of the women who are entrapped within it. Most of all, perhaps, she has learned the futility of doing anything about the state of Ireland in 1882; evictions, political murder, Land League war and, in the midst of all, this pathetic muslin world of marriage and barter. She marries a dispensary doctor and they go off to a useful life in England. Moore was once more choosing exile as the only solution in a country where the problems, and the ambiguities, seemed insoluble.

Nothing could be more different than his greatest triumph in the naturalistic style, his answer to Hardy's *Tess of the D'Urbervilles* and perhaps also his answer to the futility and frustration that dominate *A Drama in Muslin*. The novel, *Esther Waters* (1894), is still the novel by which Moore is most remembered. It is subtitled 'An English Story' although many of its readers would regard it, along with Ford Madox Ford's *The Good Soldier*, as one of the best French novels in English. Moore always patronized the English novel as something attempted by 'only the inferior or – shall we say? – the subaltern mind'.[7] No doubt he thought that a French infusion would reinvigorate it in the 1890s as an Irish one would at the turn of the century. The point is worth making only because it indicates how uneasy Moore was with the idea of any securely established tradition. Tradition was, like style, dependent on tone. The French and some of the Russians had it. In prose narrative the English did not. He would scarcely have acknowledged that the Irish had even prose narrative.

Yet, despite all these poses and snobberies, Moore produced in *Esther Waters* one of the most humane and sympathetic of all those stories of a blighted life, which are found so abundantly in late Victorian literature. Esther, an illiterate servant-girl, is seduced and deserted, then dismissed from her situation at Woodview by Mrs Barfield. She keeps her child against all odds, is partly won over to the religious views of the Plymouth Brethren, but meets up with her seducer William again and goes to live with him in his public house. His passion for gambling ruins the business and his health is broken. After his death, Esther goes back to her former position with Mrs Barfield at Woodview. The novel is naturalistic in the sense that Moore has done his homework and created the world of the bar and of the race-track with close attention to accurate detail. But it is also a psychological study of the instinctive will to survive in Esther, which overcomes the most crushing circumstances. Moore shows a sympathy with the lives of the poor, which he had kept carefully concealed up to this point. But he also displays, with that, an admiration for Esther's instincts, which is closely bound up with her illiteracy. This is no 'muslin martyr'; this is a woman who has kept her primary instincts unviolated. It is possible to see here a reordering of his attitude towards the Irish peasantry and a certain, if incipient, benevolent feudalism towards these creatures of the soil and of instinct. Even at his most humane, Moore manages to be faintly maladroit and condescending.

Celibates, a volume of three novellas published in 1895, brings Moore closer to his preoccupation with the fate of a cloistered sexuality in a sensual world. The three figures, Mildred Lawson, John Norton and Agnes Lahens, deflect their natural desires into religious cravings. Moore is moving towards his analysis of his own country's condition in his various repetitions of the psychological intimacy between spirituality and sensuality. The most astonishing novel of his early career, *Evelyn Innes* (1898), explores this intimacy against a musical and mythological background not surpassed in its elaboration until Joyce's *Ulysses* appeared. The eponymous heroine, an opera singer, finds herself forced to choose between two lovers, Sir Owen Asher, the wealthy, sensual man, and Ulick Dean, the dedicated and spiritual Irish artist, modelled very obviously on W. B. Yeats, with whom Moore had begun to collaborate on the play *Diarmuid and Grania*, based on a legend in which the heroine is faced with a similar choice. The connection between this legend and that of Tristan and Isolde is also given due prominence in a work deeply impressed by the influence of Wagner. The French novelist Edouard Dujardin, the perfect Wagnerite, had already attempted to show how the Wagnerian motifs could be used in the structuring of a novel – his was called *Les Lauriers sont coupés*, frequently cited as the novel which introduced Joyce to the so-called 'stream-of-consciousness' method. This novel is Moore's most ambitious attempt to organize his material in such a way that his supple prose would achieve cumulative effects by the repetition of phrases and ideas operating like motifs. Moore's invertebrate syntax does not help him to avoid a lushness of effect, which is often overpowering. Nevertheless, *Evelyn Innes* is a remarkable novel, in which the search for a new language and a new form is decisively extended. Moore was now beginning to produce fiction which was neither 'French' nor 'English' in its provenance. His experimentalism had opened the way to the modern novel, which, in its endless interrogation of traditional forms, was to prove so attractive to Irish writers, for whom such interrogation was a necessity if they were to write at all.

Thus Moore moved to Dublin in 1901, seeking through Yeats and Martyn refreshment from a new centre of energy and abandoning England with the abruptness which marked all his temporary enthusiasms. After *The Untilled Field*, came *The Lake* (1905). As usual, it went through revisions – minor for the second impression of 1905, substantial for the edition of 1921. (Moore's constant revising and disowning of earlier works makes him a bibliographer's nightmare.) *The Lake*, which was originally to have been one of the stories in *The Untilled Field*, was warmly acclaimed as a masterpiece. Dedicated to Dujardin, it employs the interior monologue pioneered by the dedicatee but with greater subtlety. The story is simple, the treatment complex. An Irish Catholic priest, Fr. Oliver Gogarty, expels the local schoolmistress from the parish because she is pregnant. She goes to London and, through the intervention of another priest, who reproves Gogarty for his severity, they establish a correspondence, which becomes for him a process of education. He rediscovers the passional life he has buried and forsakes the priesthood by swimming across the lake on the first stage of his journey into exile and freedom in America. He leaves his clothes neatly folded to give the impression that he has drowned. It is the development of the priest's growing consciousness which stays in the memory of most readers. It is witnessed both from his own point of view and that of others, primarily from that of Rose Leicester (or Nora Glynn as she was renamed in the 1921 edition). She has learned to see the priest's plight as an example of the evolution of historical religious belief, although she also has her own personal involvement in the business. He sees it as a personal crisis, which can be overcome with the help of her sympathy and her more objective view of the situation. The discussions which dominate the letters are fused with descriptions of the lake in its various moods, the sky which it reflects, the landscape which it dominates. As he finally escapes, Fr. Gogarty muses

'I shall never see that lake again, but I shall never forget it,' and as he dozed in the train, in a corner of an empty carriage, the spectral light of the lake awoke him, and when he arrived at Cork it seemed to him that he was being engulfed in the deep pool by the Joycetown shore. On the deck of the steamer he heard the lake's warble above the violence of the waves. 'There is a lake in every man's heart,' he said, 'and he listens to its monotonous whisper year by year, more and more attentive till at last he ungirds.'[8]

The sympathy which Moore brings to the examination of Fr. Gogarty's case is singularly absent when he treats the issues raised by religious belief in his great work of reminiscence *Hail and Farewell*. He was wise to leave Dublin before the first volume appeared, for it is a work of stylish malignance. Having used the name of Oliver St John Gogarty, the wit and friend of Joyce, in *The Lake*, he now went much further and paraded the literati of Dublin under their own names for the delectation of posterity. He wrote, as Susan Mitchell, his most acerbic critic, said, 'with a complete disregard for the feelings' of his friends, 'marvelling only that his friends should prefer immortality in any other form than that he had chosen for them'. Nevertheless, 'this new and daring form of the novel'[9] was more than an epic work of gossip, although that aspect of it remains one of its attractions, as it does of Joyce's *Ulysses*. Both writers convert Dublin from a capital city into the world's archetypal village. Edward Martyn, the type of the ascetic man, who transmutes his sensuality into the appreciation of art, and a devotion to religion, is the book's outstanding portrait. In him, Moore tries to tease out the complications of the Irish mind and the effect upon it of its contemporary social and cultural environment. Yeats too appears as a writer given to ritual and idealism of such an ethereal kind that he is unable to encompass within his work or within the movement that he led the simple, 'pagan' joys of sensual experience. Thus both men, and the country they represent, are portrayed as lacking in a deep inner vitality, which will finally have corrosive effects upon their creativity. Brooding over these is, of course, the humorous figure of George Moore himself, cast in the role of the messiah who has come to save Ireland from her spiritual and sensual disfranchisement. Like all messiahs, he is not honoured in his own country and must leave it so that it may learn more thoroughly just what it has missed. As always, Moore's fascination is with the figure of the artist and the difficulty of his role in trying to redeem society and life itself from the rigours of the self-imposed constraints with which it has been afflicted. In giving an account which will move easily from petty incident to philosophical disquisition, Moore developed further that flexible and insinuating style which can become saturated with sensations and impressions without ever quite losing its narrative, discursive drive. An intellectual crisis – his resolve to renounce Catholicism publicly and declare himself a Protestant, for instance – impels him to go on one of his walks in search of a friend to whom he can unbosom himself. The friend on this occasion is George Russell, better known as AE, the saint of the Literary revival:

I wrote for an hour and then went out in search of AE: it is essential to consult AE on every matter of importance. . . . The night was Thursday, and every Thursday night, after finishing the last pages of *The Homestead*, he goes to the Hermetic Society to teach till eleven o'clock. But the rooms were not known to me, and I must have met a member of the Society who directed me to the house in Dawson Street, a great decaying building let out in rooms, traversed by dusty passages, intersected by innumerable staircases; and through this great ramshackle I wandered, losing myself again and again. The doors were numbered, but the number I sought seemed undiscoverable. At last, at the end of a short, dusty corridor, I found the number I was seeking, and on opening the door caught sight of AE among his disciples. He was sitting at a bare table, teaching, and his disciples sat on chairs, circlewise, listening. There was a lamp on the table and it lit up his ardent, earnest face, and some of the faces of the men and

women, others were lost in shadows. He bade me welcome, and continued
to teach as if I had not been there.[10]

This is a memorable moment in this literary *flâneur's* sojourn
through Dublin. It gives a brief snapshot of all that AE stood for –
mysticism combined with the pragmatic wisdom which he provided
in the columns of his newspaper *The Irish Homestead*. We recognize
at once why AE is one of the heroes of this book. He concedes to
both the sensual and the spiritual aspects of existence. His head is in
the clouds but his feet are on the ground. No one quite captured, as
Moore did, the secret of his enormous appeal and influence. Yet the
reader who knows little or nothing of AE would recognize that, in
the economy of this work, he is the inevitable father-confessor for
someone like Moore, for Moore, in all the minuscule detail of his
volumes, has steadily dwelt on the Irish as well as his own intellectual
divisions. In this man, AE, they are harmoniously reconciled. The
portraits of individuals are, therefore, memorably unique and yet
they form part of a composite and interweaving pattern, which gives
coherence to the medley of scenes and conversations. Again it is
difficult to avoid thinking of Joyce in *Ulysses* and the manner in
which he too composed a series of recurrent motifs within a thickly
sown pattern of apparently random sensations and gossipy interludes.

Like his great contemporaries, Yeats and Joyce, Moore was
prepared to rewrite history and myth in order to ratify his quest for a
radical freedom which could be asserted in the face of all routinized
attitudes and objections. *The Brook Kerith* (1916) is his most
remarkable, *A Story-Teller's Holiday* (1918) is his most intractable
effort to do so. In the first, he tells the story of a Jesus who did not
die on the Cross, but was taken down and brought back to life and
sent to become a shepherd among the Essenes. Twenty-five years
later he meets St Paul, full of crusading zeal for the Christianity of
Christ Crucified. In the final encounter between them, St Paul
insists on continuing with his mission. He is willing to preach the
spirit against the flesh, thereby re-enacting that schism in the religious mind which Moore found simultaneously fascinating and repellent. The same separation, more brutally imposed, characterizes the
life of the famous lovers in his last large-scale work, *Heloise and
Abelard* (1921). In *A Story-Teller's Holiday*, he returns to the
treatment of specifically Irish material, telling Irish legend through
the medium of a highly improbable native story-teller, named Alec
Trusselby. Old legend and contemporary story are linked by the

recurrent theme of celibacy and the tragedies, minor or major, which flow from its enforcement. Part of the interest of the two volumes depends upon the exchange between the two narrators, Trusselby and Moore himself, described as 'a dialogue between the original and the acquired self'.[11] The Dublin Moore describes at the outset had been shelled by the British in the 1916 Rebellion. Its famous buildings 'are but phantoms', it is 'a city that has passed away'. Babylon, Pompeii and Herculaneum are called upon to give the appropriate air of transience and desolation. Yeats has left, 'having become a myth from too long brooding on myths'.[12] The world of *Hail and Farewell* has already begun to disappear, although the 'young doctor who supplies Dublin with jokes'[13] and entertained Moore on the steps of the Shelbourne Hotel – almost certainly Oliver St John Gogarty – was not far from achieving his second immortalization in fiction of a kind which would reassemble the Dublin that was now disappearing, although under a different rubric. Having been the priest of *The Lake*, he was already transformed into the Buck Mulligan of *Ulysses*. Joyce, to his chagrin, did not merit an invitation to Moore's soirées in Dublin, although Gogarty did. Now it is sometimes difficult to remember that Moore and Gogarty had any other function than to have been associated with Joyce, whose experimentation with the novel and whose fascination with Ireland, the artist, sexual repression and the dedication of the work to the restoration of sundered flesh and spirit, past and present, had all been central preoccupations of Moore's career too. The Ireland he knew was, nevertheless, fading fast. He had a premonition of the end of Moore Hall, his ancestral house:

Moore Hall will certainly fall into ruin. As soon as you have gone, the trees will be felled, and the lead taken from the roof; Moore Hall will be a ruin within a very few years; for not a great many years of life lie in front of you.[14]

Moore Hall did become a ruin. The literature that had been produced by the people of the Irish Big House was disappearing with the conditions that had initially promoted it. Yeats in his tower will always be one of its symbols; Lady Gregory and Coole Park another; George Moore and Moore Hall the most ambiguous and yet, in many ways, the most characteristic of all. But another man in another kind of tower was to dominate the history of both Irish and modern fiction. This was James Joyce in his martello tower in

Sandycove, County Dublin. Disguised as Stephen Dedalus, he was to find a new manner of walking and talking in Dublin and of making a narrative out of it.

So much has been written about James Joyce that there is no need to repeat much of it here, although it is remarkable that the commentary on his works should have turned into such an endless industry. That in itself says something about the later works in particular. *Ulysses* (1922) and *Finnegans Wake* (1939) present so many difficulties to the reader that they solicit guides and keys, dictionaries of allusion and reference, various sorts of exegetical compendia as well as interpretive essays, in which the shock of these new masterpieces is slowly absorbed and overcome. From the beginning he was opposed to the Literary Revival's cultural nationalism, believing that there had been quite enough of that already in the nineteenth century with disastrous results for the artists – like James Clarence Managan – who had been seduced by it. He looked instead to the world beyond, most especially to Europe and, among the Europeans, to Ibsen to whom he wrote on the occasion of the great dramatist's seventieth birthday, praising above all

how in your absolute indifference to public canons of art, friends, and shibboleths you walked in the light of your inward heroism.[15]

This is a suitable epigraph for Joyce's own career. Yet, for all his hostility to the reappearance of Ireland as a literary property in the years after Parnell's death, Joyce, more than anyone else, centred his work on the Ireland of that period. He shared with all his contemporaries, from Yeats and Synge to Moore and O'Casey, a preoccupation with the idea of a culture for which a wholly articulate and authentic literature had still to be found. Therefore, like them, he is deeply involved in the problems of language and of the various forms of censorship and disapproval that would deny its ultimate responsibility to truth. Like Moore, he made an artistic virtue out of his cosmopolitanism but he discovered a richer way of exploiting the analogies between his own, his country's past and the past of world history and world literature. His remembrance of things past is controlled by a variety of formal manoeuvres, which allow him to manifest them as being simultaneously present. His great synoptic narratives bring all history (everything that is crucial and much that is accidental) and all languages into the discipline of an art where everything exists in a felicitous present tense, where the most random detail can become meaningful and the most casual discovery is always *ben trovato*.

Joyce is the first and greatest of Irish urban writers. Dublin was the centre of his universe and the rapid transitions and dismembered sensations of modern urban life moulded his sensibility. Because of this, he is much more hospitable to the various kinds of popular entertainment and recreation which were a feature of the Catholic middle-class life into which he was born and from which he never entirely dissociated himself. In his writings, the Ireland of Daniel O'Connell, Thomas Moore, James Clarence Mangan and *The Spirit of the Nation* is given a new lease of life rather than the disdain which Yeats visited upon it. Yet, in his early fiction, this is a pharisaic world, coldly observed by an insider who had become estranged from it. In *Dubliners* (1914), we see another version of George Moore's Ireland, a place in which human desire and longing are frustrated by a deadening and powerful Catholicism and its social counterpart, a joyless and humiliating conformity. The opening story, *The Sisters*, first published in AE's journal, *The Irish Homestead* in 1904, introduces us in its first paragraph to the word 'paralysis'. This is a premonition of what is to come. The dead priest and the intricate bankrupt ritual of his wake are seen by a young boy who is becoming aware of the contrasting feelings within himself of attraction for this maleficent culture and rebellion against it. The desolation of the lives portrayed here rests on the abiding sense of something precious, even sacred, which has been violated – young love, the memory of Parnell, religious belief, a community's natural spirit of intimacy. The violation has produced a petrifaction of the spirit which has become institutionalized. Joyce wrote these stories in what he famously called a style of 'scrupulous meanness', making the gesture of his language the most prominent indication of his theme. Yeats's Ireland had discovered a new idealism. Joyce's Dublin has betrayed an old one – the idealism upon which the vision of a humane and living society rests. His people are driven inwards upon themselves by the pressure of their dilapidated surroundings, only to find no resource. The blankness of death covers all, as in the final vision of Gabriel Conroy in the last story, *The Dead*. The snow that falls on Dublin and extends westward to the Shannon and the grave of Michael Furey, his wife's former lover, brings the living and dead into a melancholy partnership. Just this once in *Dubliners*, we glimpse the mutual contracts that bind all together and on this sole occasion too we recognize that the wholeness of the Irish and of the human community has been perceived in the light of strong feeling. Joyce, we learn, is especially fond of such a final coda, suddenly suffusing his fiction with the retrospective power of the very energy which it had until then been denied. This closing vibrancy is, at times, sentimental. But so severe is the repudiation that precedes it that most readers find in it a solace from the unremitting bleakness that would otherwise dominate.

Joyce lived in the martello tower at Sandycove with Oliver St John Gogarty in 1904. He was by then a graduate of University College, Dublin, a student of languages and was locally known as an essayist, poet and writer of short stories. That year he also met Nora Barnacle, a chambermaid from Galway, and went away with her to Pola and then the following year to Trieste, where he began to teach English at the Berlitz school. This may have had an effect on the prose style of *Dubliners* and on that of his first novel, *Stephen Hero*, the twenty-six chapters of which he recast into the five chapters of *A Portrait of the Artist as a Young Man* in 1907–14. *Portrait* was first published in serial form in the English magazine *The Egoist* in 1915. The complete novel finally appeared in New York in 1916. Yeats and Pound were by then among his most fervent supporters and helped to get him grants from the British Royal Literary Fund and the British Treasury Fund to alleviate his appalling financial situation. Two years after moving to neutral Switzerland during the First World War, Joyce received the first of a series of munificent gifts from the wealthy and gifted Harriet Shaw Weaver, the first of many sponsors of his later career. He gradually became the centre of admiration of an inner clique of artists and avant-garde editors, especially after his move to Paris in 1920. At the same time, he began to achieve notoriety among the general public as a writer who managed to be obscene and opaque. Dublin frowned on the first two books. *The Irish Book Lover* claimed that Joyce was blind 'to the stirrings of literary and civic consciousness which give an interest and zest to social and political intercourse'[16] in the capital. Joyce, however, did not waver in his resolve to 'write a chapter of the moral history of my country',[17] seeing this as a liberating moment in the asphyxiating tradition of Irish writing. To the English publisher of *Dubliners* he wrote:

in composing my chapter of moral history in exactly the way I have composed it I have taken the first step toward the spiritual liberation of my country. Reflect for a moment on the history of the literature of Ireland as it stands at present written in the English language before you condemn this genial illusion of mine.[18]

In *Portrait*, the moral history of the development of Stephen Dedalus becomes an example of the liberation which Ireland sorely needed and implacably denied.

Portrait is not a thesis-novel. It is, in its latter part, either enriched or flawed by an ambiguity on the part of the author towards the protagonist, Stephen Dedalus, who had already figured in *Stephen Hero* as a young man entirely deserving of our sympathy and support in his struggle against the squalid morality of Irish life. It is possible to see Stephen as the greatest of all the artist heroes who had become so popular in the European novel since the 1880s. For once, we witness the growth of a consciousness which we can believe to be that of a young intellectual. Stephen begins by receiving the language of his world – nursery rhymes, Latin tags, political argument (over the fall of Parnell), hell-fire sermons, literary models. He ends by supplanting these forms of language with his own, so that the subject of the book becomes, in a formal sense, its author. In that light, the novel is a series of carefully orchestrated quotations, through which we see a young mind coming to grips with his world through an increasing mastery of language. Further, we recognize that this is a moral, not merely a formal, achievement. On the other hand, Stephen can be seen as a victim of Joyce's irony. He is the prototypical artist-aesthete, who is finally revealed to be a poseur, more gifted in theorizing about art and freedom than in producing either. It is not necessary to choose one emphasis at the expense of the other. The presence of both in the novel indicates Joyce's dissatisfaction with the limitations of the conventions of heroism, even if it be the heroism of the alienated artist in a mediocre society. This was already a worn theme by 1914. The weariness which beset it became visible in Richard Rowan, the hero of Joyce's one play, *Exiles*, written in 1915. An analyst of others, he cannot analyse his own perverse wish to have his wife betray him. Although he is an impoverished version of Stephen, Rowan does at least allow us to observe Joyce's almost neurotic fascination with treachery and betrayal, a symptom perhaps of the loneliness he felt in repudiating Ireland and in being repudiated by her.

In *Ulysses*, treachery and its accompanying loneliness is a pervasive preoccupation. Stephen Dedalus has betrayed his mother's dying request to kneel down and pray for her. His friend, Buck

Mulligan, has betrayed him by refusing to acknowledge Stephen's importance. Leopold Bloom is betrayed by his wife, who commits adultery with Blazes Boylan. As a result, the intellectual Irishman, Stephen, and the commonplace Jew, Bloom, experience profound isolation in their wanderings through Dublin during 16 June 1904. Both men are members of broken families and citizens of a broken nation. Their interwoven sojourns, fitfully modelled on the wanderings of Homer's Ulysses in his journey towards wife, son and home in Ithaca, represent, among other things, an attempt on Joyce's part to reintegrate the project of the artist hero with the spirit of the community, specifically that of Dublin but generally that of mankind, from which he has been separated. For all its faults, Dublin is no longer the centre of paralysis. It is a city of talk and song, pub and restaurant, its physical and human detail registered with an almost preternatural freshness. Stephen, armed with an astonishing array of theories which assert the ultimate independence of the individual from all parentage, tradition and history, is a son in search of a father and agonized by his betrayal of his mother. Bloom, immersed in the world of physical sensation, is seeking companionship, a community – Irish, Jewish, familial – to which he might be permitted to belong, a father searching for a substitute for the child he lost. Both are involved in an intricate series of surrogate fantasies. Bloom philanders in his mild way among real and imagined women and attaches himself to the phalanx of Dublin males, led by Simon Dedalus, Stephen's father, without ever gaining acceptance among them. Stephen ranks himself in his mind with heretical heroes and betrayed writers – Arius, Photius, Valentine, Shakespeare – or with legendary son-victims like Icarus and Telemachus. The historical and mythical shadows that haunt their minds darken the naturalistic texture of the novel, allowing us – partly through the technique of the interior monologue – to observe the endless interchange between the inner and the outer worlds, one dominated by obsessions, the other characterized by randomness. In blending all these elements together, Joyce transformed the century's conception of the novel. He reconstructed the basic forms of fiction so that myth, history, intellectual theory and naturalistic detail could coexist within a narrative frame which was flexible enough to endure vertiginous variations of style. In *Ulysses*, the modern Irish experimentation with language and form reaches a culmination. After it, the tremendous prestige of the English novel was never again so oppressive for Irish writers.

Nevertheless, the rupture with traditional practice had its own dangers. The reader of *Ulysses* might well feel betrayed after the first ten episodes when a new kind of narrative takes over and the drama of Stephen and Bloom seems to give way to a virtuoso display of literary ventriloquism. The novel caricatures its own subject – the possibility of the restoration of a community between artist and public in modern conditions – by focusing our attention on the phenomenon of the production of language rather than on the more conventional consumption of a story or theme. Analogies proliferate as in the *Oxen of the Sun* episode, where the development of English prose style and the growth of the embryo in the womb are comically dovetailed in the account of Mrs Purefoy's labour in the Holles Street Lying-In Hospital. Even more enervating is the famous and very long-winded 'catechism' of the *Itchaca* episode, in which the act of communication between Bloom and Stephen is parodied to the point of absurdity and boredom. One has the impression of great language systems beginning to break away from the central mass of the novel and turning into offshore islands inhabited by Joycean specialists, while the general population looks on. The extension of *Ulysses* towards that mythic status at which it would be able to make any one thing representative of all things was not possible within the limits of that miraculous naturalism, which is its natural basis. In order to achieve that sense of unity in diversity, of all stories being one story, one man being all men, one country being all countries, Joyce had to break with this naturalism and found his new novel in the territory of dream. Thus, we enter the world of *Finnegans Wake*.

In this fluid world of the *Wake*, the distinction between chaos and order is cancelled. Chaos simply becomes the word we give to systems of order we do not at first perceive. Order is the word we give to chaotic materials over which we feel we have gained an ephemeral mastery. Every reader becomes his own novelist in a book that was more stringently organized by its author than any other novel. Since history is envisaged in this book as a cyclic pattern of recurrences, the blurred and gigantic figures which dominate it are archetypes of human experience. HCE, or Humphry Chimpden Earwicker, the publican in Chapelizod, who is dreaming the wake is also Here Comes Everybody and he Haveth Childers Everywhere, among them Shem and Shaun, the Cain and Abel brothers who represent the eternal principle of opposition. The microcosm of Irish history contains within itself the macrocosm of world history. The Fall of Man and the Fall of Parnell are the same event in different guises. Similarly, language, especially the English spoken by Irish people, becomes, through distortion, the idea to which all other languages are approximations. Every conceivable form of fusion, pun, malapropism and displacement is employed to set off an almost infinite train of associations, references and memories, which can easily become overburdened and go out of control. The medium of this book is its subject. Myth and story are secondary to it. In fact, the narrative line or lines, when they are perceived, are little more than organizing principles which help to provide some sense of sequence and symmetry for the protean vocabularies which shift and slide under their surfaces. Many of Joyce's greatest admirers were put off by the *Wake*. Yeats should have liked it more, for, as it moved through its complex development in serial form in the pages of the magazine *transition*, under the title *Work in Progress*, he might have glimpsed in it a comic version of his own theories of Eternal Recurrence which he had published in *A Vision*. Both of them shared a capacity to organize experience into strict patterns without conceding its diversity. Thus, in the *Wake*, for all the plainness of the informing idea of history, our sense of it is enriched by language which is comically and joyfully indulging in the extravagance of the actual. No matter how omnivorous the language is, we often have a sense that there is yet more which language, even when tortured to the point of collapse, cannot confess. In *Ulysses*, the shadow of an epic hero is cast over a text full of anti-heroic or mock-heroic references and we can infer from that how much Joyce wanted us to share the modernist view that we lived in a delinquent age. But in the *Wake*, the presence that moves behind the text is the presence of the ordinary workaday world and its workaday language. The dream slippages have transformed the quotidian into the mythic and, as we read this phantom script, we are drawn to reverse the process. It seems unlikely, therefore, that Joyce was counterpointing the contemporary world against the world of myth in any disobliging manner. In fact, the curious effect of the *Wake* is to make us grateful for the particularized world we inhabit. Joyce, the master of ceremonies, transmogrifies everything for the sake of making it fresher and more endearing in its more conventional form. The introduction to the Mookse and the Gripes episode, for instance, is a perfect example of the text's yearning to be read straightforwardly, as a kind of nursery tale or music hall yarn, even though it is perversely deformed:

Gentes and laitymen, fullstoppers and semicolonials, hybreds and
lubberds!
Eins within a space and a wearywide space it wast ere wohned a Mookse.
The onesomeness wast alltolonely, archunsitslike, broady oval, and a
Mookse he would a walking go (My hood! cries Antony Romeo), so one
grandsumer evening, after a great morning and his good supper of gammon
and spittish, having flabelled his eyes, pilleoled his nostrils, vacticanated
his ears and palliumed his threats, he put on his impermeable, seized his
impugnable, harped on his crown and steeped out of his immoble *De Rure
Albo* (socolled becauld it was chalkfull of masterplasters and had borgeously
letout gardens strown with cascadas pintacostecas, herthoducts and
currycombs) and set off from Ludstown *a spasso* to see how badness was
badness in the weirdest of all pensible ways. (152)

　One of the paradoxes of Joyce's achievement is that he did in the
end give primacy to the idea of human solidarity and the ordinary
secular life of the modern city in works which have gained, because
of their extreme difficulty, a highly specialized audience. The liberal
and democratic impulse in these books has been considerably
deflected by the takeover of them by a class of experts. This indicates something ambiguous in Joyce as well as in the reception of his
work. It was there in the double vision of Stephen as hero or as
poseur in *Portrait*. It remains in *Ulysses* and in the *Wake* because the
isolation of the artist and, by extension, of the individual seems to be
too emphatic to be overcome by the emergent mass society which
Joyce saw adumbrated in the Dublin of his youth. The *Wake* is a
dream of community but it scarcely survives in the face of the
'nightmare of history' Stephen spoke of in *Ulysses*. It might be said
that Joyce found Irish history and Irish tradition so fragmented that,
in spite of his systematizing imagination, no hope for coherence
could be entertained. Such a feeling would have been widespread in
early twentieth-century Europe, when the premonitions of cultural
disintegration had become universal. The battle between disorder
and order, the individual consciousness and the communal mind, is
waged by Joyce with such a dedication and energy that he changed
the form of the traditional novel in his attempt to resolve it. He
universalized the plight in which the nineteenth-century Irish novelists had been trapped. Caught between two cultures, two languages
and two audiences, English and Irish, they had been mired by
history. Joyce, inheriting these divisions, overcame them by bringing history into the ambit of fiction and revealing thereby the

essentially linguistic and therefore ductile nature of both activities. In this respect, he emulated Yeats.

Joyce's *Ulysses* had been deemed pornographic after its publication in Paris in 1922. Eleven years passed before a New York judge cleared it of the charge and opened the way for its publication in a trade edition in the USA. By then Joyce was deeply engaged in *Work in Progress* and was gathering around him a group of disciples who would help him to complete it and help it to be received with some measure of comprehension. Samuel Beckett was one of the young recruits to the Joyce circle in 1928. His first publication was an essay on Joyce in 1929. In 1930 he helped translate the 'Anna Livia Plurabelle' section of the *Wake* into French. In 1937, the year in which his first novel, *Murphy*, was finally accepted for publication by the forty-third publisher to receive it, Beckett was involved as witness in a libel action in Dublin, taken out by a friend of his against the ineluctable Oliver St John Gogarty, who had so delighted Moore and displeased Joyce. Gogarty lost the case and left Ireland for the USA; Beckett lost face and left Ireland for France. Thereafter he visited Ireland only for family reasons. For him, as for Joyce and Moore, exile was a necessity. Like them too, language was for him a chosen rather than a naturally assumed action. After 1945, he began to write his works in French, later translating them into English himself. Thus, after his book of short stories, *More Pricks than Kicks* (1934), and his first two published novels, *Murphy* (1938) and *Watt* (1953, composed 1942–4), the works which made Beckett famous – the trilogy (*Molloy*, *Malone Meurt*, *L'Innommable*, composed 1947–9, published 1951–3), the *Nouvelles* ('La Fin', 'L'Expulsé', 'Le Calmant', 'Premier Amour', 1955) – were all written in his second language, as was the play, *En Attendant Godot*, which made him famous after its first production at the Théatre de Babylone in Paris in 1953. Beckett has so many points of contact with Joyce that it is tempting to see him as a disciple or follower. Yet, although Joyce (along with Proust) remains for Beckett one of the greatest of writers, the differences between them are too marked to allow for any glib account of their relationship.

For one thing, Beckett grew up in the Protestant upper middle class of a Dublin that had become the capital of the Irish Free State the year before he began his career as an undergraduate at Trinity College. In the year his first essay was published, the Censorship of Publications Act was passed. Ireland entered on a long period of introversion and stabilization after the stormy years of the 1920s. The atmosphere was constricting. Cultural nationalism was degraded into a species of village bigotry. Writers, in particular, fought against the prevailing ideology, partly because they were among its most prominent victims in the matter of banning books and partly because the written word had such power in Ireland. Sean O'Faolain, Frank O'Connor and Liam O'Flaherty were among the most prominent spokesmen for the writers and for a general liberalization of the ethos of the new state. Beckett, however, played a little part in this dispute. He was certainly affected by the disenchantment and nullity of the Irish situation but, locked in his own personal depressions, was not disposed to do much about it other than escaping from it. Going to Paris and becoming involved in the Joyce circle and in the Verticalist movement which was then associated with the journal *transition*, only confirmed his sense that he and his generation had nothing left but that 'integral pessimism' of which *transition* made such a fuss. Beckett had come after the Revival and after the great age of European modernism. The rich and multifarious world of Joyce's fiction had been replaced by the pure poverty of a world where only Habit ruled:

Habit is a compromise effected between the individual and his environment, or between the individual and his own organic eccentricities, the guarantee of a dull inviolability, the lightning-conductor of his existence. Habit is the ballast that chains the dog to his vomit. Breathing is habit. Life is habit.[19]

Ireland, we may say, functions in Beckett's work as a mode of absence. It is the anonymous landscape of the trilogy and of some of the later plays and fictions such as *All That Fall* and *First Love*. Within this vacuous space a series of meditations take place, the materials for which are sometimes stories, sometimes philosophical problems. But the stories lead nowhere and the problems are rendered ridiculous. Beckett's two languages of disquisition and of narrative are worked hard, to the point of exhaustion. When they resume, they carry with them an air of futility and resignation. Language aches to give up, to reach the silence which would signify death. But as long as consciousness remains, language proceeds. Two authors cast their shadows on all that he has written – Descartes and Dante. The Cartesian method of radical doubt is adapted, but the Cartesian premises are denied. *Cogito ergo sum* and *sum res cogitans* are declarations which, in Beckett's world, would appear ineffably smug. But the method by which everything inessential is pared away until the ultimate primary essence remains appeals to him, even though the paring away process will obviously be infinite for someone who does not or cannot believe in any primary essence. The effect of Cartesianism, its emotional consequence on Beckett's heroes, is deadening. They all suffer from an apathy of sublime proportions. They recognize the futility of existence and regard with venom anyone who dares to gloss it otherwise. So deep is their depression that it becomes the basis for a coherent and perfectly rational vision of the torment of everyday life. Here the Dante of the *Purgatorio* appears as the epic literary mentor and, particularly the figure of Belacqua from the ante-Purgatory, the epitome of Sloth, living or rather reliving the whole period of his life again under the shadow of a rock. Thus Beckett's novels and plays contain intellectually brilliant practitioners of the Cartesian method of radical doubt who are also stunned depressives, emotionally crippled by the vision of the meaninglessness of a life which must be lived and relived.

Belacqua Shuah is the odd name of the first Beckett hero, the ataraxic eccentric of *More Pricks than Kicks*. The ten stories in this volume are a record of his grotesque existence in Dublin, his marriages, his accidental death and his burial on the day his house is burned down. Except for the first of them, 'Dante and the Lobster', they are exercises in undergraduate affectation and humour. But the first novel, *Murphy*, is almost free of the excessive inkhorn extravagance of the short stories. Its hero has a 'Belacqua fantasy' – to escape from time. To that end, he practises various techniques of concentration, taking pleasure in the governance of his own mind just as he is goaded into displeasure by the requirements of the external world, represented by Celia, a prostitute who loves Murphy and wants him to find a job as a condition of her staying with him. Murphy does settle for a job in a lunatic asylum, where he feels more at home than elsewhere, especially with his chess-playing schizophrenic friend, Mr Endon. However, Murphy cannot gain full admission to the inner world of the insane and returns to his apartment to meet an untimely death in a gas explosion. Thus Beckett brings to a comic end the story of his gang of Irish misfits in London, dominated by the philosophic Murphy who had almost reached that state in which mind and body, self and world were happily and totally sundered from one another. This division, normally seen as tragic, is here viewed as desirable but tragic because not attainable. The novel rests firmly on this inconoclastic inversion.

In *Watt*, the power of the mind expresses itself in logic; the helplessness of the body is expressed in humiliation. Empirical data are frozen into analytic set-pieces which rob them of their natural interconnecting fluency. So Watt's manner of walking is described in such a manner that it becomes impossibly complicated; and yet he walks. Watt's stay in Mr Knott's house is dictated by a systematic arrangement which makes no sense; and yet it works. Beckett seems here to be stretching language to the point at which its connection with a meaningful world is broken, thereby indicating the possibility that the world is meaningless or that language is competent only to render meaningless what would otherwise be taken for granted. His favourite devices of the inventory and the series – exhaustive schema which include everything and mean nothing – are elaborated in this instance with a merciless rigour, which can sometimes be trying and sometimes comic. The story may be a parable or an allegory of Man confronting the Void, armed with his useless gift of ratiocination. But its irritable, obsessive turnings and twistings do not make it amenable to such translations. Mr Knott, for instance, appears to Watt differently each day. On each of eighty-one occasions he merits four descriptive epithets out of a total range of twelve possible. The listing takes two pages. There are numerous examples of the same manic cataloguing of the infinite choices which a novel, or language, or consciousness can make when faced with a presence which is an absence like Mr Knott. Occam's razor was never so badly needed nor so little used.

The difficulty of writing about people whose lives are completely internalized was solved when Beckett adopted the monologue as the dramatic form for the great trilogy he composed in the late forties. *Molloy*, *Malone Dies* and *The Unnamable* are narratives in which an orphic voice flows on relentlessly, unencumbered by the necessity to obey the usual conventions of fiction, which had so severely intruded upon Murphy's experimental journey into the fastness of his own mind. Physically bound or disabled, they become talking heads. Their inertia is deeper than anything imagined by Joyce or Moore. It is metaphysically, not socially, dictated. Story is almost abandoned, but figures and names from earlier writings are introduced as though the character in the novel had been their creator. This is fiction vengefully representing as reality other fictions. Molloy and Moran, in the first of these novels, are writing reports about their pointless journeys into immobility. Molloy is the 'Irish', Moran the 'French' aspect of Beckett. One begins in despair, the other in confidence. Both end in ruin. Malone takes an unconscionably long time to die in his bedroom, tormented by memories, stories, the peremptory demands of his useless body. The Unnamable is limbless, trapped in an urn, condemned to talk until he goes almost berserk with grief and frustration at the endlessness of his plight. Language becomes more and more as reality becomes less and less. Everything is exact and measured and yet nothing has a boundary or limit. Journeys are undertaken by cripples. Escape is impossible so repetition is inescapable. The wish to be dead is countered by the wish that one had never been born. The desire for silence can only be expressed in words. With all these paradoxes and contradictions undermining the activity of language, it comes as no surprise to find that Beckett's prose, laden as always with pedantry and humour, is characterized by ramifying digressions, reservations, corrections and cancellations. Nothing can be said straightforwardly, including that last remark. The logic that had driven Murphy and Watt to the asylum now informs the structure of the sentences themselves. They dislocate sense by adhering rigidly to the strategies of formal analysis. The complications of these texts are intensified when their author translates them from their original French into English. One text becomes two, and although they are substantially the same, a host of minor differences seems to demand new emphases; altered cadences change the colour of feeling in particular passages. Language reproduces itself and finds that it has become different while remaining the same. The process of reading Beckett becomes labyrinthine.

Nouvelles et textes pour rien (1955, *Stories and Texts for Nothing* 1967) and *From An Abandoned Work* (1956) reveal even in their titles the extreme to which Beckett had brought the writing of fiction. *Waiting for Godot* and the radio play *All That Fall* (1957) remain within the tragic and neurotic zones explored in the fiction but the dramatic form liberates him in his treatment of it. As a dramatist, Beckett has more affinities with Yeats than with any other Irish writer. The stylized stage sets, the ritualized actions and speeches, the repudiation of the commercial theatre's idea of plot and its replacement by the monologues and dialogues of people who are 'mindtight' in a world which is 'bodytight' – these are all recognizable Yeatsian gestures. Wilde (with his Salomé, written in French), Synge, Moore, Joyce and Yeats had all paid their obeisance to France. Beckett made the interchange so intimate that he became a great Irish as well as a great French writer. In that sense, he broke the always dangerous connection between nationality and literature, although from another point of view it could be argued that he confirmed the ambition of the most important writers of the Revival to Europeanize Irish writing and thereby escape from insularity. The fondness of Irish dramatists in particular for vagrant or delinquent characters is a further symptom of their sceptical or disenchanted vision of established social forms, something common enough among oppressed peoples who feel that their communal experience is misrepresented by being regarded as peripheral. But Beckett excavates these rather inarticulate feelings with such vigour that they are re-presented in his writings as centrally human experiences. His drama has been particularly successful in this regard. Dramatic forms which had been associated with experimental theatre are refashioned by him into the norms of popular theatre.

The popularity of *Waiting for Godot* is partly explained by the fact that it combines the routines of slapstick comedy perfected in the music-hall and in the early cinema with the gestures of tragic theatre. The religious and philosophical references, the shadowy presence of the tragic (and therefore meaningful) death of the Crucifixion and the more substantial memories of attempted suicide by the clownish couple Vladimir and Estragon with their comic turns, their soliloquizing, their duets of despair and their anguished quartets with Pozzo and Lucky create a sense of the anomalous in the audience when the feeling deepens, as much as when it lightens. Categories like comedy and tragedy are as useless here as in O'Casey. The subtle mixture of tones can suddenly transform itself into sharp contrasts in the polarized light of a single speech, like Pozzo's outburst at the end. Then it resumes itself in the antiphonal response of Vladimir:

> Astride of a grave and a difficult birth. Down in the hole, lingeringly, the grave-digger puts on the forceps. We have time to grow old. The air is full of our cries. (*He listens*) But habit is a great deadener.[20]

In *Endgame* and *Krapp's Last Tape* (both 1958) the waiting for someone or something to come is modified into a waiting for the past to return to give purpose or meaning to the desiccated present. The immobility of the personages in these plays is both the stillness of those who wait and the paralysis of those who have begun to die. Even in *All That Fall*, the first work originally written in English since 1945, Mrs Rooney staggering to the railway station near Dublin has difficulty in keeping the impression of death out of her vigorous words. Her husband remarks that 'one would think you were struggling with a dead language'. To this she gives the famous and hilarious – yet almost melancholy – response:

> Well, you know, it will be dead in time, just like our own poor dear Gaelic, there is that to be said.
> *Urgent baa*.[21]

The lamb's bleat gives a delicious Special Effect to the remark.

The drama had its repercussion on Beckett's fiction. It helped him get rid of that neutered 'I' that had been the voice source in the trilogy. Instead, the later fictions or narratives, finally disembarrassed of plot, are voices in empty space, late night transmissions picked up through a cloud of static on some high-frequency wavelength. They come out of the silence abruptly and fade back just as suddenly. Yet for all the accidental and occasional aspect of pieces like *Ping* (1967) or *Lessness* (1970), *For To End Yet Again and Other Fizzles* (1976), they retain, even intensify, the lucid, systematic rationale of inquiry, which the works of the 1930s and 1940s had more generously provided. As in Joyce, the random and the highly organized elements within a text are played against one another in a phantom chess-game. Sometimes, as in *Ping*, almost every organizing principle – punctuation, syntax, grammar, story – has vanished and we have only flickering images and the word 'Ping' itself to control the obsessive, wholly impersonal and yet totally confessional outpourings. Beckett seems to have gone as far as possible in abolishing from his writing the dimension of time. He wants neither sequence nor simultaneity but some intercalatory dimension in which the tension between the two is forgone entirely. These formal manoeuvres are the artifices for the control of those feelings which he blends in such estranging and disturbing ways. Feeling remains authentic as long as it remains intransitive. To find a language for it is to betray it. It is, therefore, appropriate that this inhabitant of Ireland, the 'Elysium of the roofless'[22] should live in two languages, French and English, and still be able to say, 'Tears and laughter, they are so much Gaelic to me'.[23]

Gaelic was no mystery to Flann O'Brien, who wrote one novel *An Béal Bocht (The Poor Mouth*, 1941, translated 1964) in that language. It is, characteristically, an outright attack on the various and misguided attempts to revive it. O'Brien, whose real name was Brian O'Nolan (or Ó Nualláin), is even better known as Myles, short for Myles na gCopaleen, the pen-name he used for the weekly column he wrote for *The Irish Times* between 1940 and 1966. Even Beckett's remorseless hilarity cannot quite match the humour of O'Brien's deadpan prose. But O'Brien achieved his best effects in only two novels – *An Béal Bocht* and *At-Swim-Two-Birds* (1939) – and in his newspaper column, now published in a useful selection, *The Best of Myles* (1968). Although his other novels have their attractions and brilliancies – especially *The Third Policeman* (completed 1940, published 1967) – they are flawed by the intermittent failure of that delicate balance between logic and fantasy which makes his early fiction so remarkable. *The Hard Life* (1961) and *The Dalkey Archive* (1964) are ingenious reworkings of the earlier novels, lacking the autonomy and finish of their predecessors. For this, James Joyce is to blame. O'Brien's reaction to Joyce's work and, later, to Joyce's fame is one of the most astonishing examples of the 'anxiety of influence' to be found, even in Ireland where the closeness of the small literary community stimulates fiction and friction of varied quality and unvaried regularity. At first, there was admiration and respect. Then, as the books on Joyce began to proliferate, especially in the USA, a certain modification occurred. In 1951, O'Brien declared that

the true fascination of Joyce lies in his secretiveness, his ambiguity (his polyguity, perhaps?), his leg-pulling, his dishonesties, his technical skill, his attraction for Americans.[24]

The publisher's refusal of *The Third Policeman* in 1940, the outbreak of war and the intense local Dublin-based cult of Myles na gCopaleen among the readers of *The Irish Times* served to enhance the contrast between O'Brien's fortunes and those of Joyce. O'Brien could see that he and Beckett, along with Denis Devlin and Brian Coffey, were the only considerable writers of their generation to have escaped the wearisome enchantments of the Revival. He was not among the group Beckett christened 'the Antiquarians', who still lived parasitically off the cultural nationalism created by Ferguson, O'Grady and Yeats.[25] O'Brien knew Old and Modern Irish. He admired the terseness and precision of the language and consequently found it distasteful to see these qualities transmogrified into Romantic vagueness and dishevelled dreaminess by people whose ignorance of the language was almost perfect. Yet there he was, in his 'homebased exile', shut off from the world by war, shut in with Ireland by his notoriety. The problem of provincialism and cosmopolitanism which he embodied (and which was to exercise so many of his contemporaries, like Patrick Kavanagh and Sean O'Faolain, who felt the burden of the 1940s, in Ireland in a similar way) was projected for him in the reception of Joyce, the most profoundly local of writers, who had now the most international of reputations. Thus the absorption of Joyce in the early novels, which led to their enrichment, declined into a running battle with his reputation in his later work, leading to its impoverishment. The culmination comes in *The Dalkey Archive*, where Joyce appears as a very religious curate serving in a pub twenty miles north of Dublin, anxious to become a Jesuit and horrified to hear that he is regarded as the author of *Ulysses*, 'that dirty book, that collection of smut'.[26] As for *Finnegans Wake*, Joyce thinks it is still no more than a song.[27]

The humour of this is darkened by the fact that this most unheroic Joyce has a counterpart in the idiot-genius de Selby, transposed now from *The Third Policeman* to the village of Dalkey, as far south of Dublin as Skerries, Joyce's refuge, is north. De Selby (whose name puns on the German *das Selbst*, the Self) has created a concoction which will destroy the world by relieving the atmosphere of its oxygen. Its intermediate use, so to speak, abolishes serial time and enables de Selby to converse with a number of figures from past history, all of them early fathers of the Church, including St Augustine. Their concerns, most of them heretical, are remarkably similar to those of James Augustine Joyce in *Ulysses*. (The comic and the more serious treatment of the anti-heroic theme, which depends on the fiction of a 'dead' here being alive in circumstances which make heroism suspect, had already been explored by Lennox Robinson's play *The Lost Leader* (1918), where Parnell is the victim, and in Moore's *The Book Kerith*.) The man whose (finally aborted) ambition is to bring de Selby and Joyce together is one Mick Shaughnessy, 'a lowly civil servant', who wants to stop the destruction of the world by the former and wonders if it could be done

by bringing together de Selby and Joyce and inducing both to devote their considerable brains in consultation to some recondite, involuted and incomprehensible literary project, ending in publication of a book which would be commonly ignored and thus be no menace to universal sanity?[28]

'Universal sanity' is, in fact, the ideal of O'Brien's writing. It is threatened by two forces. One is folly, the other self-involvement. Folly comes in every conceivable guise and is hunted down in his newspaper column with such exquisite precision that the joy of the reader is provoked by the manner more than the object of the pursuit. The educational system, the language revival, government policies in general and a host of other samples of human folly are converted into mechanistic schemes for the suppression of the human element by a satirist who is himself a contriver of schemes and machines more elaborate than any ever devised. He defends ordinary common sense by using the weapons of its opponents. But in the case of Joyce (or Beckett), the inhuman element is created by the excessive concentration on the autonomous world of the work of art at the expense of common experience. Such a degree of self-involvement is the deepest form of exile. While O'Brien is more able than either to take pleasure in the self-enclosed world of art, he retains a suspicion that its relation to and effect on ordinary life is damaging. It is, therefore, appropriate to find that his fiction moves simultaneously in two directions – one towards a realism which is exaggeratedly squalid, the other towards a fantasy which is exaggeratedly pure. The transition from one to the other is always unforced and rapid because both are registered in a prose which is uniform in tone and economy. As in Swift, the plain style is ultimately more shocking in its effect than any virtuoso display could be.

The Third Policeman brings the worlds of realism and fantasy together in a particularly eerie manner. It begins with the murder of an old man called Mathers by the hero and his companion John Divney. It ends with the reappearance of the hero on Divney's threshold sixteen years later. This proves fatally upsetting for Divney, because he had murdered our hero sixteen years before so that he could keep Mathers' money and a farm and pub for himself. Now that both are dead, they can meet again in the de Selbian universe of lost souls, which our hero had just left after a series of strange adventures therein with the policemen Sergeant Pluck, Constable McCruiskeen and the third policeman himself, Fox. We can take it that the cycle (literally) of events will recur endlessly. These men are locked in a carefully arranged hell. Its 'reality' is confirmed by the theories of de Selby which proliferate in the footnotes and which open every chapter other than the first and last. Equally, its 'reality' is undermined by the disputes, recorded in the footnotes, which rage among the commentators on de Selby's works. (The application to Joyce needs no emphasizing.) Within the de Selbian world, there are various but cognate threats to be faced. The sergeant is obsessed with the fear that all the inhabitants of the parish are slowly turning into the bicycles which they ride, by a process of molecular interchange. The constable is obsessed with the theory of infinite recession, which he embodies in a series of boxes, which he makes with fanatical precision to fit one inside the other until they pass beyond the point of visibility – and beyond. Eternity is a machine run by the third policeman to keep the other two occupied. Even the landscape is a strictly composed illusion. Over all broods the de Selbian obsession with omnium – i.e. omniscience – and, typically, it is envisaged as something in a box which is also a bomb, which kills the hero and leads him into the phantom hell of the self. The moral parable is clear enough at one level. To seek omniscience is to concede to fantasy. We can also infer that the 'Joycean' world of aesthetic completeness is another version of such a search and has the same deplorable results, commentaries within commentaries *ad infinitum*. But the narrator, although his greed for money as well as his study of de Selby lead him through murder into these phantasmal punishments, belongs by nature in a very different world – that of sheer ordinariness. De Selby's world is the inverse of that. (The fact that the novel is a parody of the famous French novel, *A Rebours*, by J. K. Huysmans – one known to Moore, Wilde and Joyce – emphasizes the satiric parable on aesthetic self-containment and on the perversion associated with it.) The fact too that de Selby's world is controlled by policemen (prominent also in *The Dalkey Archive*) reminds us further of the connection between sinister fantasy and the world of officialdom – of government and its uniformed minions. Their wonderful malaprop jargon is redolent of the officialese, which O'Brien, as a civil servant, knew so well that he parodied it in his newspaper column into something which had its own unearthly beauty. However, any beauty that was unearthly was condemned on that account. O'Brien's protagonists are so deeply immersed in, so native to, the world of the slothful and ordinary that we finally give that world of the bed, the pub, the living-room, a moral priority over all the glittering alternatives of the mind's fictions. In *The Hard Life*, the young schoolboy hero Finbarr watches the obsessions of his older brother Manus and his half-uncle Mr Collopy grow into monstrous but comic fantasies while he remains rooted in the squalid quotidian world of the actual.

However, their worlds become so grotesque that his final reaction to the latest development in his brother's mania is 'a tidal surge of vomit'. O'Brien's reaction to the monotony of human monomania became increasingly violent.

However, in his masterpiece, *At-Swim-Two-Birds*, delight is the dominant emotion. It is impossible to describe either the complications of its interwoven plots or the freshness of feeling, which remains intact through all the sophisticated parodies which are episodically developed with a casual aplomb. The book opens with four beginnings – the narrator, chewing bread and giving us examples of three separate openings for the novel he is about to write. He is an undergraduate at University College, Dublin. His life at home with his uncle and at college as an impecunious scholar-drunkard forms one narrative. Another is formed by his burlesque account of the legendary Gaelic heroes, Finn McCool and Mad Sweeney. The third consists of the story of Dermot Trellis, who is writing a novel, the characters of which lead an independent life while Trellis is asleep and revenge themselves upon him by writing a novel in which he is a character. All three narratives blend into one another until they fuse in the 'Conclusion of the book, ultimate'. The epigraph, from *Hercules furens*, is sweetly ironic; it means, 'For all proper things do stand out distinct from one another'. Yet the medley of styles and characters which we meet with here has not the imperious claim upon our admiration which we find in *Ulysses*. The narrator tells us that, 'The novel, in the hands of an unscrupulous writer, could be despotic'. He then goes on to propound his own theory of radical freedom in fiction. Author, reader and character are all free. The despotism of the monomaniac author (like Joyce) is disallowed. His self-involvement is replaced by extroversion. The commonplace and the fantastic become two aspects of the one thing in a genial if closed universe of interchangeable parts:

In reply to an inquiry, it was explained that a satisfactory novel should be a self-evident sham to which the reader could regulate at will the degree of his credulity. It was undemocratic to compel characters to be uniformly good or bad or poor or rich. Each should be allowed a private life, self-determination and a decent standard of living. This would make for self-respect, contentment and better service. It would be incorrect to say that it would lead to chaos. Characters should be interchangeable as between one book and another. The entire corpus of existing literature should be regarded as a limbo from which the discerning authors could draw their characters as required, creating only when they failed to find a suitable existing puppet. The modern novel should be largely a work of reference. Most authors spend their time saying what has been said before – usually said much better. A wealth of references to existing works would acquaint the reader instantaneously with the nature of each character, would obviate tiresome explanations and would effectively preclude mountebanks, upstarts, thimbleriggers and persons of inferior education from an understanding of contemporary literature.[29]

This is a description of what *At-Swim-Two-Birds* is and what *Ulysses* and the *Wake*, the chief works of the Joycean egotistical sublime, are not. And yet the kinship between these novels is close and acknowledged to be so. O'Brien is making a gentle distinction, which allows him to absorb rather than be absorbed into Joyce's achievement. After this novel, that balance and irony were lost.

It would therefore be insulting to see O'Brien as nothing more than a Joycean disciple, even though he became as obsessed by Joyce as the most throughgoing de Selbian commentator ever did with de Selby. It is ironic that he never moved out of the shadow thrown by Joyce's reputation because he, along with Beckett, had found his way to the anti-novel as the ideal form in which the romantic conception of the artist-as-hero could finally be dismantled. He suspected the despotism of the Joycean artist but was vanquished by the despotism of the posthumous reputation he achieved. Although his failure can be attributed to the demands of his thrice-weekly column, to the misfortunes of the war, to the lack of a wider audience for his novels and to his excessive drinking, its roots were probably deeper. He gave way to the introversion which he had always countered by the precise evocation of the actualities of Dublin life. In *The Dalkey Archive*, the fantasy of Joyce and de Selby coming together is never seriously entertained because Mick, the pallid go-between, does not live in a sufficiently real world to give that fantasy a ground and a meaning. The fading of that genial realism made the fantasy thin and thereby revealed how paradoxically vital it was for O'Brien's (as it was for Beckett's) avant-garde fiction. Joyce, above all authors, could only be outfaced by a writer who, among all his other gifts, needed to register everything 'with perfection of detail and event'.[30]

This is precisely what is lacking in other experimental fantasy-fictions of the period. The Revival had created a habit of mind which found the conjunction between myths of the past and the actualities of the present an appealing structural device both in poetry and in fiction. Few authors, however, found it possible to make the conjunction effective within a single work, with the result that their writing became polarized between the extremes of fantasy and the extremes of realism. Thus the same author produces fantasies of a peculiarly whimsical purity and realistic novels of a determined grimness. Among the outstanding examples of this schismatic division between two modes of writing are Eimar O'Duffy, Brinsley McNamara, Mervyn Wall and, above all, James Stephens. O'Duffy's first novel, *The Wasted Island*, is a bitter record of the ferment that preceded the 1916 rising and the disenchantment that came immediately after it. His best-known work, *King Goshawk and the Birds* (1926), the first in what is known as the Cuandine trilogy, is a strange mixture of satire and romance, relating the adventures of a mythic hero Cuandine in the degraded worlds of contemporary Ireland and England. Brinsley McNamara's first novel, *The Valley of the Squinting Windows* (1918), is one of the first and one of the most effective exposures of the narrow meanness of village life, sufficiently wounding to provoke the villagers concerned to burn the book publicly and hound his father from their midst. In contrast, *The Various Lives of Marcus Igoe* (1929) is a meditation on the autonomy of literature, elaborated in a fey and whimsical style. Mervyn Wall's two famous novels about a medieval Irish monk – *The Unfortunate Fursey* (1946) and *The Return of Fursey* (1948) – are among the subtlest and funniest of all modern Irish fantasies. But they too are countered by the unrelenting realism of *Leaves for the Burning* (1952), in which a journey undertaken by a group of friends to Sligo for the re-internment of the body of W. B. Yeats is offered as an image of the essential squalor of Irish society. The case of James Stephens is, perhaps, the most exemplary of all. At one time Joyce appointed him as the author who would finish the *Wake* in case Joyce should die before doing so. When we read Stephens's work we can see some method in this Joycean madness. The main novels – *The Charwoman's Daughter* (1912), *The Crock of Gold* (1912), *The Demi-Gods* (1914), *Irish Fairy Tales* (1920), *Deirdre* (1923) and *In The Land of Youth* (1924) – all achieve, though in different ratios, the intermingling of the fantastic or mythic and the realistic. But Stephens's realism is of a particularly powerful, because sober and understated, kind. (He also wrote one of the best eye-witness accounts of the Easter Rising, *The Insurrection in Dublin* 1916.) His world of gods and demi-gods, philosophers and leprechauns, is one of sunlit wisdom and instinctive happiness. The social world he depicts is dominated by the most unfeeling cruelties and selfishness, where the greatest crime is poverty. The opening of *The Charwoman's Daughter* is a well known instance of his plain exactitude:

Mary Makebelieve lived with her mother in a small room at the very top of a big, dingy house in a Dublin back street. As long as she could remember she had lived in that top back room. She knew every crack in the ceiling, and they were numerous and of strange shapes. Every spot of mildew on the ancient wallpaper was familiar. She had, indeed, watched the growth of most from a greyish shade to a dark stain, from a spot to a great blob, and the holes in the skirting of the walls out of which at night time the cockroaches came rattling, she knew also. There was but one window in the room, and when she wished to look out of it she had to push the window up, because the grime of many years had so encrusted the glass that it was of no more than the demi-semi-transparency of thin horn. When she did look there was nothing to see but a bulky array of chimney-pots crowning a next-door house, and these continually hurled jays of soot against her window; therefore, she did not care to look out often, for each time that she did so she was forced to wash herself, and as water had to be carried from the very bottom of the five-storey house up hundreds and hundreds of stairs to her room, she disliked having to use too much water.[31]

Comparing that with the opening of *The Crock of Gold* helps to give an impression of the distance between the two worlds in Stephens's fiction:

In the centre of the pine wood called Coilla Doraca there lived not long ago two Philosophers. They were wiser than anything else in the world except the Salmon who lies in the pool of Glyn Cagny into which the nuts of knowledge fall from the hazel bush on its bank. He, of course, is the most profound of living creatures, but the two Philosophers are next to him in wisdom. Their faces looked as though they were made of parchment, there was ink under their nails, and every difficulty that was submitted to them, even by women, they were able instantly to resolve. The Grey Woman of Dun Gortin and the Thin Woman of Inis Magrath asked them the three questions which nobody had ever been able to answer, and they were able to answer them.[32]

This is close to Flann O'Brien's parodies in *At-Swim-Two-Birds* but Stephens does not find that sustained ironic tone which subverts the O'Brien narrative and makes the activity of writing itself the subject of amused scrutiny. The repeated attempts on his part and on that of others to conjoin these worlds of Gaelic myth and Irish reality is, of course, a symptom of the increasing strain to which the heroicizing impulse of the Revival was subjected, especially in the aftermath of the political settlement of 1922. The society itself made the discrepancy between mythological grandeurs and quotidian pettiness so severe that it became impossible to incorporate them satisfactorily in fiction. Modern literature had exploited the discordant relationship between a vision of an integrated past and a disintegrated present to the point of exhaustion by the 1930s. The ambition to do so lingered in Ireland, partly because of the achievements of Yeats and Joyce and partly because the dream of a cultural revival was only reluctantly surrendered by a generation which was too vulnerable to accept its demise. However, when that acceptance was made, the savagery of the disillusion, the bitterness of the repudiation was, on occasion, quite awesome. Austin Clarke, for instance, became the scourge of the new Ireland of the 1950s and 1960s, even though no one had been more entranced by the possibility of calling in the old world of Gaelic civilization to balance and chasten the vulgarities of the oppressive present. His Celtic-Romanesque romances, *The Bright Temptation* (1932) and *The Singing Men at Cashel* (1936), or even the verse-drama *The Son of Learning* (1927), dedicated to George Moore and giving central prominence to the artist hero in a contest between Church and State, bespeak a faith in the idiom and the ideals of the Revival which he never entirely lost. The dangers of whimsy, undisciplined extravagance and folksy fake-wisdom were always in close attendance upon such writings. Perhaps Jack Yeats, the painter and brother of the poet, otherwise so 'rooted' a man, gave in to these dangers more helplessly than others when he turned to writing. *The Charmed Life* (1938), *Ah Well* (1942) and *And to You Also* (1944) are such flimsy affairs that they expose the vacuity that lay at the heart of the fantasy fictions of the long period from early to mid-century. The emptiness is in part social, but it is also the emptiness of a literary form which had outlived its usefulness. Moore, Joyce and O'Brien had exhausted the possibilities in prose, as had Yeats in poetry and Synge in drama, for the confrontation between mythological energy and contemporary penury of spirit. The theme was rewritten many times but it could not endure the disappearance of heroic ideals, which the new Catholic-bourgeois state so quickly and efficiently dispelled in the first three decades of its existence. Nationalism had certainly helped to create a new idea of Ireland, which had great and liberating consequences. But it also created a version of Irishness – compounded of whimsy, romantic populism, Celtic nativity heroisms, and a belief in the salience of the artist in political as well as cultural affairs – which was as restricting and as subject to caricature as the old colonialism had been. This was not surprising since the nationalism was a response to the colonialism and since it had been led by the Anglo-Irish section of the people, the colonials themselves. The long and lingering death of this nationalism became the aggrieved theme of much Irish writing of the middle decades of the century. It was a neo-colonial plight and it took the customary form of a battle between provincialism and cosmopolitanism, inwardness and outgoingness, native traditions and foreign importations. The Censorship was an expression of nationalism as much as was the literature it suppressed. Both were posited on an idea of Irishness, so much so that they sometimes forgot that literature could be quite distinct from it or any allegiance to it.

The more conventional fiction of the modern period, in Ireland as elsewhere, escaped most of the experimental novel's dizzy self-questionings and dislocations by assuming the existence of a scale of values which was expressed in a set of social attitudes or structures which could claim some degree of general assent. Among these, the most enduring social constellation in Irish fiction was represented by the Big House, the home of the landed gentry, which dominated the life of the Irish countryside from the eighteenth century. Its only serious competitor was the Roman Catholic Church but it did not, in modern times, have the same appeal, partly because it was too powerful and pervasive a presence ever to play the role of representative image of a brilliant but threatened civilization, for which the Big House was so perfectly endowed. When Catholicism gained that sad eminence, it was usually in the form of the ideal construct it once had been in some distant past – generally the Celtic Church of the seventh to the ninth centuries or some other pre-Reformation image. Alternatively, Catholicism was often treated in a powerfully negative manner. It could be viewed as the organizing force which quelled the vibrant pagan personality of the race; or as the handmaiden of British imperial guile which helped to destroy late eighteenth-century and later forms of radicalism or liberalism; or it could be seen as the religion of the rabble, which established itself by keeping its congregation ignorant and civilization at bay. It is curious that so few Irish writers have shown any imaginative sympathy for Catholicism as such. This is, perhaps, a comment on the strong anti-intellectual features of a religion which was compelled by circumstances to minister to the oppressed and uneducated and was then unable to adapt in any effective way to the new forces released by the alleviation of these disadvantages. At any rate, it is clear that Irish literature has shown a marked predilection for idealized versions of civilization as they are represented in institutions which, like the Church or the Big House, arouse deeply felt ambivalences in the audience which reads about them. They are, of course, in a simple and direct sense, Catholic and Protestant images, but their sectarian distinctness does not preclude – indeed it demands – a recognition of the intimate animosities which they fostered in the enclosed conditions of rural life. By the close of the nineteenth century, it was clear that the Big House had no future in the new economic and political climate. It was at that point that it entered upon its long Indian summer as a cultural memory and myth, reproducing in a curious way the metamorphosis of the Irish language at the point of its disappearance some fifty years earlier. Irish literature sometimes reads like a series of studies in dying cultures; the moment of political death is the dawn of cultural life. Perhaps that is the ultimate reason for the anomalous position of Catholicism in Irish writing. When or if it ever reaches the moment of extinction, it will gain a literary respectability without which it is content to flourish in the meantime.

Edith Somerville and Violet Martin, known to literature as Somerville and Ross, anticipated the tragic cadence of the Big House novels (and, of course, of Yeats's poems on the Big Houses he immortalized) in a remarkable novel which is not about the Big House at all – *The Real Charlotte* (1894). It is a close and concentrated study of the destructive power of hatred within the confines of an Irish Protestant middle-class society which takes its tone from and looks up to the local Big House. The centre of attention is Charlotte Mullen and her victim, the young and beautiful Francie Fitzpatrick. But the Big House family of the Dysarts is stricken by all the ills that a too-refined aristocratic flesh is heir to – most especially the ill luck to have all the grace but none of the pressure of personality needed to give the society a moral as well as a social example. The financial frailty of this society, based on horses, land

and an increasingly uncooperative tenantry, exacerbates the sensibilities of its inhabitants to the point of breakdown. The sinister element in their personalities is the incapacity to develop. They are all transfixed by circumstances. Like Charlotte, they have movements of feeling, but 'cannot be said to possess the power of development'.[33] Such fixity of mind can be heroic, as in the case of Shibby Pindy in *The Big House of Inver* (1925), by Violet Martin (Martin Ross), whose Herculean efforts to save the Prendiville house and fortunes end in disaster with the burning of the Big House and the death in the fire of her helpless father. Since the nineteenth century, the decay of Anglo-Irish society had been expressed in novels of an increasingly sinister tone. Ruined houses consorted well with stories of hauntings, ghostly presences were readily available images of guilt and loneliness. Sheridan Le Fanu was the great Victorian master of this genre, although its most hysterical and popular development was achieved in Bram Stoker's *Dracula* (1897), which extends and vulgarizes the vampire motif Le Fanu had already introduced in his short story 'Carmilla' (1872). The living dead of the aristocratic vampire's tribe are victims of an historical crime from which the very bourgeois living – like Mina Harkness, the heroine – must be released by a joint Anglo-American assault, fortified by 'the wonderful power of money'.[34] This is the power which Anglo-Irish landowners and middle classes sadly lacked. They were caught in an historical crisis from which there was no escape. In Elizabeth Bowen, the Le Fanu and the Somerville and Ross heritage is combined, especially in *The Last September* (1929), yet another tale of Big House life ending in the destruction both of the building and the way of life it represented. The central relationship between the daughter of the house, Lois Naylor, and the young English officer, Gerald Lesworth, is doomed by the stifling and disintegrating world of Ascendency snobbery, as much as by the War of Independence fought by the IRA against the British army. Gerald is killed in an ambush, and the three great houses of the district are burnt to the ground in a night.

At Danielstown, half way up the avenue under the beeches, the thin iron gate twanged (missed its latch, remained swinging aghast) as the last unlit car slid out with the executioners bland from accomplished duty. The sound of the last car widened, gave itself to the open and empty country and was demolished. Then the first wave of a silence that was to be ultimate flowed back confidently to the steps. The door stood open hospitably upon a furnace.[35]

Some of Bowen's best stories are set in London of the Second World War, a place similarly threatened by destruction and containing within itself the terrors which crisis precipitates. Her heroines are displaced people – orphans, divorcees – and her world is disoriented, a sequence of broken surfaces, perceptions, accidents. Sometimes there is a laboured attempt to confirm the possibility of a natural promise in the midst of threat. At the end of *The Heat of the Day* (1949), as the Second World War ends, a mother gathers up her child from the pram to let him see three swans flying west across a sky just traversed by homecoming bomber planes. But *The Death of the Heart* (1938) and *Eva Trout* (1969) both end with an abruptness which is both shocking and familiar, for this is a world in which the likelihood of emotional and cultural amputation is bitterly strong. Elizabeth Bowen is the writer in whom the internal as well as the external collapse of an Irish and of an English civilization is finally registered. The strange death of liberal England included the stranger death of Ascendency Ireland. With her work, the last remnant of social faith disappeared from Irish fiction – that is, faith in the enduring power of contemporary society to confer meaning on the individual life. Although the Big House continued to reappear in novels from 1930 to the present day, its function was largely a nostalgic one; it was an image of memory, an indication of political conservatism, even an expression of cultural disdain for the contemporary moment. But, in all essentials, it had become one of the many Romantic ruins of the European mind.

As the Protestant and Anglo-Irish world lost its political and economic power in the new Free State (although not in the new Northern statelet), it also began to suffer cultural exclusions. In literature, the most fully developed statement came from Daniel Corkery, Professor of English at University College, Cork, in his book *Synge and Anglo-Irish Literature* (1931). This was a sequel to his earlier *The Hidden Ireland* (1925), in which he had tried to define the essence of the Gaelic literature of the eighteenth century and make that the basis for the quintessentially Irish spirit. Although he allows Synge into the Irish fold (just), he excludes almost everything and everyone else in the Revival and, beyond that, in the English language tradition in Ireland. In seeing the development of Irish society and literature in this way he was, at one level, expressing the triumphalism of the new-found state and its satisfaction at having finally destroyed the hegemony of the landowning class. He was also recognizing the harsh reality of the

Protestant/Catholic distinction and attempting to find a literary gloss for it. The result is not bigotry, as many have said; for Yeats's defence of the Protestant tradition in his Senate speeches is of the same stripe. Both are acts of repossession which come too late. They are both assertions that Irish experience contains opposed elements, but their sponsorship of one over the other lacks charity, a fact dictated by the circumstances of the period rather than by a personal failure in generosity. There was and would continue to be a species of apartheid in Irish society. Elizabeth Bowen, remembering her young years in the Dublin of the 1890s, spoke of it in *Seven Winters: Memories of a Dublin Childhood* (1943):

It was not until after the end of those seven winters that I understood that we Protestants were a minority, and that the unquestioned rules of our being came, in fact, from the closeness of a minority world. Roman Catholics were spoken of by my father and mother with a courteous detachment that gave them, even, no myth. I took the existence of Roman Catholics for granted but met few and was not interested in them. They were, simply 'the others', whose world lay alongside ours but never touched. As to the difference between the two religions, I was too discreet to ask questions – if I wanted to know. This appeared to share a delicate awkward aura with those two other differences – of sex, of class. So quickly, in a child's mind, does prudery seed itself and make growth that I remember, even, an almost sexual shyness on the subject of Roman Catholics.[36]

By the 1930s, the position had been transformed. The Protestant minority was now on the outside. The society remained divided. In Frank O'Connor's story 'My First Protestant' (1951), the narrator, Dan Hogan, says of a former girlfriend,

'She was my first Protestant. There were a number of them in our locality, but they kept to themselves.'[37]

That was published a quarter of a century after Lennox Robinson's play *The Big House* was staged at the Abbey, stimulating AE to speak of the 'liberating thrill' the final and defiant outburst of the Protestant heroine, Kate Alcock, gave him as she asserted her Anglo-Irish difference in the midst of yet another burned out mansion. (Between 1921 and 1923, 192 Big Houses were destroyed.) AE's aspiration towards 'the balancing of our diversities in a wide tolerance' in place of a stagnant uniformity remained no more than that, despite the heroic efforts of his journal *The Irish Statesman*.[38] The Republican writers of the 1930s – O'Connor, Liam O'Flaherty, Peadar O'Donnell and Sean O'Faolain – were particularly disillusioned by the endurance of the old divisions. For, after all, the revolution had been fought. Yet everything seemed the same, the same utterly, only worse. The Revival and the Revolution had, between them, mobilized energies on behalf of a carefully selective image of Ireland's past. In doing so, they had concentrated so much attention on the phantom national spirit that they took little account of the actual dilapidation and provincialism which this, in the name of tradition, could encourage. Irish fiction transformed this situation into a scrutiny of the narrative convention of representation, for, where there was nothing to represent in fiction then fiction could be taught to represent nothingness. Equally, it could represent the long declension into nullity. After the revival and the Revolution, this declension remained, in the eyes of a new generation, a theme of unremitting fascination. For these new writers, the exit from the labyrinth of Irishness, the old essentialism, lay in modernization, the creation of a possible future rather than the recreation of an impossible past.

Notes

1   *A Communication to My Friends*, p. 83.
2   Malcom Brown, *George Moore: A Reconsideration* (Seattle, 1955), pp. 184–90; Graham Owens, 'The Melodic Line in Narrative', in *George Moore's Mind and Art*, ed. Graham Owens (Edinburgh, 1968), pp. 99–121.
3   *The Untilled Field*.
4   ibid.
5   *Parnell and His Island* (London, 1887), p. 6.
6   *A Drama in Muslin*.
7   *Avowals* (New York, 1926), p. 12.
8   *The Lake* (Gerrards Cross, 1980), p. 179.
9   Susan L. Mitchell, *George Moore* (Dublin 1916), p. 80.
10 *Hail and Farewell*.
11 Ernest Longworth, Preface to *A Story-Teller's Holiday*, 2 vols (London 1928), I, p. viii.
12 *A Story-Teller's Holiday* I, pp. 9–11.
13 ibid., p. 8.
14 ibid., II, p. 261.

15 *Letters of James Joyce*, ed. S. Gilbert (1957), p. 52.
16 Quoted in *The Egoist* (June, 1917), p. 74; reprinted in notes to *A Portrait of the Artist As a Young Man*, ed. Chester G. Anderson (New York, 1968), p. 337.
17 *Letters* II, ed. R. Ellmann, p. 134.
18 *Letters* I, pp. 62–3.
19 Quoted by A. Alvarez in *Beckett* (London, 1973), p. 21.
20 *Waiting for Godot* (New York, 1954), p. 58.
21 *All That Fall* (London, 1957), p. 35.
22 *First Love* (London, 1973), p. 31.
23 *Molloy*, p. 37.
24 'A Bash in the Tunnel', *Envoy* V, April 1951, p. 11.
25 Andrew Belis (Samuel Beckett), 'Recent Irish Poetry', *The Bookman* LXXXVI, August 1934, pp. 235–6.
26 *The Dalkey Archive* (London, 1968), p. 191.
27 ibid., p. 147.
28 ibid., p. 129.
29 *At-Swim-Two-Birds* (London, 1968), p. 33.
30 ibid., p. 69.
31 *The Charwoman's Daughter* (Dublin, 1912), p. 3.
32 *The Crock of Gold* (London, 1946), p. 283.
33 *The Real Charlotte* (London, 1973), p. 391.
34 *Dracula*.
35 *The Last September* (London, 1948), p. 283.
36 *Seven Winters*, p. 44.
37 Frank O'Connor, *Collection Two* (London, 1964), p. 113.
38 Quoted in Terence Brown, *Ireland: A Social and Cultural History 1922–79* (Fontana, 1981), p. 120.

8 Contemporary literature, 1940–80

Fiction

In the thirties and forties of this century, a number of writers emerge whose careers as artists are indistinguishable from their crusades as men of letters against the philistinism and parochialism of the new state. Sean O'Faolain is the outstanding personality in a group which includes Austin Clarke, Patrick Kavanagh, Frank O'Connor, Peadar O'Donnell and Sean O'Casey. O'Faolain was editor of a literary magazine *The Bell* from 1940 to 1946; Peadar O'Donnell gave it a more emphatic left-wing orientation during his editorship from 1946 until the last number in 1954. *The Bell* followed the example of George Russell's (AE) magazines, *The Irish Homestead* (1905–23) and *The Irish Statesman* (1923–30), by becoming a focus for new writing and for the dissenting voices which sought to articulate a critique of Irish social and political life. The literature of this generation thus combines, in a curious way, the emotions of commitment to and of alienation from Ireland, alternatively formulated in utopian and iconoclastic versions of what the country could be and what it actually was. Along with the more specifically literary and scholarly *The Dublin Magazine* (1923–58), edited by Seumas O'Sullivan, *The Bell* attempted to resituate Ireland in a wider and less oppressively devotional context than that provided by the long-standing effects of the late nineteenth-century 'Devotional Revolution' among the Catholic beneficiaries of the Land War, whose descendants also became the chief beneficiaries of the Irish revolution.[1] The recrudescence of this narrow, triumphalist Catholicism promoted the popularity of novels like those of Canon Sheehan (1852–1913), particularly *My New Curate* (1900), while it also contributed to the extinction, as far as reputation was concerned, of Gerald O'Donovan's novels about the death of liberal Catholicism, *Father Ralph* (1913) and *Waiting* (1914). The crisis in Irish Catholicism was precipitated by the First Vatican Council's identification of 'modernism' as the enemy of all that was Christian.

From the decade of the 1870s, Irish Catholicism adopted this view with a remarkable wholeheartedness, reinforced by the cultural nationalism which sought to specify the uniqueness of Irish-Celtic civilization in modern Europe.[2] By the 1920s, with the triumph of the Irish Catholic middle classes, nationalism had begun to yield so entirely to this anti-modernist Catholicism, that legislation such as the Censorship Act of 1929 was regarded by most people as a defence of both Irishness and Christianity. This fusion of powerful forces distressed the anti-modernist Yeats, who proceeded to formulate, rather belatedly, his own version of an essentially Irish hostility to the modern world, which had a distinctively Protestant, Ascendancy origin in the eighteenth century. But its Protestantism was also an element in its European, non-provincial nature. The debate in which O'Faolain and his contemporaries were later engaged had its terms dictated by these developments. The only antidote available to Catholic provincialism appeared to be some reintroduction into Irish life of the European heritage and background. By 1932, the year of the Eucharistic Congress in Dublin, celebrating 1500 years of Christianity in Ireland, and the year in which Eamon de Valera assumed power, the alliance between an anti-modernist Church and an introverted state and culture had been consolidated. It was, thereafter, to reach paranoiac proportions at times. Even Ireland's neutrality during the Second World War, a considerable diplomatic achievement and a genuine declaration of independence, was widely interpreted (and still is) as yet another symptom of the society's fear of and repudiation of the modern world.[3] On occasion, the search for a less constricting vision of Catholicism would have its moments of literary triumph – in poetry, Denis Devlin's *Lough Derg and Other Poems* (1946), Austin Clarke's *Pilgrimage* (1929), *Night and Morning* (1938) and *Ancient Lights* (1955), and in fiction, some of O'Faolain's short stories, particularly 'Lovers of the Lake' (1958), and Francis MacManus's *The Greatest of These* (1943), a novel set in late nineteenth-century Kilkenny in which the relationship between a Bishop and a renegade priest is a paradigm of the battle between authority and rebellion which Ireland had decided in favour of the former. In 1971, Thomas Kilroy, in *The Big Chapel*, reinterpreted the Kilkenny episode on which MacManus's novel had been based as a parable on the mutual failure of both authority and rebellion. It is appropriate that this novel should have appeared then to remind us that the debates of the forties and fifties had their origins in the

1870s; the new state had not invented triumphalist Catholicism; it merely gave it an opportunity to establish itself in a nationalist mould. In opposing this phenomenon in 1940, O'Faolain was facing a mentality which had been formed in two centuries of Catholic humiliation and one of Catholic triumph. His awareness of this is manifest in his two famous biographies. *The King of the Beggars* (1938), a life of Daniel O'Connell, the great nineteenth-century creator of the Irish Catholic nation, and *The Great O'Neill* (1942), the leader of Catholic Ireland in the days of Elizabeth I of England. In these men, he inscribes a version of the contemporary Irish conflict between the forces of a sectarian nationalism and a more generous adaptable internationalism (or 'modernism'). The ambiguity of their positions becomes for him an emblem of the vacillation of the Irish mind between these two destinies. These two books contain, *in parvo*, the chief preoccupations of O'Faolain's own fiction and of the debates on the relationship between Irish nationalism and Catholicism, which continue to the present day.

The title of O'Faolain's volume of critical essays, *The Vanishing Hero* (1956), serves as an appropriate epigraph to his three novels, *A Nest of Simple Folk* (1934), *Bird Alone* (1936) and *Come Back to Erin* (1940). The protagonist in each of them is dominated by a heroic and revolutionary past, to which he is bound by affection and tradition, which exercises a fatal attraction. The titanism of the will exemplified by the heroes of the preceding generations is an insufficient heritage for those who must live in the more complex and pragmatic world of the post-revolutionary era.[4] On the other hand, the mixture of joyless religion, greed and respectability with which the middle classes have replaced that heroic rebelliousness is unsatisfactory too. O'Faolain's people seek the attractions of an advanced, varied civilization, while remaining attached to a belief in the certainties of a simpler, morally decisive world. But his elaboration of this well known contrast becomes increasingly subtle, especially in his short stories. There is in them an increasing admiration for the confident, secular world of material success and cultural enrichment, which he frowningly compares with the impoverished and restricted world of Ireland in the thirties and forties. Yet the admiration for a cosmopolitan, ethically governed society is countered by his nostalgia for that sense of liberation which he had experienced as a youth during his participation in the Irish revolution and which he merges with the passionate experience of an instinctive, sexual love. These two aspects of experience – the organized and conceptual, and the rebellious and intuitive – are the imaginative modes in which he realizes the cultural debate between modernism and provincialism, unable to give up or to give in entirely to either. His preoccupation with style and form in the short story was an even deeper symptom of this tension. Although, like O'Connor, he looked to Flaubert, Chekhov and de Maupassant as his models, he also reacted with hostility to the 'besotted realists' like Zola and even Joyce. He wanted the purity of control but did not want to lose the richness of extravagance in his writing. The celebration of sexual love as a revolutionary liberation and of a cosmopolitan society as a civilized ideal left the bleak, sexually repressive and Jansenist contemporary society of Ireland as the worst of all possible worlds. Yet his stories are rarely so schematic as this description might indicate. In 'Lovers of the Lake', two adulterous lovers from the rich and successful middle class find themselves on Lough Derg, an ancient site of pilgrimage and penance. Jenny, the woman who has come here in search of the faith that will enable her to become morally decisive and put an end to the relationship, is pursued by her highly sceptical lover Bobby, who is determined to confront this superstitious foolishness with his love. Neither ancient nor modern Ireland wins this particular battle. The desire for clarity and faith remains part of the confusion of actual living, not separable but distinct from it. The fierceness of the spiritual life and the durability of the secular life are incorporated in this story with such tact that neither is satirized as extremism. Harsh doctrinal condemnation and flaccid hedonism are both caricature descriptions of the attitudes represented here.

Frank O'Connor's short stories, translations and other writings are so comfortably addressed to an audience that the initial sense of community established by their confident and confiding tone often outlasts the substantial impression of loneliness and alienation which they contemplate. Even in his most eloquent denunciations of orthodox behaviour and attitudes, there is a softening element of camaraderie between him and his audience, which bespeaks the intimacy of a culture in which it is easy to be knowing because everything is familiar and known. He has the poise of a man who belongs and the pose of a man who is an outcast. The contradiction is energetically exploited but seldom explored. Like O'Faolain, O'Connor wanted the risks of modern individuality and the consolations of traditional community. The new Ireland provided neither. So, he fulminated against its unenviable achievement in losing the first and refusing the other while settling instead for a bogus piety and a slavish conformism. Naturally he made enemies, had his books banned and was compelled, in 1952, to go to the United States where his inclination towards bluff sentimentality was enhanced by exile and fame. The charm of the world of his stories is so potent that the most desperate situations can never be taken seriously. All his disappointed lovers and disillusioned revolutionaries and shopkeepers have a vulnerable and endearing aspect to them, which is confirmed for the reader by the sententiousness of the author. Yet, there are stories, like 'The Bridal Night' (from *Crab Apple Jelly*, 1944) in which the voice and the tale co-operate to create a solitude the more poignant for the communal source out of which it has arisen. In this instance an old woman is telling the story of her only son who went mad for love of a girl who was beyond him. On the night before he is taken to the asylum, the girl comes and lies with him to ease his agony, while the mother and a neighbour sit in the kitchen. Thereafter, the community can't do enough for her and the mother treasures the son's departing moment of peace. The lonely setting, at dusk beside the Atlantic, the woman's monologue and the narrator's marginal, listening presence show O'Connor's economy and restraint at its best. But the story itself is an emblem of his work and his time. A close society, an unbearable loneliness and a narrator caught between the fascination of both provide a telling image of the sense of displacement which characterized his most lasting work, a sense for which his calculated charm was an insufficient consolation.

O'Faolain and O'Connor were both children of the Civil War, pupils of the fiercely nationalist Daniel Corkery and, on both accounts, prone to disillusion as the phantom of a renovated Ireland receded during the bitter decades of the thirties and forties. Nevertheless, they continued to strive for a reconciliation between their vision of Ireland's possibilities and its diminished reality. O'Faolain found a way towards it in his 'conversion' to Roman Catholicism after a sojourn in Italy in 1946. But for Francis Stuart, who also fought on the Republican side in the Civil War, there was no possibility of reconciliation. From the outset of his strange career in 1923 to the present, Stuart has consistently adhered to an evangelical belief in the importance of a chosen few, from whom the possibility of a new preternatural tenderness of feeling and awareness would be nurtured to the point at which it would replace the existing subnormal world. The necessary prelude to this new dispensation was suffering and disgrace; the scapegoat figure, who would assume the burden of pain, was the artist. In Stuart, therefore, the religious sensibility is dominant and peremptory to a degree not known before in Irish writing. In his autobiographical novel *Black List Section H* (1971), Stuart tells of his rediscovery of the Bible during his married life in County Wicklow with Iseult, the daughter of Maud Gonne, Yeats's beloved:

Christ had held the most forward position of His time for several hours. And it would fall to the condemned, the sick-unto-death and perhaps a handful of unregarded artists to defend these areas of consciousness in the coming days as best they could. (ch. 20, p. 119)

Later, at dinner with Yeats, he expands on his ideas in relation to the Irish censorship laws:

H didn't share the sense of outrage of Yeats and his fellow intellectuals at the censorship law. It was a matter of indifference to him. The Irish censorship would catch the smaller fish but if a really big one was to swim into view it would be set on by far more ferocious foes than any Irish ones.

'If somebody somewhere writes a book which is so radical and original,' H announced. . . 'that it would burst the present literary setup wide open, that writer will be treated with a polite contempt by the critical and academic authorities that will discourage further mention of him. He'll raise deeper, more subconscious hostility than sectarian ones and he'll be destroyed far more effectively by enlightened neglect than anything we would do to him here.'

Yeats had lifted his head and was regarding H intently.

'You believe that the artist is bound to be rejected? You equate him with the prophet?' (ch. 20, p. 121)

In 1940, Stuart accepted a position as lecturer in the University of Berlin. He stayed in Germany throughout the war and broadcast to Ireland once a week from 1942 to 1944, encouraging the policy of Irish neutrality and expressing sympathy for IRA prisoners, North and South. He had spent a year in jail in Ireland in 1922–3 and, after the war, was detained for a further year by the French authorities. He had sought disgrace and had found it. Between 1947 and 1950 he wrote a trilogy of novels – *The Pillar of Cloud*, *Redemption*, and *The Flowering Cross* – which (like Beckett's trilogy at the same time) fell dead from the press. These, along with *Black List* and the later novels – *Memorial* (1973), *A Hole in the Head* (1977) and *The High Consistory* (1981) – are the central works among his twenty-two novels. His deliberate alliance with Germany and, later, with the paramilitaries in the North of Ireland was a declaration of freedom from the powerful pieties of convention. He is like O'Faolain, O'Connor and Beckett in his wish to reintegrate his Irish experience with the European crisis and his work, as much as theirs, is an implicit critique of Ireland's failure to sustain its earlier engagement with the world at large. Stuart, imaginatively obsessed with the figure of dishonour, and Beckett, equally entranced by the figure of inertia, go further than their contemporaries in thus ratifying their social delinquency, making contact and even identification with a community of outcasts the central preoccupation of their work. Because of the war, the outcasts were numerous but without cohesion as a group. They were bonded by isolation. This allowed Stuart to preserve his belief in the radical isolation of the artist and, at the same time, the necessity for the artist to make contact with the outcast and despised.

Born into Northern unionism, he married into the Irish revival and took the Republican side in the Civil War. Whatever cause he joined he left it when it became successful. His element is risk; anything which calcifies into a categorical attitude – moral, social, political – is anathema to him. As guerilla, poultry farmer, gambler, philanderer, prisoner, refugee, German sympathizer, unsung artist, he risks all kinds of destruction in order to see what survives. His search is for holiness through sin. This holiness is inexplicable unless Stuart's repeated references to the New Testament are taken into account. It is the holiness represented by the innocent scapegoat figure who is put to death by a coalition of the established powers and of the people for a crime he did not commit. The artist is like Christ in this respect. He is a permanent victim of the mechanism by which the community attempts to rid itself of innocence for the sake of preserving its solidarity. There is, therefore, in Stuart's fiction a variety of attempts, some of them desperate indeed, to embody in a person the idea of a total innocence which is, nevertheless, politically and socially criminal. His meditation upon this leads him to give a fully serious treatment to the action of violence in society, something which, remarkably, no other Irish writer has done.

Women bear the brunt of this violence and are physically or psychologically mutilated by it. Yet, through it, they enter a territory of feeling which is beyond sentimentality or sexual desire or what is generally called love. They become practitioners of charity and have a redemptive capacity, which Stuart, with an evangelical longing, sees as a condition of the appearance of the new world and the disappearance of the old. Thus, in *The Pillar of Cloud*, set in post-war Germany, Dominique Malone is saved by the Mayerski sisters, who have suffered terribly in the war; in *Redemption*, set in Ireland after the war, Ezra Arrigho is finally granted spiritual peace by the reappearance of Margareta, and the imprisoned Louis Clancy in *The Flowering Cross* wins freedom through his love for the blind girl, Alyse. The two 'Northern Ireland' novels, *Memorial* and *A Hole in the Head*, are dominated by the relationship between a writer – Sugrue and Barnaby Shane respectively – and a woman – Herra and Emily Brontë – which is characterized by extreme neurosis and, simultaneously, by a tenderness not available to the normal world, where violence reigns. Violence is the climate of the institutional life; peace is the climate of the redeemed life. They are conjoined by the suffering of the scapegoat, in which evil attempts to destroy innocence but, unwittingly, makes it active and redemptive.

Few Irish novels of this period escape the stereotyped confrontation between the enervation of the social life and the desire for freedom and plenitude, which characterizes the increasingly introverted private consciousness. Because religion was so pervasive and influential in almost all aspects of existence, most emphatically so in its attitudes towards sexual matters, the heroism of the individual life tended to be expressed in an increasingly secular idiom, with sexuality celebrated as the deepest form of liberation. Further, in reaction to the various idealizations of Irish life, which had been popular during the Irish revival and which were thereafter transmuted into an ideology of Catholic Ireland, novelists tended to use all the resources of naturalism in order to present a bleak and unforgiving counter to the current propaganda.[5] Although there were some remarkable successes, the polemical impulse in these novels was often dependent on the circumstances they were designed to combat. There is something dated both about the issues and about the forms in which they were engaged. The operation of the censorship ensured that novels would be noticed to the degree that they broached subjects which were under social taboo and not for any more enduring or interesting innovation in form. In a curious way, censorship retarded the effects in Ireland of experimental work like that of Joyce, Beckett and O'Brien. Books which earned the notoriety of being banned were books which were likely to be understood, because of the familiarity of the naturalistic form. Equally, to challenge the status quo, writers felt an obligation to do so with a certain directness. As is often the case, naturalism became the mode favoured by those who regarded themselves as committed, or as interested, in the facts of common life. Like all the current European versions of 'socialist realism', the central intimation of such novels was the existence of an authentic solidarity and community hidden below the autocratic and life-denying forms and fictions of the official order. Stuart was remarkable in his almost anarchic acceptance of a permanently deforming Pharisaic system, within which there would survive a perpetually redemptive band of apostles. For others, the enduring truths were those of the authentic community, which were taken as 'natural'; the ephemeral, if powerful, inauthenticity belonged to the 'unnatural' external world of regulated society.

As a consequence, a number of complete but submerged and quarantined worlds emerge in Irish fiction, each claiming for itself an autonomy and a reality greater than that which environs it. Forrest Reid's *Peter Waring* (1937, a rewriting of *Following Darkness*, 1912) identifies one of them as the enchanted universe of adolescence as it revealed itself in the North of Ireland in the last decades of the nineteenth century. Bounded on one side by a dreary puritanism and the squalor of Protestant Belfast, his sensibility seeks satisfaction in a spacious, light-filled mansion, Derryaghy House, owned by a motherly and understanding widow. Reid's unremitting delicacy is rebuked by the contrast with the almost brutal vigour of Liam O'Flaherty's novels in the most typical of which – *Skerrett* (1932), *Famine* (1937) and *Land* (1946) – the will to survive overcomes all other forces in a merciless struggle. O'Flaherty's insistence on the elemental nature of existence, his concentration on the primitive and on the primary forces by which his islanders, peasants and revolutionaries are moved, contribute to the impression that the realism here is in service to the most melodramatic of all the myths of solidarity, namely that the only enemy is finally the fear of defeat itself. No greater contrast could be imagined than the fiction – primarily the short stories – of Mary Lavin. From 1942, when *Tales from Bective Bridge* appeared, she has established a deserved reputation as one of the most fearsomely economical of the Irish writers. Her work, largely concentrated on the experience of love lost but still treasured, articulates communal

values in terms of individual experiences. At first sight, her stories
are deceptively simple and subdued, but once the reader becomes
acclimatized to the nefarious sweetness of the narrator's voice, the
illusion of comfort disappears and is replaced by a deeply disturbed
sense of the frailty of human values in a smug and complacent
middle-class society. Only the world of love, represented by the
ethereal and dislocated young woman who appears so often in the
best stories, retains a final authenticity, even though the critique of
the surrounding society is gently implied rather than loudly
enforced. A more specific and aggressive advocacy for an oppressed
grouping appeared in novels like James Plunkett's *Strumpet City*
(1969), in which the working people of Dublin are stimulated to
consciousness by the Labour leader James Larkin and confronted
by their employer enemies, with the Catholic clergy ambiguously
caught in the conflict; or in Patrick Kavanagh's two versions of
pastoral, *The Green Fool* (1938), the soft version, and *Tarry Flynn*
(1948), the harsh version, in which the rural region and its populace
are rescued from illusory stereotyping. A variation on the elemental
theme is played by Benedict Kiely in novels like *The Captain with
the Whiskers* (1960) and *Dogs Enjoy the Morning* (1971), in which
the only real world is that about which the most extraordinary,
legendary anecdotes can be told. The violent and alienated life of an
urban and politically unstable present is time and again set against a
place or a time in which values were unquestioned and a sense of
community securely assumed. Michael McLaverty's *Call my
Brother Back* (1939) is one of the most tender evocations of this
experience, with Rathlin island and sectarian Belfast as its polarized
arenas. Janet McNeill's *The Maiden Dinosaur* (1964) records the
plight of a lost Protestant gentility which looks back to the twenties
as the period of stability which has suddenly yielded to the coarser
present. It is not surprising that contrasts of this kind should be
more discordant in the North, given its history of strife and its deep
hunger for a healing security. In the novels of Brian Moore, this
realism of the submerged life in the corrupt system finds its
apotheosis.

Moore's first novel *Judith Hearne* (1955; republished as *The
Lonely Passion of Judith Hearne*, 1959) is written with an economy
that hovers between elegance and meanness. There is no attempt to
charm the reader into an appreciation of the endearing uniqueness
of this wretched woman's life. There is no gesture towards the
presence of elemental forces, either in the community or in the

individual. All the detail is damning. Even where there is pathos, there is no dignity. It is a world without aura, an Ireland unenhanced by a pronounced style, its atmosphere fumigated of the scents of heroism, myth, historical crisis, nostalgia for a better time. Judith Hearne's life is a pathetic, loveless business, hemmed in by religion, class, woebegone gentilities and inexorable social and physical decay. Her dream life is her only exit but it is finally chastised by the nullity of her daily existence and she sinks into a graceless senility, a victim of deadening circumstance. The story of Diarmuid Devine in *The Feast of Lupercal* (1957; reprinted as *A Moment of Love*, 1965) is similarly humiliating. Devine, like Judith Hearne, has his growth as a person violently aborted by a punitive, fear-ridden society. It is only when Moore leaves Northern Ireland and moves, first to Canada and then to the United States, that the fascination with society's victimization of these lonely lives undergoes a modification. In *The Luck of Ginger Coffey* (1960), Ginger almost goes under but finally survives the pressures of making his incompetent way in the New World. He even furnishes himself with a rudimentary ethic of endurance. But it is in *An Answer from Limbo* (1962) that Moore begins to free himself from the *simplisme* of the battle between the aspiring individual and the stifling social form. The devoutly Catholic Mrs Tierney, who finds herself transplanted to New York as a baby-minder for her writer-son Brendan and his Jewish wife Jane, dies in utter isolation after a vain attempt to re-establish some form of spiritual values in her son's shallow and godless household. In this instance, it is the free, secular life of New York that is disobligingly seen in contrast to her narrow but potent faith. Escape from the restrictions of Belfast also means a loss of communal and spiritual values, which arise from a complex of forces richer than the merely predatory sexual-commercial universe of American success. By the early seventies, Moore had begun the search for a new form which would allow him to inquire more thoroughly into the question of the values which religious belief can provide and which the loss of that belief demands. There is here an element of the exile's characteristic crisis – the desire to belong cancelled by the repudiation of the demand that he belong to a system of failure and repression. But Moore goes further than this. He wants to investigate the sources of the desire to belong and, in doing so, finds himself obliged to challenge novelistic naturalism as a sufficient form.

The result is an astonishing sequence of parables – *Catholics*

(1972), *The Great Victorian Collection* (1975), *The Mangan Inheritance* (1979) and *The Cold Heaven* (1983). Even those novels which remain within the context of naturalism – *The Doctor's Wife* (1976) and *The Temptation of Eileen Hughes* (1981), both of them direct descendants of *I am Mary Dunne* (1968) – have a new obsessional quality whereby the women who dominate them seek through love and sexual experience something other than an escape from their conventional lives. They seem to have a hunger for something appetite cannot satisfy, for a sense of transcendence, on the way to which the rediscovery of personal identity is only a first step. Their surroundings are no longer squalid, but comfortable and even wealthy. The consumer world has now replaced late Victorian Belfast as the physical site of the conflict. But the fulfilment, the hedonism of their lives is for them as great a pressure as poverty and the lack of sexual fulfilment had been for Judith Hearne. In the fables, this other world is identified with ancestral belief and longing. It is not just nostalgia, although that too is there. It is a radical dissatisfaction with the actual that leads in the end to either the acceptance of or the recognized possibility of miracle, an irruption into the complex, secular world of hotels, motels, affairs, professions and cosmopolitan ease. Moore's allegiance to the actual world does not waver. Instead it learns to coexist with the possibility of another, apocalyptic place, in which the simple can wholeheartedly believe and which the sophisticated dread to accept other than as a psychic disturbance or metaphor. Thus he pushes his naturalism to the breaking point, but never permits it to disintegrate. At the end of *The Cold Heaven*, Marie, who was witness to an apparition of the Virgin on the shores of California, surrenders it to the semi-reluctant Church and turns towards 'that ordinary, muddled life of falling in love and leaving her husband and starting over again'. Belief remains a powerful force that must be refused, and yet the effects of which in the ordinary run of experience cannot be denied. To put it in Catholic terms, Moore's people lack the gift of grace partly because it is mediated to them through a culture and through a Church, which is, in the aesthetic and in the moral sense, graceless. One has the impression that this may be an explanation but is not an excuse.

John McGahern's first three books, *The Barracks* (1963), *The Dark* (1965) and *Nightlines* (1973), are as implacably bleak as anything to be found in Moore's early work. The psychic isolation which they describe is rendered with an actuarial tidiness, the precision of the recorded details tinged at all points with a faint, cello sadness. Even in the most casual moments, there is a conscious emphasis on bleakness, which never quite cancels an incipient tenderness:

The line of black cattle trailed all that winter round the fields in search of grass, only small patches in the shelter; always a funeral of little winter birds in their wake in the hope that the rocking hooves would loosen the frozen earth down to the worms. And in the evenings they'd crowd at the gate to low with steaming breaths for their fodder. (*The Dark*, ch. 9, p. 47)

In McGahern's crepuscular world, the deep energies of life have been occluded and turned poisonous. In their secret decay they are clouded by shame. Sex, cancer, drink, lovelessness are known by those who are afflicted by them to be the pathological inversions of their truly human alternatives – love, health, rationality, generosity. McGahern's people find it as difficult to live with themselves as with others. They are caught in a curious dilemma. Disdaining the usual and entrapping fictions which surround human relationships, the saccharine and oppressive notions of love and marriage most prominent among them, they look for a more candid freedom by testing experience in relation to the senses and then by scrutinizing the feelings which such a testing generates. But there are two chief kinds of physical testing. One is the sensual experience of sex, the other is the sensual experience of illness. Each develops in unexpected directions. Sexual experience, which involves another, leads to self-enclosure; illness, which is private and involves one's own body exclusively, leads to an opening out towards others.

There is no religious feeling in these novels, although there is a feeling for the force of religion in Irish social life. McGahern's world is almost entirely bereft of anything beyond the horizon of empirical experience. The melancholy discipline of his writing is most successful within that specifically secular zone. When he attempts to depart from it, as in *The Leavetaking* (1974), his control tends to waver and he allows his strict tenderness to degenerate into sentimentality. Even though he rewrote the last pages of this novel, he cannot quite find a convincing idiom for the description of a successful love affair. The link between sexuality and love is problematic. One can be clinically observed to such an extent that the other must appear almost absurd in comparison. This is an issue which he finally confronted directly in *The Pornographer* (1979).

Here McGahern polarizes the forces which have been dominating his work, the better to see them and the more courageously to interrogate their mutual relationship. The hero is a writer of pornography for a journal run by an ex-poet, Maloney. He has invented two characters, Mavis and Colonel Grimshaw, whose sexual appetites are as inexhaustible as their ways of satisfying them are ingenious. He meets a woman at a dance in Dublin, they become lovers and she becomes infatuated with and pregnant by him. She goes to London to have the baby. By this time, he is backing away from the relationship as fast as he can, despite the loud disapproval of his boss Maloney and her Irish friends in London. During this time his aunt is dying in a Dublin hospital, his uncle is visiting her regularly and his provincial childhood life is constantly being interwoven again with his self-encased metropolitan existence. The girl has the baby, he abandons her, is beaten up for doing so and goes to his aunt's funeral scarred by the punishment. Finally, the exemplary courage and magnanimity of his aunt is brought home to him as he realizes how it survived the helpless selfishness of her own family. Her shrewd charity is not, he realizes, a practical gift. It is a spiritual achievement. Her illness has clarified the nature of love, his love affair has clarified the nature of selfishness. At that point, he decides to leave Dublin, come home to the farm and propose marriage to the girl. He is redeemed. Pornography is shown to be the literary equivalent of unfeeling selfishness, illness the final opportunity to confirm values that go beyond the welfare of the self. The customary bleakness finally gives way to a pervasive tenderness, which will not deny but equally will not be denied by its chill alternative. In this novel, McGahern enriches without softening his vision of the lives of quiet desperation, which are lived out in an Ireland in which the compatability between sexuality and illness is a frighteningly natural phenomenon.

With the appearance of John Banville's *Long Lankin* (1970) and *Nightspawn* (1971), it was obvious that an important writer had arrived, although in what his importance consisted was not clear until the publication of *Birchwood* in 1973. This is one of the most startling of the century's varied achievements in Irish writing. It is a narrative, told by Gabriel Godkin, the child of an incestuous relationship, of the hero's quest for his twin sister in an Ireland which is by turn that of the Civil War period and that of the nineteenth-century famine. The Godkin house and estate, both in fairly ruinous condition, have their counterpart in Prospero's travelling circus, a medley of freaks, mutants and sinister cruelty, the natural home of the twin brother Michael. (There is no twin sister.) The extreme condition of breakdown, which characterizes this society, ravaged by war and famine, undermined by incest, violence, and insanity, drives Godkin back upon himself to such a degree that he lives only by the laws of his own consciousness, even though he queries its reality too. Everywhere we hear echoes of other writers and other worlds – Dostoevsky, Beckett, le Fanu, Nabokov, Flann O'Brien, Maria Edgeworth, Herman Hesse. The intensity of this self-consciousness is increased by the fact that Gabriel is writing the novel as a memoir, arranging the pieces of his past experience in the hope of discovering a design which he nevertheless knows either does not exist or will exist only because he has invented it. Thus the novel plays with a series of conventions and a sequence of puns on names. The Gothic elements are frankly borrowed. Incidents, like the death of Granny Godkin from spontaneous combustion, are stolen from Dickens's *Bleak House*. There is an insistence on our remembering that the story is a series of literary conventions. Prospero's Magic Circus stirs memories of, say, the Magic Theatre in Hesse's *Steppenwolf* (1929), but the correspondence is by no means exact. In the same way, this novel is one of the many Irish fictions about the decline of the Big House, but it wears its conventional rue with a difference. The world of Elizabeth Bowen has become interfused with that of Sheridan Le Fanu, yet neither is fully present. Banville uses literary echoes as a reminder that the essential activity is the act of writing itself and that the essential futility is manifest in the gap between a discrete, discontinuous experience and the formed plots and arranged motifs which are a necessary feature of literature. He is fascinated by the idea of the lost twin, partly for the metaphorical opportunities it offers in the way of rendering a quest for the lost or the other self, partly because it encapsulates the anguish of a consciousness which, in recognizing itself, recognizes its inescapable otherness. To tell the story of one's life is almost to become someone other than oneself. Writing is the strange activity which bridges and opens this gap. All of Banville's subsequent novels – *Copernicus* (1976), *Kepler* (1981), *The Newton Letter* (1983) – elaborate upon this perception with great brilliance. The three scientists mentioned in the titles are men who have a coherent and splendid vision of the order of the universe, which contrasts very sharply with the disorder of the worlds in which they live. Yet this disorder is not external to them; they participate in it and even conspire with its dishevelment in order to produce the crystalline systems by which they are remembered. Banville is interested here in the centrally flawed relationship between order and disorder, opposites which are really twins. In *The Newton Letter*, perhaps the most subversive of all his works, he carefully dismantles the historically received idea of Newton, of order, of the Irish fictional convention of the Big House, of the convention of fiction itself (there is a parodic relationship with Goethe's *Elective Affinities*), of the representational function of words, until the reader is compelled to recognize that this is writing in pursuit of its own nature. Banville thus restores to Irish fiction the principle of radical doubt, which governs the work of predecessors like Beckett and Flann O'Brien. Like them, he writes with the virtuosity of someone who is both entranced and aggravated by the phenomenon of language itself and the ever receding mystery of its relationship to actual experience.

No other novelists of this period have the penetrative power of Stuart, Moore, McGahern or Banville. The Big House novel, given a new lease of life by Yeats's poetry, continued to attract writers because of its attractive, if archaic, confrontation between civility (of the old, *ancien régime* kind) and philistinism (of the contemporary, *arriviste* kind). There were strange, powerful interventions from English novelists like Henry Green in his novel *Loving* (1933) and J. G. Farrell with *Troubles* (1972). In each case the spectacle of decay in the Irish Big House setting was part of a wider vision of lives marginalized by the slow internal collapse of the British Empire. Among Irish novelists, Aidan Higgins in *Langrishe Go Down* (1966) gave the genre a remarkable resuscitation by resiting it in the 1930s and writing of it with an almost incandescent lyricism. But Higgins thereafter turned to a more experimental and, one might say, self-indulgent kind of fiction, leaving Jennifer Johnston to find new resources within this well established format. In *The Captains and the Kings* (1972), *The Gates* (1973), *How Many Miles to Babylon?* (1974) and *The Old Jest* (1979), she uses the social distinctions which separate people as a means to discriminate more subtly among them in moral terms. This is made more possible by the decline of the Ascendancy class, most marked after the First World War and further accelerated after the foundation of the new Irish state. As the economic distinctions weaken, the conventions of social behaviour begin to give way and individuals are thrown back upon their own personal resources to survive the conflict and isolation which succeed so quickly upon their world's collapse. Jennifer Johnston's world is, morally speaking, simpler than those of McGahern or Moore. Her very style is crisp and decisive, entirely appropriate for someone who still has such affection for the secure world whose disappearance she understands and laments. But the humane clarities of this attitude do not easily survive the very different complexities of the contemporary Northern Irish troubles. In trying to come to terms with that situation in *Shadows on our Skin* (1977), she revealed how closely dependent upon the genre of Big House fiction such a stalwart morality is.

Almost all Irish novelists are concerned with the varieties of social or political dislocation which are an inevitable product of the country's history. William Trevor is as skilled in the depiction of the phenomenon in English as in Irish circumstances and he brings to it a sinister quality, which has more in common with Graham Greene's *Brighton Rock* than with his more exotically melodramatic Anglo-Irish forebears. The pervading gloom of novels like *Mrs Eckdorf in O'Neill's Hotel* (1969), *The Boarding House* (1965), *The Children of Dynmouth* (1976) is upset rather than relieved by a number of comic sequences, which are perhaps too grotesque to be effective in such a subdued and controlled environment. Trevor does have a sense of the evil that lives in dreariness and this element lends to his slightly musty prose an edge of danger and threat which is cumulatively disturbing. But it is as a short-story writer that he is most distinguished. *The Ballroom of Romance and Other Stories* (1972) is an acknowledged classic, especially in the title story; so too is *Lovers of Their Time* (1978). Both volumes are, in a way, about the banality of evil and the evil of banality, but they are so deeply recessed in their time and in their apparent diffidence that their power is not immediately obvious. Trevor has a polite Anglican outdatedness, which tends to disguise his very real apprehension of contemporary blights and disjunctions.

An anecdote, recounted by Oliver MacDonagh, gives a particular insight to the growing sense of dislocation and of introverted solidarity, which was to take on such drastic forms in the Northern Irish statelet and was a continuous pressure on the novels of this period. In 1906, the Anglican Canon George Hannay, who wrote under the pseudonym George Birmingham, was excluded from taking part in Gaelic League functions by the local Roman Catholic parish priest. Hannay was a member of the Gaelic League, but he was excluded on the ground that he was unIrish.[6] Hannay was also the author of a premonitory novel *The Red Hand of Ulster*, published in the year of the Home Rule Crisis, 1912. This novel is certainly the earliest and perhaps the best account of the Northern Loyalist's sense of dislocation. Although Hannay sees a solution in British withdrawal, the political importance of his work is in the analysis of the Loyalist mentality. Riven by ambiguity, it is, like much in the Irish literary and political traditions, unable to be at peace with itself. It feels excluded and wants to be included, but not by those (British or Irish) who excluded it in the first place. It is an alienated but not an alien mentality. Its homelessness is a condition much brooded upon in Irish novels, although since Hannay few novelists have attempted to come to terms with this particularly northern version of dispossession. That was left to the poets and the dramatists.

Poetry

Poets from the North of Ireland have recently dominated the Irish, and even the English, literary scene to such an extent that the long interval between the death of Yeats in 1939 and of Joyce in 1941 and the appearance of Seamus Heaney, Derek Mahon, Michael Longley, James Simmons in the mid-sixties has tended to be looked upon as an interregnum. As a consequence, poets who had struggled against isolation and obscurity in that interval have had to undergo again the loss or reduction of public attention for their work. Some have been so effectively ignored that their names are barely known. Brian Coffey, Padraic Fallon and Denis Devlin are the most gifted in this group; others like Austin Clarke, achieved only a brief independence between playing the role of an epigon of Yeats and a precursor of others. Thomas Kinsella began by winning an audience and then, as his poetry became more difficult and as the 'Northern Poets' simultaneously appeared, he lost it. John Montague shared his initial audience with Kinsella and his later audience with the northern newcomers. Patrick Kavanagh forced his way out of obscurity into a local prominence. Since then, he has been regarded as a father figure to the Northern revival and, more specifically, to Seamus Heaney. Even though the founding of the Dolmen Press by Liam Miller in Dublin in 1951 inaugurated a new era in Irish publishing, most especially for poetry, it remained difficult for Irish writers to achieve visibility in the English-speaking world. Possibly, Irish neutrality during the Second World War was a contributory factor in this and the general decline in Ireland's historical role, which neutrality accentuated and economic failure confirmed, made the sense of estrangement between Ireland and the rest of the world extreme. Anthony Cronin's brilliant memoir *Dead as Doornails* (1976) gives the best account of the period. Dublin in the late forties.

was an odd and, in many respects, unhappy place. The malaise that seems to have affected everywhere in the aftermath of war took strange forms there, perhaps for the reason that the war itself had been a ghastly unreality. Neutrality had left a wound, set up complexes in many, including myself, which the post war did little to cure.[7]

Cronin's own poetry is beset by the aggressions, the bitterness and the boredom which were the occupational hazards of the residual bohemian life the city had then to offer. Although he can offer an ironic variation on Yeats in a poem of self-reconciliation, there is no avoiding the sense of a city and a culture as well as of a person wounded or disabled by circumstances: 'Not that he has, but that he is, such friends.'[8] Such friends as Cronin had, like Brendan Behan or Patrick Kavanagh, had to devote a good deal of their energies to finding a way to make a living, for writing could not then do it for them. Austin Clarke spent too much of his time in hack reviewing and in marking examination papers. In all the memoirs of the period there is a persistent sense of the sheer grind that had to be endured for the sake of enough money to live on and to write on. Flann O'Brien, Clarke, Cronin, Kavanagh dissipated much of their talent in a society which permitted little else in the way of rejection. It is unsurprising to find that so many of these artists assumed personae in their serious and in their occasional writings, as well as in their personal lives, in which wastefulness was an important element. Talent, time, money could be wasted, drunkenness and unemployment could be given moral status and, finally, the writing itself would become imbued with something of this spirit of subversive squalor. O'Brien's novels, Kavanagh's satiric poems, Behan's plays and Cronin's varied writings, including his poems and his novels, *The Life of Riley* (1964) and *Identity Papers* (1979), all manifest this spirit, countering the very real grimness of the general situation with a comic verve that is often generated by the camaraderie of an outcast group. A degree of incestuous, intramural coding in these works excludes a larger audience, but their total effect was beneficial in that they acted as a constant reminder of an alternative possibility to the existing order of things. As such, they linked up in natural alliance with journals such as *The Bell*, John Ryan's *Envoy*, David Marcus's *Poetry Ireland* and the brief, if memorable *Kavanagh's Weekly* of 1952. In Belfast, journals like *Lagan* (1943–7) and *Rann* (1948–53) provided a focus for writers like John Hewitt, W. R. Rodgers, Roy McFadden, Sam Hanna Bell, Maurice Craig and Robert Greacen. The founding of the Lyric Theatre by Mary O'Malley in 1951, followed six years later by the first number of its magazines *Threshold* was, along with the appearance of the Dolmen Press and a national Arts Council, a sign of a new energy, North and South. But the climate was still oppressive and the fifties saw the death of more journals than any other decade before or since. Ireland was still losing its young through emigration and driving its writers into internal or external exile through denigration.

One of the most potent of Irish exiles was Louis MacNeice, who seems at first sight to represent in a particularly hesitant manner many of the dogged issues of provincialism and escape, commitment and evasion. The Protestant son of a Home Rule clerical household in Carrickfergus with deep connections in the West of Ireland, MacNeice became one of the left-wing poets of the English thirties, associated in the general mind with Auden and Stephen Spender. He loved Ireland, North and South, but could stand the oppressions and pettiness of neither one. Yet he did not make his mixed alienation and attachment the material of a defined or defining pose. His *The Poetry of W. B. Yeats* (1941), an important work in the reception of Yeats, cast a critical eye on the poet's systematizing passion and aristocratic posturings. Yet he saw in Yeats a dynamic ambition to co-ordinate scattered experience into ordered shape and in this respect found a response in his own work. MacNeice was more sceptical than Yeats, less inclined to see in the flux of empirical experience or in the apocalypse of war the indications of a tragic denouement to a brilliant opportunity. His poetry is sufficiently beset by dread and marked by repudiation of the coarse aspects of the modern world, but it retains at its heart an abiding patience with the ultimate nature of the human condition. Belfast is a hard city, Dublin a place of soft light, the West a pastoral dream; between them the imagination negotiates, asking Ireland to make a truce with the harsher and more actual world of London, the Second World War, the new urban dreariness of a broken down Europe.[9] *Autumn Journal* (1939), Section XVI, is his challenge to a country that is maimed by its separation from the world and yet is seductive because

> on this tiny stage with luck a man
> Might see the end of one particular action.

That too is a deception. Ireland is both of the world and not of it. It is commercial Belfast, Augustan Dublin, Celtic Mayo, a sequence of actual identities that are always tinged with unreality, because these characteristics are part of the lore of place and of pastness, always out of key with the plain, observable realities of the lives lived within them. MacNeice is the harbinger of a secular sensibility that retains a fondness for the sweet charms of myth but prefers the plainer, starker truths of poetry.

Two other poets – Austin Clarke and Patrick Kavanagh – represent in their work a similar blend of the emotion of alienation from the society and of commitment to its improvement. Clarke began his career very much in the shadow of Yeats. When his *Collected Poems* were published in 1936, only a few poems (from the 1929 volume *Pilgrimage*) escaped the lush seductions of the Celtic Twilight idiom, which the young Yeats had patented so successfully. But with the appearance of *Night and Morning* (1938) and, above all, of *Ancient Lights*, published by Dolmen in 1955, Clarke moved out of the magnetic field of Yeatsian influence and established his own voice. This finally became audible to a wider public with Dolmen's publication in 1961 of *Later Poems*. Thereafter, obscurity and publishing difficulties overcome, Clarke became the Angry Old Man of Irish letters, concentrating his fire on Irish clericalism and the sexual repression which was its main preoccupation and achievement. As with so many of his contemporaries – O'Faolain and Kavanagh – he was a crusader whose career was both limited and stimulated by the crusading instinct. He found the climate of the new Ireland hostile but necessary. He opposed it by calling in another Ireland to redress the balance. His world of medieval monasticism became a metaphor of the integrated culture, the disintegration of which he traces through the Reformation, the Counter Reformation and the Renaissance, emphasizing throughout one obsessive theme – the formation of attitudes towards sexuality and the link between these and freedom or the loss of it. This historical perspective is, however, no more than a background to his own experience, for which history provides an ordering and analytic principle. Clarke's greatest poems are energized by the conflict between freedom and imprisonment understood in terms of a battle between body and soul, between art's liberation and the Church's oppression. The extraordinary power generated in the best of his work is sourced in his gift for finding a compatability between history and autobiography and the consequent discovery of a public language for private griefs and torments. The blending of these elements was achieved with infinite craft and care. Clarke drew on the elaborate assonantal and alliterative patterns of Gaelic poetry to achieve the rich harmonics which give such resonance to his best work. He converts contemporary social stress, which led to his own isolation, into psychological distress, the analysis of which in historical and religious terms led to his late emergence as a poet. Poems like 'Ancient Lights', 'Tenebrae', 'Martha Blake', 'Repentance', 'The Straying Student' are among his most memorable, although it must be said that his assumption of the role of Ireland's literary conscience also stimulated him to produce verses of a merely local importance, tiresome in their spry and self-conscious humour. Nevertheless, Clarke's adoption of the function of a social commentator and his nurturing of the minority and adversarial stance is an important and characteristic example of the crusading commitment which, however uncomfortably or clumsily achieved, was a consistent feature of the Irish writer's conception of his role in and relation to a deeply flawed society.[10]

Clarke's preoccupation with the hostility between the prescriptions of religion and the desires of the body and imagination is rebuked in the work of Denis Devlin. A diplomat and intellectual who spent most of his time outside Ireland, Devlin is in some respects less amenable to incorporation within the tradition of modern Irish poetry than any other. He began publishing his poems in 1930, achieved some recognition with *Lough Derg and Other Poems* in 1946, died five years later and had a brief posthumous reputation restored in 1963 and 1964 with the publication of his *Collected Poems*. As much as Clarke, Devlin concentrates on the relationship between belief and sexual love; but in him their association is a benign one, displaying a slowly discovered and intricate mutuality, which is perceived finally in the experience of oneness to which each is complementary. He also has affinity with Clarke in his fascination with the European Catholic tradition and its devotional Irish counterpart, seeing both as having been effectively shattered by the wars of the early century and assuming to himself the imaginative effort of reconstituting them into a few and refreshed integration. 'Lough Derg' is the poem in which this attempt is most clearly undertaken, but also in other poems such as 'The Passion of Christ', 'The Colours of Love' and, above all, in 'The Heavenly Foreigner', his long, central work. Devlin attempted (under the influence of contemporary French poets like Paul Eluard and St John Perse) to achieve a poetry in which the fission between word and referent would be cancelled or overcome and to offer this as an analogue of the experience of love in which lover and beloved would be freed of their subject–object relationship and become the living and unifying principle of love itself, this too being a further analogue for religious faith in which the believer and that in which his faith is vested become incarnated in one. This is a rare instance of a metaphysical poetry in the symbolist mode and its uniqueness in Ireland emphasizes the rarity of a specifically Christian poetry in a country where the traditional modern relationship between poetry and belief has been fraught with tension and suspicion. Despite this, we can see in Devlin a positive vision of what is so fruitfully negative in Clarke. In 'The Colours of Love' the end of a love-affair is the prelude to another kind of love, as the lights of Paris melt into the Irish rainflowers:

At the Bar du Départ drink farewell
And say no word you'll be remembered by;
Nor Prince nor President can ever tell
Where love ends or when it does or why.

Down the boulevard the lights come forth
Like my rainflowers trembling all through Spring,
Blue and Yellow in the Celtic North. . .
The stone's ripple weakens, ring by ring.

Better no love than love, which, through loving
Leads to no love. The ripples come to rest. . .
Ah me! how all that young year I was moving
To take her dissolution to my breast!

Yet if Devlin in some sense rebukes Clarke, he himself is even more powerfully rebuked by Kavanagh. Against Devlin's cosmopolitanism and intellectuality Kavanagh counterposes the most aggressive localism and natural instinct. Again the contrast is more apparent than real, for Kavanagh, like Devlin, is a religious poet in his search for 'casualness', that state of spiritual leisure in which the experience of separateness is replaced by that of oneness. But such a state belongs to the poetry after 1955, when Kavanagh was convalescent after a serious illness. First he had to go through a series of iconoclastic battlings and manoeuvrings, the point of which was to establish for himself a clear ground for poetry, a ground not colonized by Yeats or Yeatsians, by politics or provincials, by Dublin literary types or by clergy. In a surprising manner, Kavanagh is the poet-laureate of the Free State, as it was first called. That is to say, he is at odds with the spiritual heroics of the foundation period of the State and is perfectly in accord with the general desire to climb down from the dizzy heights of mythology, the glories of battle, elaborate readings of tradition and labyrinthine pursuits of Irishness and to concentrate instead on the stony, grey soil of his native Monaghan and the actualities of living in the here and now. But, with all that, he was a believer in the miraculous power of poetry to reveal the essential quality of experience, although for him the miracle had to take place directly without all the liturgical and hieratic ceremonies of the Yeatsian mysteries. As a consequence, he spoke more candidly and audibly to his audience, especially the audience of writers, allowing them to be, in John Montague's famous phrase, 'liberated into ignorance'. Kavanagh led Irish poetry away from Yeats and the Revival to a new sense of the importance of the regional, the territory known through folklore, sensual experience, daily life, besetting memories. His famous hegira to a life of initial poverty and obscurity in Dublin, his longing for recognition for this new poetry, also became part and parcel of the next generation's attitude towards the need for the public recognition of poetry as something neither arcane nor embarrassing, but accessible and real. Through his example John Montague and Seamus Heaney came to a recognition of their own powers and the availability to poetry and to a public of their own experience.[11]

It is difficult to estimate Kavanagh's importance because there is a discrepancy between his influence, which was great, and his achievement, which was uneven. Beside him, Clarke and Devlin and Coffey, not to mention Yeats, seem dedicated craftsmen, remote from the banalities and casualness which disfigure so many of Kavanagh's poems and make his satiric pieces appear now so puerile. But these are the necessary defects of his virtues. Kavanagh's candour, the very naïvety with which he looked at his Monaghan world, helped to name the anonymous experience of the small farmer, the quiet corner of a field, the muddy lanes and the dull gossipings of a townland that suddenly became known anew to an audience that realized it had known that experience and that place all along. This maieutic power in Kavanagh's verse is, perhaps, its greatest distinction. It represented the power of poetry to make one actually see the world that had, until its arrival, only been looked at. His best poems, therefore, are revelations of the ordinary.

Kavanagh's first volume, *Ploughman and Other Poems*, was published in 1936, the same year as Clarke's *Collected Poems*. His last volume, *Come Dance with Kitty Stobling*, came out in 1960. Compared to Clarke, who began publishing in 1917 and continued until 1974, it was a relatively brief career. Yet Kavanagh managed in that quarter of a century to lift the burden of Irish and world history from the stooping shoulders of the Irish poet. In its place he put

> the spirit-shocking
> Wonder in a black slanting Ulster hill.

His local places – Shancoduff, Glasdrummond, Mucker – made no pretence of being microcosmic versions of the world beyond. The Second World War was 'the year of the Munich bother':

> Which
> Was more important? I inclined
> To lose my faith in Ballyrush and Gortin
> Till Homer's ghost came whispering to my mind.
> He said: I made the Iliad from such
> A local row. Gods make their own importance.

It is tempting to exaggerate the anti-literary aspect of Kavanagh's work in order to define its novelty and directness. But he was indeed conscious of what, in the recent literary tradition, he had to reject. To that end, he produced several versions of anti-pastoral, as a corrective to the Revival's idealization of the peasant and the 'natural' life. His autobiographical novels, *The Green Fool* (1938) and *Tarry Flynn* (1948), and, above all, his long poem *The Great Hunger* (1942) are the most notable, although the sentiment of rejection and refusal to be found in these does not disappear until the mid-fifties. *The Great Hunger* is a bitter account of the spiritual famine of the Irish small farmer. Paddy Maguire's life is compressed by poverty, religion, the despotism of convention. It has its pathos but never has dignity. Kavanagh later rejected this poem because it incriminated him too much with social and moral issues and coerced him towards a tragic account of existence. Instead, after his rebirth on leaving hospital, he espoused an ethic of 'not caring', of learning to 'lie/At the heart of the emotion', of waiting for the miracle to arrive:

> God cannot catch us
> Unless we stay in the unconscious room
> Of our hearts.

The patience and charity of Kavanagh's best poems – 'Canal Bank Walk', 'Innocence', 'Peace', 'Shancoduff', 'Father Mat', 'Question to Life', 'Epic' – make a remarkable contrast to the bitterness and violence of his public personality. The contrast is instructive in its power of reminding us of the struggle by Kavanagh and his contemporaries to gain acknowledgement for literature in an indifferent society and to find a public (and a publisher) for it. Although there were signs that such a public was beginning to emerge by the mid-fifties, Kavanagh, Clarke, Devlin, Coffey and many others spent the formative parts of their lives as writers in isolation or in the almost equally dangerous embrace of a small coterie of friends. With the appearance of Thomas Kinsella and John Montague this atmosphere of enclosure and struggle began to change.

Standish O'Grady once said that 'the history of one generation became the poetry of the next'.[12] This remark was made in the context of his study of ancient Irish myths and history. It was ratified by Yeats's adaptation of O'Grady's own eccentric version of early Irish myth and history into his own poetry but, more importantly, it called attention to the recurrent tendency of Irish poetry to avail of antiquarian and historical research into the past as it sought for a principle of continuity with which to ally itself. This search was itself a symptom of the Irish writer's sense of disorientation in relation to a past which seemed hopelessly fragmented and discontinuous. No Irish poet has been more alert to this sense of incompletion than Thomas Kinsella, nor more determined to come to terms with it. Modern poetry as such provided some exemplary instances of the confrontation between poetry as a system of order and history as a spectacle of disorder. American poets, especially Ezra Pound and, later, William Carlos Williams, impressed Kinsella by their achievement in this respect, although Joyce was the great, native exemplar. His earlier volumes – *Poems* (1956), *Another September* (1958), *Moralities* (1960), *Downstream* (1962), *Wormwood* (1966) and *Nightwalker and Other Poems* (1968) – all published by Dolmen, with whom Kinsella was to have a permanent and fruitful relationship – show a readiness to break out of the smug peripherality of Irish experience and face up to the violent heritage of the post-war world. (Kinsella was a civil servant in the Department of Finance which produced the Economic Programme, which opened Ireland up to world trade and economic revival in the early sixties.) Time and time again he challenges himself to sup on horrors:

> when that story thrust
> Pungent horror and an actual mess
> Into my very face, and taste I must. ('Downstream')

The 'mess' must be consumed and absorbed so that it can be reproduced as structure. This is a basic image throughout his work. It indicates the fascination with the incorporation of that which is repellent and disintegrated for the sake of a more comprehensive system of order in which the disorder will be subsumed. However, what distinguishes Kinsella in this pursuit is the intensity with which he realizes disorder. His country's history, her language, the Second World War, his own family experience are dominated by violence and illness of such atrocious severity that the assertion of order can not at first be much more than marginal or rhetorical. His language vacillates between a measured eloquence and a mutilated incoherence. In the early seventies, he turned back to Irish mythology and, simultaneously, to theories of evolutionary development and Jungian psychology to provide the structuring motifs which would thereafter dominate his work and give it the consistency of a sustained, analytic investigation, in which biological, mythological, historical and psychological experiences would operate analogically, one for the other. At the heart of this investigation was the conviction that the instinct towards order and development persists through failure, abortion, illness, violence. Out of mess comes crystalline structure, even though other versions of structure might try to replace this authentic thing. Colonial rule, institutional religion would be two such characteristic and deeply known forms of false structure. They too would disintegrate and yield to the radical drive towards true culture, culture being what the imagination achieves in transforming nature. From *Notes From the Land of the Dead* (1973) through to *One* (1974), *A Technical Supplement* (1976), *Song of the Night and Other Poems* and *The Messenger* (1978), Kinsella has pursued this awesome programme of supplying a total architecture to replace the rubble of post-war experience. In doing so, he has lost a substantial part of the audience he commanded up to 1968. The reasons for this are perfectly clear. In the first place, the poems depend for much of their resonance and interlinkages on difficult and obscure sources – the Irish Book of Invasions, Darwin, Jung, Renan, Pound. In the second place, Kinsella has sacrificed the elegance and orotundities of his early verse for a much more experimental and apparently haphazard mode of writing, in which he attempts to transmit the process of consciousness on the way to that point at which it will become its own object. In the third place, in publishing much of this later work in pamphlet form through his own Peppercanister Press, he has implicitly appealed to a fit audience, though few, and repudiated the larger audience which wants its poets to be as charmingly accessible as possible – or, if not accessible, at least charming. Yet, for all that, Kinsella is by now the most formidable presence in Irish poetry, a man whose work has achieved a continuity and sustained power, which is all the more impressive when we look at the comparatively scattered and broken achievements of predecessors like Devlin, Clarke and Kavanagh.

Richard Murphy, like Kinsella, began to publish with Dolmen Press. *The Archaeology of Love* appeared in 1955; but it was not until the collection *Sailing to an Island* appeared in 1963 that he began to gain recognition as one of the most notable poets of his generation. *The Battle of Aughrim* (1968), *High Island* (1974), *Selected Poems* (1979) and *The Price of Stone* (1985) consolidated his position, although his presence was more often acknowledged than was his quality defined. Murphy, the son of a family devoted to the colonial service, spent part of his early life in Ceylon, was educated at Oxford and yet remained rooted in his native west of Ireland which became for him a home and, in some respects, a chosen site for his enterprise as a poet. This has characteristically Irish obsessions at its heart. Living in his 'High Island', Cleggan, off the west coast, he became both a house-builder and a boat-builder, a man who practised a conscious architectural craft to combat the wild elements in which he lived. Against this superficially Anglo-Irish vocation to create structures of civilization, he contrasted a native Irish form of nomadic unstructured restlessness, represented for him by the wandering tinkers. The relationship thus established became for him a personal analogue of the contrast between the decay of Anglo-Ireland and the encroaching consumerism of a gross middle- or lower-middle-class Ireland, as hostile to the tinkers as to its Anglo-Irish remnant and, of course, to the poet's ideal of a creativity which would give enduring forms to itinerant freedoms. It is, therefore, no surprise to find that Murphy's poetry is as distinguished by its craftsmanship as it is beset by loneliness. The loneliness is actually enhanced, not appeased, by the craftsmanship; for everything that is made – ships, buildings, artefacts, love affairs – inclines towards the nullity out of which they initially arose. The sequence of fifty sonnets in *The Price of Stone* is Murphy's most sustained contemplation on these issues, ending in his address to his new-born son ('Natural Son'), an admission that no final defence can be provided against the loneliness of being alive:

> No house we build could hope to satisfy
> Every small need, now that you've made this move
> To share our loneliness, much as we try
> Our vocal skill to wall you round with love.

Murphy invests his sense of history in things or in people; but they are all remembered perfections, not living actualities. His nostalgia is thus always tinged by a certain disdain for what is. The energy of his language is not matched by an answering rhythmical variation in his music. An intense perception is subdued by a metrical staidness; his sense of formality is ultimately stronger than his sense of risk. Yet the constant attempt to embody in poetry the ancient battle between disjointedness and coherence is the central engagement of his generation. In this respect he is at one with both Kinsella and Montague and, like them, he has the power to make the issue applicable beyond the circumstances of his own historical situation.

With John Montague, the North as it is now known, becomes the crucial territory in Irish poetry. From the outset, Montague had a markedly irredentist attitude towards it, a wish to recover it from its separation and solitude and bring it back within the horizon of literature. Kavanagh had already done this for Monaghan but Montague expanded the ambition when he turned to his own native county of Tyrone and sought, through local, familial and national history, to rediscover it as a fertile rather than a narrow and barren ground. His first four volumes – *Forms of Exile* (1958), *Poisoned Lands* (1961), *A Chosen Light* (1967) and *Tides* (1970) – revealed a double domination of his imagination. On the one hand there was old Ireland, from the mythological figures who came ashore in the Book of Invasions to the local old people who shadowed his childhood in 'Like Dolmens Round My Childhood, The Old People'.

> Ancient Ireland, indeed! I was reared by her bedside,
> The rune and the chant, evil eye and averted head,
> Fomorian fierceness of family and local feud,
> Gaunt figures of fear and of friendliness,
> For years they trespassed on my dreams,
> Until once, in a standing circle of stones,
> I felt their shadows pass
> Into that dark permanence of ancient forms.

This was a petrifying inheritance. The Gorgon stare of those old people and of the Irish history and folklore they embodied would have been inescapable if a more benign attraction had not pulled Montague's gaze away. This was the appeal of the sensual, the sexual, the living landscape. Experiences of this kind tend to be secret and private, whereas everything else is publicly known and gossiped. From the early poems, then, we can observe the tentative arrangement of a series of very fragile truces between these two worlds, their fragility enhanced by the severe formality and courtesy of the poems, which with their elegance and leanness are about as far away from the more farouche Kinsella's language as they could possibly be. But it was not until the collapse of the Northern statelet that Montague turned fully towards it. Until then, in America and in Paris, he had dallied with his sexual and political experiences in a leisurely if sophisticated manner, as if wondering how two zones of such extreme dissimilarity could possibly coexist. But in *The Rough Field* (1972), he provides an elaborate collage of new and old poems, woodcuts, quotations and epigraphs from various sources, in an effort to identify his discovered theme – the breakdown and death of a civilization. Or, more exactly, the breakdown of two civilizations, that of Gaelic and that of Planter Ulster. The breakdown is both tragic and wounding; it is also liberating, for it permits him to see a synchronous relationship between the disjunctions in his own life (the break-up of his first marriage) and of his own native area. Thereafter, in *A Slow Dance* (1975), *The Great Cloak* (1978) and *The Dead Kingdom* (1984), Montague intensifies the sense of poignancy and risk which always lies at the heart of his love poetry and etches it the more clearly against the background of a widespread but understandable contemporary violence. The besetting responsibility of wanting to do something, to intrude into the violent political arena, is countered by the very nature of the deep privacies of love, which he wants to cherish. In a recent poem, 'Mount Eagle', he sighs for the 'lost freedom' which the loss of his aloofness will involve. It is as though he were preparing for another public poem like *The Rough Field*.

What Montague discovered in Tyrone, Seamus Heaney rediscovered in County Derry. At first, the discovery was harmless enough, although the eloquence with which it was done was in itself remarkable. Heaney lamented lost innocence in *Death of a Naturalist* (1966) but then in *Door into the Dark* (1968) he rediscovered ways of dramatizing his meditations upon that loss. His fascination with the processes of decay and rot, with the simmering slime and mud and soil of his local farmland areas is reverential. Earth, air and water are his elements, the forces which appeal to the illiteracies of instinct before they are controlled into the literacies of verse. Heaney is fond of this kind of contrast. A Herculean strength in air, an Antaeus-like beseeching of the earth, image perfectly the process of bringing the ooze and midden of history and nature into a tangible form. His poetry is saturated with the love for deliquescent nature, the primary flow of earth and water; but, equally, it reveals a prehensile hunger for the form which that deliquescence achieves when it is converted into a human artifact. In the dark rite of passage between the two states he discovers an analogue for the movement in himself from unreflective to reflective consciousness. This is well established by the close of *Door into the Dark* and then, in a manner entirely characteristic of Irish poetry, it seeks further confirmation and expansion by looking to history or, in Heaney's case, prehistory, the formless soil out of which the forms of history spring. *Wintering Out* (1972) is the moment at which Heaney departs from the Kavanagh-inspired theme of innocence towards a deeper incrimination in history and a consequent deeper research into the mysteries of poetry itself. Once again, as we see him give an historical gloss to vowels and consonants, the sexual identification of each reminds us of the poet's readiness to see something formed (a poem) break down into words and syllables before being reconstituted as itself again. Clearly Heaney has found a way to inspect his Northern past, which is also a way of inspecting the nature of his own imagination. The combination of these quests is as rare as it is powerful. Yet the power remains compressed inside the rather squat stanza forms he favours. They allow for the registration of great physical accuracies, but they provide almost no space for a discursive development. In *North* (1975), Heaney begins to break out of this formal mould as well and to bring his poetry under the twin pressures of the archaeologically remote past of Vikings and Norsemen and the savage present of British soldiers and internecine warfare. Seeing one as a function of the other, he takes the pressure of both into his verse

> with the actual weight
> of each hooded victim,
> slashed and dumped. ('The Grauballe Man')

With *Field Work* (1979) and *Station Island* (1984) there came further developments. Briefly, the earthbound, archaeologically mythologized world, so dominant up until then, began to disappear. In its place there emerged a more specifically human world, still full of victims of violence, but no longer the objects of a contemplative grief. In *Field Work*, the dead have voices. Voices, prophetic and sibylline, the voices of O'Riada, Lowell, Colum McCartney, Ledwidge and, above all, the voices of married lovers are orchestrated with the poet's own. This is his first populated book. Heaney has taken the great risk of having shed an enabling myth after going to all the considerable trouble of creating one. He is dramatizing the play of his consciousness and the pain of his conscience against that of others. In some respects, this is a sign of great confidence, understandably assured after the reception given to his work, but most especially to *North*. But it is also the sign of his new sense of freedom. After all the pother with history and politics and even the historicizing and politicizing of language, he is now seeking a world elsewhere, language is visionary, not a medium tensed between mighty oppositions:

> Breasting the mist, in sowers' aprons
> My ghosts come striding into their spring stations.
> The dream grain whirls like freakish Easter snows.

> (Glanmore Sonnets, I)

The translation of the old Irish text *Buile Shuibhne* as *Sweeney Astray* (1983) was a further indication of Heaney's longing for an increased range and freedom. Sweeney, turned into a bird by a saint's curse, flies from his native North all over Ireland and, in his isolation, sings his woe and comment upon the worlds he visits. *Station Island* has a section of Sweeney-derived lyrics, which intimate the kind of dense, brilliant but less accessible lyric form Heaney is gravitating towards. The title poem is itself a staking of a claim to a place in the Irish tradition of Carleton, Joyce and others; it is also a plea for forgiveness to all whom he must abandon to their political and social fates as he pursues his dedicated art, under Joyce's blessing. Heaney has moved so far beyond the regional territory opened by Kavanagh that it is at first difficult to see their intimacy. His achievement, like that of Kinsella, is still far from completion even though it is already remarkable.

Heaney is by far the best known of a group of poets, all Northerners, who have appeared on the scene in the last twenty years. Derek Mahon, Michael Longley, Paul Muldoon and Tom Paulin are the most notable, although Frank Ormsby, James Simmons, Medbh McGuckian, Ciaran Carson and several others are still in the process of establishing what is in effect a new revival. In Mahon two major presences exercise the anxiety of their influence – Louis MacNeice and Samuel Beckett. In a strange sense, Mahon has recovered MacNeice for the local tradition. His scepticism, his complex of loyalties and disloyalties towards Ireland and England, his bright modernism and wit are all reinstated in Mahon, although Mahon has brought the mandarin pose to a pitch of elegance that MacNeice never attained, not even in *Autumn Journal* (1939). He has also exceeded MacNeice in his capacity to transmit, through a simple catalogue of things, a sense of dread and of an ending that is half desired, wholly deserved. For Mahon's essential landscape is Belfast and he constantly turns it, in poem after poem, into a bombed site, a vision of what it will all be like when the war is over and only the rubble has a voice. But, although there is an apocalyptic note in all of Mahon's poetry, it never becomes melodramatic. Instead he turns towards the most exquisite reductions, paring everything down until its existence is vestigial. At that point, his eloquence begins so that, as in Beckett, one has the sense of language which is always in excess of the occasion which engendered it and is yet always controlled, expert. *Night-Crossing* (1968), *Lives* (1972), *The Snow Party* (1975), *The Hunt By Night* (1982) all meditate on the isolation of the artistic sensibility, which the Northern violence emphasizes but does not violate. He listens to but does not finally attend to the voices

> Demanding that I inhabit,
> Like them, a world of
> Sirens, bin-lids
> And bricked-up windows.

His loyalty is elsewhere, to the voiceless, to the forgotten, to the poets wrecked by circumstance and by their gift, to the inanimate and vegetable worlds, which speak so heartbreakingly in his most famous poem, 'A Disused Shed in County Wexford' (derived from J. G. Farrell's novel *Troubles*):

> They are begging us, you see, in their wordless way
> To do something, to speak on their behalf
> Or at least not to close the door again.
> Lost people of Treblinka and Pompeii!
> 'Save us, save us,' they seem to say,
> 'Let the god not abandon us
> Who have come so far in darkness and in pain.
> We too had our lives to live.
> You with your light meter and relaxed itinerary,
> Let not our naive labours have been in vain!!

Derek Mahon and Michael Longley are close friends, but their poetry seems to be based on quite different assumptions. Longley's is, or was, the most English or the most civil poetry of the Northern group because it betrayed no covert or explicit sympathy for the notion that political violence and imaginative intensity might be more intimately related than one would like to admit. In fact, a companionable decency lives at the heart of Longley's early work, especially *No Continuing City* (1969) and *An Exploded View* (1973), although less so in his third and fourth volumes *Man Lying on a Wall* (1976) and *The Echo Gate* (1981). Yet, although this lowers the temperature of his poems, none of which have Mahon's ruthless elegance, it allows for a more hospitable tenderness, a serene melancholy of the sort we associate with a collector of specimens. The objects in his poems are turned slowly round for consideration, handled by the words until they are known thoroughly and almost, but not quite, domesticated. However, increasingly, the political crisis in the North impinges upon his work, forcing it towards pathos and the larger questions of identity. The civility remains but the equilibrium of the early poems is now struggled for; there is a powerful unease. On the birth of a child, he writes to three fellow poets (Simmons, Mahon, Heaney):

> For yours, then, and the child's sake
> I who have heard the waters break
> Claim this my country, though today
> *Timor mortis conturbat me*. ('Letters'; *An Exploded View*)

James Simmons founded *The Honest Ulsterman* in 1968 and has generally been master of ceremonies for the Northern revival. His rather anarchic liberalism governs his poetry which transmits, for the most part, an air of relaxed friendliness or articulates the passage from sentiment to opinion with an enviable ease and aplomb. Since *Judy Garland and the Cold War*, his poetry has been less inclined towards a performance art, in which he presented himself for recognition to others, and more solemnly (and seriously) directed towards himself, preoccupied now with a consciousness of himself. This alteration is characteristic of the effects of the Northern crisis and its increasing demands on the writer as it prolongs itself from their youth into their middle age. But in the generation behind Simmons a more complex and intriguing battle is being fought out between Paul Muldoon and Tom Paulin. Stated briefly, it is a battle between a poetry of denial (Muldoon) and of commitment (Paulin). Muldoon's resource is apparently inexhaustible; even Mahon sometimes appears unsophisticated in comparison. He blends the most improbable elements – an old Celtic quest journey, the Immram, with a Raymond Chandler idiom, the trickster cycles of the Winnebago Indians with an account of an IRA gunman's peregrinations in Belfast. But he refuses to be locked into any of the expectations raised by the narrative categories he invokes. By disorienting expectation, he turns his poetry into a magical process of shape changing, allowing words to exist and then to fade before conceding to other worlds. Anything like a fixed view, a positive beginning or ending, is anathema to him. He wants a freedom for poetry that would be intolerable in any other activity and yet is *the* only necessity poetry seeks. *New Weather* (1973), *Mules* (1977), *Why Brownlee Left* (1980) and the grimly comic *Quoof* (1984) mark progressive stages in the attainment of this pure space in which Muldoon's brilliant *écriture* can be inscribed. Tom Paulin, on the other hand, in his three volumes, *A State of Justice* (1973), *The Strange Museum* (1980) and *The Liberty Tree* (1983), is more forthright in his demand that poetry should be grounded in a political reality and contribute to an enriched sense of community. He calls out his enemies, without hesitation: Paisley

> his cult
> of Bunyan and of blood
> in blind dumps like Doagh and Boardmills –
> that's the enemy. ('And Where Do You Stand on the National
>   Question?', *Liberty Tree*)

His poetry takes up dialect, academic speech, various argots and jargons, demanding of them a discipline, a behavioural stability, which will be both a cause of and a symptom of a more general liberation from factional politics. The degradation of the Protestant Republican tradition into Orange bigotry is, for him, the most tragic decline of modern Irish politics. As a poet, he wants to find a conciliation between the old free speech of classical eighteenth-century liberty and the demotic speech of contemporary fanaticism. This is the

> > dream
> of that sweet
> equal republic

which is the foundation of his poetic and political vision. Paulin and Muldoon dominate the ground on which the next phase of the Northern revival will emerge.

There is no point in pretending that this summary would serve as a rudimentary history of modern Irish poetry. Too many poets have been omitted – Brian Coffey, Brendan Kennelly, Padraic Fiacc, John Hewitt and, among the younger poets, Eavann Boland, Elaine Ni Chuilleanáin, Medbh McGuckian, Aidan Matthews, Gerard Dawe, Paul Durcan and many others. The general pattern, although subject to severe modifications in relation to any one of these poets, is nevertheless established. Irish poetry cannot entirely evade a confrontation with Irish history although it finds various strategies of deflection and even of escape in order to preserve some

vestige of independence from it. Yeats and Joyce both set a formidable example and all the writers considered here had to find a way
out of their shadow before they could find the freedom to write
unburdened by an unpayable debt. Kavanagh released Irish poetry
from that bondage and, since then, the interchange with history has
taken on more protean and varied forms. The heroic impulse of the
earlier literature has faded or has been altogether renounced. With
it went some of the more statuesque poses of the Revival and a more
nervous, exploratory set of attitudes came to replace it. What makes
this poetry important, however, is not its success in disengaging
from its early century exemplars. Like them, it too has been compelled to take upon itself the whole burden of culture, the interrogation
of the links that connect us to or, in breaking, disconnect us from the
idea of a social community.

Drama

In drama, three playwrights dominate the contemporary period –
Brian Friel, Thomas Murphy and Thomas Kilroy. Friel is closer
than Murphy to the preoccupations of the poets. His northern
community is subverted by a deep sense of failure, which expresses
itself in emigration, violence, lovelessness. His plays – most notably
Philadelphia, Here I Come! (1964), *The Freedom of the City* (1973),
Volunteers (1975), *Living Quarters* (1975), *Aristocrats* (1979),
Faith Healer (1980) and *Translations* (1981) – investigate the historical and psychological causes and consequences of that failure.
The Northern crisis crystallized these preoccupations in a startling
way. Faced with the spectacle of a broken community living in the
twilight zone of a war, Friel was stimulated to bring this experience
into the heart of his drama. As a result, his plays seemed to co-
ordinate with the poetry of Heaney and Montague in the elaboration of a long analysis of the politics of language, the language of
politics and their relationship to the language of poetry and drama.
This process in Friel culminated in the widely acknowledged masterpiece, *Translations*, in which the linguistic crisis which saw the
disappearance of Gaelic and its replacement by English becomes
the focus through which questions of authority and failure, love and
treachery, culture and its disintegration are examined. Friel's
achievement is on such a scale that through him we are enabled to
re-read the plays of Behan, O'Casey and Synge, Beckett and the
late Yeats. He provides an insight into the deep roots of the elo-

quent Irish stereotype and its inarticulate companion which the Revival had successfully exploited but had unthinkingly accepted.

Thomas Murphy has remained largely unaffected in his work by the Northern crisis but, like Friel, he casts a wicked eye on the squalor of small-town provincial life and derides its incarcerating and institutionalized repressions. The almost brutal realism of his plays was modified by the influence of Tennessee Williams, first visible in *A Crucial Week in the Life of A Grocer's Assistant* (1969) and further developed in *The Morning After Optimism* (1971). However, with *The Gigli Concert* (1984), Murphy had an indisputable triumph. Here he finds a means of demonstrating the subtle accord between actuality and fantasy and, in doing so, reminding us of the alliance between the drama and the Irish novel. Murphy's conception of freedom is Dionysiac; his conception of repression is totalitarian. The ferocity of the collision between them has often led him into exaggeration and melodrama, but in *The Gigli Concert* he avoids these pitfalls and provides a tragic parable of entrapment within both actuality and fantasy.

Thomas Kilroy's best-known plays, *The Death and Resurrection of Mr. Roche* (1969) and *Talbot's Box* (1979) cast a very cold eye on the deficiencies of an Irish, more particularly a Dublin, social system which still bears the stigmata of the Joycean paralysis in its attitudes towards sexuality, money, and in the moral cowardice of its inhabitants when faced with serious personal or social issues. But in each play the central figure – a homosexual and a religious *dévot* who is transformed after his death into a saint by interests who see how useful he can be to them – is, like the protagonist of Kilroy's novel, *The Big Chapel*, someone in whom a radical solitude is projected. The relationship of an outcast individual to the community may be cast in the form of an attack upon that community's narrowness, its failure to incorporate anything that is not uniform, conventional or deemed to be respectable. But Kilroy, while he moves in the direction of such a critique, is more interested in the solitude intself, in the quality of courage needed to sustain it, and in the possibility that it is only in such solitude, not in any social relationship, that freedom can be known. Like Friel and Murphy, he finds no ground in his inherited experience for the treatment of shared authentic values; instead, like them, he is driven to consider the question of value in the lonely space created by the individual for himself, even (or perhaps especially) if that space can only be constructed by people who are driven into oddity, difference, even treachery, by their hunger for something more than the official pieties of a failed or hypocritical society. All of Kilroy's dramatic work has been dominated by the search for a way of presenting the solitude of such people in relation to the society from which they have withdrawn. His definitive work on this theme has yet to come.

Epilogue

One of the recurrent paradoxes of Irish writing is its continuous preoccupation with the experience of discontinuity. This, in itself, would be enough to allow us to speak of the existence of a tradition, however elusive that term may be when it comes under investigation. But, in addition, the discontinuity has been the product of unique historical circumstances, not matched in Western Europe. For three, perhaps four centuries, Irish literature has lived in the shadow of political and economic breakdowns of distressing frequency. It has lived between two languages and two cultures, it has competed with antiquarian and historical research, with political theory and clerical polemics in its attempt to identify the existence of a cultural community in which the possibility of freedom might be won. In the twentieth century in particular, these experiences, and the habituation of the Irish mind and sensibility to them, have given the literature of the country a prominence never known before. It is, in many ways, a specifically modern literature bred out of the most dishevelled and improbable circumstances. By now, it is neither Gaelic nor Anglo-Irish writing which is central. The conciliation between the two, although by no means complete, is sufficiently advanced to allow the use of the phrase 'Irish writing' without fear of its being misunderstood or recruited to any particular group or sect. That, at least, is one symptom of a fundamental and hopeful change.

Notes

1   Nicholas Canny, 'Fusion and Faction in Modern Ireland', *Comparative Studies in Society and History*, vol. 26, no. 2 (April, 1984), pp. 364–5.
2   Cf. Oliver MacDonagh, *States of Mind: A Study of Anglo-Irish Conflict 1780–1980* (London, 1983), pp. 113–16.
3   See Terence Brown, *Ireland: A Social and Cultural History 1922–79* (London, 1981), pp. 141–210; Augustine Martin, 'Literature and

Society, 1938–51' in *Ireland in the War Years and After, 1939–51*, (Dublin, 1969), pp. 167–84.

4   See Conor C. O'Brien, 'The Parnellism of Sean O'Faolain' in *Maria Cross: Imaginative Patterns in a group of Catholic Writers* (new ed., London, 1963), pp. 87–108; Benedict Kiely, *Modern Irish Fiction – A Critique* (Dublin, 1950), pp. 113–21.

5   Cf. Maurice Harmon, 'Generations Apart: 1925–1975' in P. Rafroidi and M. Harmon (eds.), *The Irish Novel in our Time* (Lille, 1975–6), pp. 49–65.

6   *States of Mind*, p. 114.

7   Anthony Cronin, *Dead as Doornails* (Dublin and London, 1976), p. 2.

8   Anthony Cronin, *Collected Poems* (Dublin, 1973); the last line of the poem 'Familiar', p. 89.

9   See Derek Mahon, 'MacNeice in England and Ireland', in T. Brown and A. Reid (eds.), *Time Was Away: The World of Louis MacNeice* (Dublin, 1974), pp. 113–22; Edna Longley, 'Louis MacNeice: "The Walls are Flowing" ', in *Across a Roaring Hill: The Protestant Imagination in Modern Ireland* (Belfast, 1985), pp. 99–123.

10   See my 'Austin Clarke's Irelands', *Times Literary Supplement* (8 December, 1972), pp. 1013–15.

11   For a more detailed account of the situation in modern Irish poetry, see Dillon Johnston, *Irish Poetry After Joyce* (Notre Dame, 1985), and my *Celtic Revivals: Essays in Modern Irish Literature* (London, 1985).

12   Standish O'Grady, *History of Ireland* (London, 1880), p. 6.

Select bibliography

Note: Individual works are noted in the text and footnotes. The aim of the bibliography is to provide a list of general works which will help to establish a background to the study of Irish literature.

Bibliographies

R. I. Best, *Bibliography of Irish Philology and of Printed Irish Literature* (Dublin 1913)

R. I. Best, *Bibliography of Irish Philology and Manuscript Literature: Publications 1913–1941* (Dublin 1942)

R. Baumgarten, *Bibliography of Irish Linguistics and Literature, 1942–71* (Dublin 1980)

S. J. Brown, *Ireland in Fiction: a guide to Irish novels tales romances and folklore* (2nd edn 1919; repr. Shannon 1969)

S. J. Brown, *A Guide to Books on Ireland* (Dublin 1912)

A. Eager, *A Guide to Irish Bibliographical Material* (London 1964)

R. Finneran, *Anglo-Irish Literature: A Review of Research* (New York 1976)

R. J. Hayes, *Manuscript Sources for the history of Irish Civilisation*, 11 vols., (Boston 1965)

R. J. Hayes, *Sources for the History of Irish Civilisation: Articles in Irish Periodicals*, 9 vols., (Boston 1970)

M. Harmon, *Select Bibliography for the study of Anglo-Irish Literature and its backgrounds* (Dublin 1977)

E. H. Mikhail, *A Bibliography of Modern Irish Drama 1899–1970* (London 1972)

B. McKenna, *Irish Literature, 1800–1875: A Guide to Information Sources* (Detroit 1978)

General works: literary histories, surveys, collections of essays

R. K. Alspach, *Anglo-Irish Poetry from the English Invasion to 1798* (Philadelphia 1943; 2nd rev. edn, 1960)

J. C. Beckett, *The Anglo-Irish Tradition* (London, 1976)

S. H. Bell, *The Theatre in Ulster: a survey of the dramatic movement in Ulster from 1902 to the present day* (Dublin 1972)

E. A. Boyd, *Ireland's Literary Renaissance* (Dublin 1916; rev. edn, 1922; Dublin 1969)

M. Brown, *The Politics of Irish Literature: from Thomas Davis to W. B. Yeats* (Seattle and London 1972)

T. Brown, *Ireland: A Social and Cultural History 1922–79* (London 1981)

T. Brown, *Northern Voices: Poets from Ulster* (Dublin 1975)

A. de Blacam, *Gaelic Literature Surveyed* (Dublin 1929; rev. edn New York 1974)

A. Bliss, *Spoken English in Ireland 1600–1740* (Dublin 1979)

J. Cahalan, *Great Hatred, Little Room: The Irish Historical Novel* (New York 1984)

J. Carney (ed.), *Early Irish Poetry* (Cork 1954)

A. Carpenter (ed.), *Place, Personality and the Irish Writer* (Gerrard's Cross and New York 1977)

W. S. Clark, *The Early Irish Stage: The Beginnings to 1720* (Oxford 1955)

P. Connolly (ed.), *Literature and the Changing Ireland* (London and New Jersey 1982)

D. Corkery, *The Hidden Ireland: A Study of Gaelic Munster in the Eighteenth Century* (Cork 1924; Dublin 1967)

D. Corkery, *Synge and Anglo-Irish Literature* (Cork 1931)

P. Costello, *The Heart Grown Brutal: The Irish Revolution in Literature from Parnell to the death of Yeats, 1891–1939* (Dublin and New Jersey 1978)

A. Cronin, *Heritage Now: Irish Literature in the English Language* (Dingle 1982)

J. Cronin, *The Anglo-Irish Novel; the Nineteenth Century* (Belfast 1980)

G. Dawe and E. Longley (eds.), *Across A Roaring Hill; the Protestant Imagination in Modern Ireland* (Belfast 1985)

S. Deane, *Celtic Revivals: Essays in Modern Irish Literature, 1880–1980* (London 1985)

M. Dillon (ed.), *Early Irish Society* (Cork 1954)

D. C. Duggan, *The Stage Irishman: a history of the Irish play and stage characters from earliest times* (Dublin 1937)

D. Dunn (ed.), *Two Decades of Irish Writing* (Cheadle Hulme 1975)

U. Ellis-Fermor, *The Irish Dramatic Movement* (London 1939; rev. ed. 1954)

R. Fallis, *The Irish Renaissance: An Introduction to Anglo-Irish Literature* (Syracuse 1977; Dublin 1978)

T. Flanagan, *The Irish Novelists, 1800–1850* (New York 1959)

R. Flower, *The Irish Tradition* (Oxford 1947)

J. W. Foster, *Forces and Themes in Ulster Fiction* (Dublin 1974)

A. Gregory, *Our Irish Theatre* (New York and London 1914; enlarged edn, Gerrards Cross 1973)

S. Gwynn, *Irish Literature and Drama* (New York 1936)

R. Hogan, *After the Renaissance: a critical history of Irish Drama since 'The Plough and the Stars'* (Minneapolis 1967; London 1968)

R. Hogan (ed.), *Dictionary of Irish Literature* (Connecticut 1979; Dublin 1980)

R. Hogan (ed.), *Modern Irish Drama*, 4 vols., (Dublin 1975–9)

H. Howarth, *The Irish Writers, 1880–1940* (London 1958)

H. Hunt, *The Abbey, Ireland's National Theatre, 1904–1979* (Dublin 1979)

D. Hyde, *A Literary History of Ireland* (London 1899; rev. edn London 1967; 1980)

A. N. Jeffares, *Anglo-Irish Literature* (London 1982)

D. Johnston, *Irish Poetry After Joyce* (Notre Dame and Dublin 1985)

R. M. Kain, *Dublin In The Age of William Butler Yeats and James Joyce* (Oklahoma 1962; Newton Abbot, 1972)

R. Kearney (ed.), *The Irish Mind: Exploring Intellectual Traditions* (Dublin 1985)

H. Kenner, *A Colder Eye: The Modern Irish Writers* (New York 1983)

B. Kiely, *Modern Irish Fiction: A Critique* (Dublin 1950)

R. Loftus, *Nationalism in Modern Irish Poetry* (Madison 1969)

F. S. L. Lyons, *Culture and Anarchy in Ireland 1890–1939* (Oxford 1979)

P. MacCana, *Celtic Mythology* (London 1970)

W. J. McCormack, *Ascendancy and Tradition in Anglo-Irish Literary History from 1789 to 1939* (Oxford 1985)

R. McHugh and M. Harmon, *Anglo-Irish Literature* (Dublin 1982)

S. MacRéamoinn (ed.), *The Pleasures of Gaelic Poetry* (London 1981)

A. E. Malone, *The Irish Drama 1896–1928* (London 1929)

A. Martin, *Anglo-Irish Literature* (Dublin 1980)

A. Martin (ed.), *The Genius of Irish Prose* (Cork and Dublin 1984)

D. E. S. Maxwell, *Modern Irish Drama 1891–1980* (Cambridge 1985)

V. Mercier, *The Irish Comic Tradition* (Oxford 1962)

C. C. O'Brien (ed.), *The Shaping of Modern Ireland* (London 1960)

U. O'Connor, *Celtic Dawn: A Portrait of the Irish Literary Renaissance* (London 1984)

B. O. Cuiv, *Literary Creation and Irish Historical Tradition* London 1964)

B. O. Cuiv (ed.), *Seven Centuries of Irish Learning, 1000–1700* (Dublin 1961)

T. O'Raifeartaigh (ed.), *The Royal Irish Academy: a bicentennial history, 1785–1985* (Dublin 1985)

T. Paulin, *Ireland and the English Crisis* (Newcastle upon Tyne 1984)

R. Porter and J. D. Brophy (eds.), *Modern Irish Literature: Essays in honour of William York Tindall* (New York 1972)

P. Rafroidi, *Irish Literature in English: The Romantic Period*, 2 vols. (Gerrards Cross 1980)

P. Rafroidi and M. Harmon (eds.), *The Irish Novel in Our Time* (Lille 1976)

P. Rafroidi and T. Brown, *The Irish Short Story* (Gerrards Cross 1979)
L. Robinson, *Ireland's Abbey Theatre: A History 1899–1951* (London 1951)
J. Ronsley (ed.), *Myth and Reality in Irish Literature* (Waterloo 1977)
R. Welch, *Irish Poetry from Moore to Yeats* (Gerrards Cross 1980)
K. Worth, *The Irish Drama of Europe from Yeats to Beckett* (New Jersey 1978)

Anthologies

Anon., *The Spirit of the Nation: Ballads and Songs by the writers of the Nation with Original and Ancient Music* (Dublin 1845; 2nd enl. edn Dublin and London 1882)
A. Bradley (ed.), *Contemporary Irish Poetry: An Anthology* (Berkeley, California 1980)
S. A. Brooke and T. W. Rolleston (eds.), *A Treasury of Irish Poetry in the English Tongue* (London 1900)
D. Carroll (ed.), *New Poets of Ireland* (Denver 1963)
G. Dawe (ed.), *The Younger Irish Poets* (Belfast 1982)
C. Brooke, *Reliques of Irish Poetry* (London 1789)
C. G. Duffy, *The Ballad Poetry of Ireland* (Dublin 1845)
P. Fallon and S. Golden (eds.), *Soft Day: A Miscellany of Contemporary Irish Writing* (Notre Dame and Dublin 1981)
D. A. Garrity (ed.), *The Mentor Book of Irish Poetry* (New York 1965)
D. H. Greene (ed.), *An Anthology of Irish Literature* (New York 1954)
J. Hardiman (ed.), *Irish Minstrelsy; or, Bardic Remains of Ireland; with English Poetical Translations*, 2 vols. (London 1831; repr. New York 1971)
M. Harmon (ed.), *Irish Poetry After Yeats* (Dublin and Boston 1979)
K. Hoagland (ed.), *1000 Years of Irish Poetry* (New York 1947)
J. Keefe (trans.), *Irish Poems: from Cromwell to the Famine; A Miscellany* (Lewisburg and London 1977)
B. Kennelly (ed.), *The Penguin Book of Irish Verse* (Harmondsworth 1979)
E. Knott, *Irish Syllabic Poetry 1200–1600* (2nd edn, Dublin 1957)
S. Lucy (ed.), *Love Poems of the Irish* (Cork 1967)
D. MacDonagh and L. Robinson (eds.), *The Oxford Book of Irish Verse XVIIth Century–XXth Century* (Oxford 1958)
D. Mahon (ed.), *The Sphere Book of Modern Irish Poetry* (London 1972)
J. C. Mangan and J. O'Daly, *The Poets and Poetry of Munster* (Dublin 1849)
D. Marcus (ed.), *Irish Poets 1924–1974* (London 1975)
V. Mercier and D. Greene (eds.), *1000 Years of Irish Poetry* (New York 1953)

V. Mercier and D. Greene (eds.), *1000 Years of Irish Prose: The Literary Revival* (New York 1952; 1961)
J. Montague (ed.), *The Faber Book of Irish Verse* (London 1974, 1978); retitled *The Book of Irish Verse* (New York 1976)
J. McCarthy and C. Welsh (eds.), *Irish Literature*, 10 vols. (Philadelphia 1904)
G. Murphy (ed.), *Early Irish Lyrics* (Oxford 1956)
J. O'Daly (trans. and ed.), *Reliques of Irish Jacobite Poetry* (Dublin, 1844)
J. O'Daly (trans. and ed.) *Fenian Poems* (Dublin 1859; 2nd series, Dublin 1861)
T. F. O'Rahilly (ed.), *Danta Gradh* (Dublin 1916)
T. F. O'Rahilly (ed.), *Measgra Danta: Miscellaneous Irish Poems* (Dublin and Cork 1927)
F. Ormsby (ed.), *Poets from the North of Ireland* (Belfast 1979)
S. O. Tuama and T. Kinsella (eds.), *An Duanaire 1600–1900: Poems of the Dispossessed* (Dublin 1981)
C. A. Read (ed.) *The Cabinet of Irish Literature*, 4 vols. (London, 1879–80; rev. and enl. edn by K. Tynan Hinkson, 3 vols., London 1905)
L. Robinson (ed.), *A Golden Treasury of Irish Verse* (London 1925)
D. Russell (ed.), *The Portable Irish Reader* (New York 1946)
G. B. Saul (ed.), *The Age of Yeats* (New York 1963)
G. Sigerson (ed.), *Bards of the Gael and Gall* (London 1897; rev. edn 1907)
G. Taylor (ed.), *Irish Poets of the Nineteenth Century* (London 1951)
W. B. Yeats, *The Oxford Book of Modern Verse* (Oxford 1936)

Historical background

J. C. Beckett, *A Short History of Ireland* (London 1952)
J. C. Beckett, *The Making of Modern Ireland 1603–1923* (London 1966)
N. Canny, 'Edmund Spenser and the Development of an Anglo-Irish Identity', *The Yearbook of English Studies* 13 (1983), 1–19
N. Canny, 'The Formation of the Irish Mind: Religion, Politic and Gaelic Irish Literature 1580–1750', *Past and Present*, no. 95 (May 1982), 91–116.
M. J. Craig, *Dublin 1660–1860* (Dublin 1969)
E. Curtis, *A History of Ireland* (London 1936)
B. Inglis, *The Story of Ireland* (London 1956; 2nd edn 1965)
R. Kee, *The Green Flag* (London 1972)
J. Lydon and M. MacCurtain (eds.), *The Gill History of Ireland*, 10 vols. (Dublin 1972–4)
F. S. L. Lyons, *Ireland Since the Famine* (London 1971; 2nd rev. edn 1973)
O. MacDonagh, *Ireland* (Englewood Cliffs 1968), retitled *Ireland: The Union and its Aftermath* (London 1977)
O. MacDonagh, *States of Mind: A Study of Anglo-Irish Conflict 1780–1980* (London 1983; 1985)

N. Mansergh, *The Irish Question 1840–1922* (London 1965; rev. edn 1975)

T. W. Moody and F. X. Martin (eds.), *The Course of Irish History* (Cork 1967)

T. W. Moody, F. X. Martin and F. J. Byrne (eds.), *A New History of Ireland*, 10 vols. (Oxford, 1978–), vols. III, *Early Modern Ireland (1534–1691)*, and VIII, *A Chronology of Irish History to 1976* have appeared so far.

Chronology of important dates from 1550–1980

1550–1603

Ireland and England

First printing press in Ireland 1550
The Book of Common Prayer first book printed in Ireland 1551
plantation of Leix and Offaly 1556
Mary I of England dies, succeeded by Elizabeth I 1558
Shane O'Neill's rebellion, submission and death, 1561–7
first book printed in Gaelic, transl. of Book of Common Order, at Edinburgh, 1567
John Kearney's *Gaelic Alphabet and Catechism* first book in Irish printed in Ireland, 1571
rebellion of Fitzgeralds of Desmond 1569
Elizabeth I excommunicated 1570
Richard Stanihurst, *Treatise containing a Plaine and Perfect Description of Ireland*, 1577
Raphael Holinshed's *Chronicles of England, Scotland and Ireland* 1577
plantation of Munster, Edmund Spenser, secretary to Lord Deputy, *The Faerie Queene*, pts. 1 & 2
A View of the Present State of Ireland, 1586–96
Tadgh Dall O hUiginn, one of the greatest Irish bardic poets, d. 1590
University of Dublin (Trinity College) f. 1591
Spenser's castle in Co. Cork burned 1598
Hugh O'Neill, earl of Tyrone (1587), proclaimed traitor 1595, at war with English forces under Mountjoy, defeated at Battle of Kinsale, 1601, submits 1603
New Testament translated into Irish, 1603.

Ireland, England and Europe

Literary Events
More's *Utopia* trans. into English 1551
Ronsard's *Amours*, 1552
Sir Walter Raleigh b. 1554
Castiglione's *The Courtier* trans. into English, Francis Bacon
b. 1561
Foxe's *Book of Martyrs*, St John of the Cross d. 1563
term 'Puritan' first used, John Calvin d. Roman Index of Prohibited
Books published, 1564
Camoens *The Lusiads*, John Donne, Ben Jonson b. 1572
Tasso's *Gerusalemme Liberata* 1575
Montaigne's *Essays* 1580
Sir Philip Sidney d. 1586
Marlowe's *Tamburlaine*, Hakluyt's *Voyages*, Casaubon's edition of
Strabo, 1587
Marlowe's *Doctor Faustus*, Thomas Hobbes b. Vatican Library
opened, 1588
Shakespeare's early plays, *Henry VI–Twelfth Night*, 1590–1600
Descartes b. 1596
Bacon's *Essays*, 1597
Spenser d. 1599.

History and politics
French wars of religion, including St Bartholomew's Day Massacre
1572, end soon after coronation of first Bourbon, Henry IV, 1594
Spanish Armada defeated, 1588
James VI of Scotland becomes James I of England and Ireland.

1603–95

Ireland and England
The Flight of the Earls to Spain, 1607
Plantation of Ulster begun, 1608–9
St Anthony's Franciscan College at Louvain f. 1606
Book of Common Prayer trans. into Irish, 1608
O'Hussey's *The Teaching of Christ* 1611
Sir John Davies, *Discovery of the true causes why Ireland was never
entirely subdued until the beginning of his majesty's happy reign*
1612
F. Conry's *Desiderius*, 1616

Hugh MacCaghwell's *The Mirror of the Sacrament of Penance* 1617
F. Morison, *Itinerary* 1619
P. O'Sullivan Beare *Historicae catholicae Iberniae compendium* 1621
J. Ussher *Discourse of the religion anciently professed by the Irish and Scottish* 1622
collection of Irish poems, *Duanaire Finn* transcribed, 1627
2nd collection, *Book of O'Conor Don*, 1629–30
Sir James Ware (ed.), *The History of Ireland* 1633
Geoffrey Keating completes *Foras Feasa ar Eirinn (Basis of Knowledge About Ireland)*, 1634
Michael O'Clery and others complete *Annals of the Four Masters* 1636.

Catholic rebellion in Ulster, 1641
Civil War begins in England, 1642
Charles I executed, Cromwellian campaigns and massacres in Ireland 1649–51
suppression and confiscations
restoration of Stuarts, Charles II, 1660
Navigation Act against Irish trade, 1667
The Popish Plot, 1678
James II crowned 1685
siege of Derry 1689
William of Orange wins Battle of the Boyne 1690
Treaty of Limerick 1691
Penal Laws against Catholics begin, 1695.

Devotional and political works in Gaelic and Latin continue to be published by Irish exiles in Europe, 1639–95
Sir John Temple *The Irish Rebellion* 1641
G. Boate *Ireland's Natural History* 1652
pamphlets on transplantation of Catholic Irish, 1655
Robert Boyle *The Sceptical Chymist* 1661
Irish-Latin dictionary, 1662
William King *State of the Protestants in Ireland*
Sir William Petty *Political Anatomy of Ireland* 1691.

England and Europe

Literary events
Shakespeare, *Hamlet–The Tempest* 1603–12

Cervantes, *Don Quixote* Part I 1605, Part II 1615
Jonson, the Metaphysical Poets, the Jacobean dramatists
fl. 1603–40
Milton, *Shorter Poems* 1645, *Paradise Lost* 1667
Bunyan *Pilgrim's Progress I* 1678
Molière *Le Misanthrope* 1666
Racine *Phedre* 1677
Dryden *Absalom and Achitophel* I & II 1681–2
Locke *An Essay Concerning Human Understanding* 1690.

1695–1800

Ireland and England
Robert Molesworth *An Account of Denmark* 1694
John Toland *Christianity not Mysterious* 1696
Daibhi O Bruadair d., Farquhar's *Love and A Bottle* 1698
Swift *Tale of A Tub* 1704
Berkeley *The Principles of Human Knowledge* 1710
R. Steele *The Conscious Lovers* 1722
Swift *Drapier's Letters* 1724, *Gulliver's Travels* 1726, *A Modest Proposal* 1729
Aogan O Rathaille d.1729
F. Hutcheson *An Inquiry into the Original of our Ideas of Beauty and Virtue* 1725, English–Irish dictionary 1732
Irish poet Seamas Dall Mac Cuarta d. 1733
Charles O'Conor *Dissertations on the ancient history of Ireland* 1753
Edmund Burke *The Sublime and the Beautiful* 1756
Oliver Goldsmith *The Citizen of the World* 1764
The Vicar of Wakefield, Henry Brooke *The Fool of Quality* 1766
Goldsmith *The Deserted Village* 1770
She Stoops To Conquer 1773
Sylvester O'Halloran *A General History of Ireland* 1774
Burke *Speech on Conciliation with America*, Sheridan *The Rivals* 1775, *The School for Scandal* 1777
Royal Irish Academy f. 1785
J. C. Walker *Historical Memoirs of the Irish Bards* 1786
Charlotte Brooke *Reliques of Irish Poetry* 1789
Burke *Reflections on the French Revolution* 1790, *Letter to Sir Hercules Langrishe* 1792 and 1795
Edward Bunting *General Collection of Ancient Irish Music* 1796
Maria Edgeworth *Castle Rackrent* 1800.

Penal Laws against Catholics, 1695–1725
rule of the 'undertakers' in Ireland, 1725–60
emergence of patriot opposition 1760
abolition of penal laws begins 1771
Irish Parliamentary Independence 1782
formation of United Irishmen 1791
the rebellion of 1798
Act of Union 1800

Establishment of Hanoverian dynasty on English throne from 1714
Jacobite Rebellion 1745
War of the Austrian Succession 1740–8
Seven Years' War 1756–63
War of American Independence 1775–83
War against the French Revolution 1793–1802.

England and Europe
Literary events
Pope *The Rape of the Lock* 1712
Defoe *Robinson Crusoe* 1719
Pope, the first *Dunciad*
Gay *The Beggar's Opera* 1728
Voltaire in England 1726–9
Marivaux *Le Jeu de L'Amour et du Hasard* 1730
Prevost *Manon Lescaut* 1731
Richardson *Pamela* 1740
Fielding *Tom Jones*, Diderot *Lettre sur les Aveugles* 1749
Gray, *Elegy in A Country Churchyard*, Rousseau, first *Discours*
    1750
Montesquieu *L'Esprit des Lois* 1751
Wincklemann *Thoughts on Greek Works of Painting and Sculpture*
    1755
MacPherson's *Ossian* 1760
Sterne *Tristram Shandy* 1759–67
de Laclos *Les Liaisons Dangereuses* 1772
Goethe *The Sorrows of Young Werther* 1774
S. Johnson *Lives of the Poets* 1779
Blake *Poetical Sketches* 1783
Kant *Critique of Practical Reason* 1788
Wordsworth and Coleridge *The Lyrical Ballads* 1798 and 1800.

1801–91

Ireland and England

Lady Morgan *The Wild Irish Girl* 1806

Thomas Moore *Irish Melodies* 1807–34

Edgeworth *The Absentee* 1812, *Ormond* 1817

C. Maturin *Melmoth the Wanderer* 1820

J. and M. Banim *Tales of the O'Hara Family* 1825–6

T. C. Croker *Fairy Legends and Traditions of the South of Ireland* 1825

G. Griffin *The Collegians* 1829

W. Carleton *Traits and Stories of the Irish Peasantry* 1830–3

C. Lever *Confessions of Harry Lorrequer* 1839

J. C. Mangan *The Poets and Poetry of Munster* 1849

John Mitchel *Jail Journal* 1854

D. Boucicault *The Colleen Bawn* 1860

E. O'Curry *Lectures and Manuscript Materials of Ancient Irish History* 1861

W. Allingham *Laurence Bloomfield in Ireland*, S. Le Fanu *Uncle Silas* 1864

Sir Samuel Ferguson *Lays of the Western Gael* 1865

S. O'Grady *History of Ireland: Heroic Period* 1878–80

C. Kickham *Knocknagow* 1879

Oscar Wilde *Poems* 1881

G. Moore *A Drama in Muslin* 1886

Yeats *Mosada* 1886

The Wanderings of Oisin 1889

Wilde *The Picture of Dorian Gray*, Shaw *The Quintessence of Ibsenism* 1891.

Catholic Emancipation, 1829

Reform Bill 1832

Tithe War 1830s

Daniel O'Connell's Repeal Campaign 1840–2

break with Young Ireland 1846

the Great Famine 1845–7

The Fenian Brotherhood formed 1858

outbreak of American Civil War 1861

Gladstone's First Land Act 1870

Parnell's parliamentary career 1875–91

Land League formed 1879

Home Rule Bill 1886

Land Purchase Act of 1891 establishes Congested Districts Board
Irish Literary Society of London f. 1891 at house of W. B. Yeats.

England and Europe
Literary events
Romantic authors – Wordsworth, Coleridge, Blake, Byron, Shelley,
    Keats, Scott, Hazlitt, Peacock, Lamb fl. 1800–25
J. Austen fl. 1811–18
Dickens' novels 1836–70
Thackeray's novels 1844–60;
G. Eliot's novels 1858–78
Hardy's novels, 1872–96
Tennyson *In Memoriam* 1850
Darwin *On the Origin of Species* 1859
J. S. Mill *On Liberty* 1859
Arnold *Essays on Criticism* 1865
On the Study of Celtic Literature, Marx *Das Kapital* I, 1867
Browning *The Ring and the Book* 1868
Nietzsche *The Birth of Tragedy* 1872
Newman *The Idea of a University* 1873
H. James *The Portrait of a Lady* 1881
Huysmans *A Rebours* 1884
Zola *Germinal* 1885
Stevenson *Dr. Jekyll and Mr. Hyde* 1886
Gilbert and Sullivan *The Gondoliers* 1889
W. James *Principles of Psychology* 1890
G. Gissing *New Grub Street* 1891.

1892–1940

Ireland and England
Wilde *Salome, Lady Windermere's Fan*
Shaw *Widowers' Houses*, Yeats *The Countess Kathleen* 1892
Hyde *Love Songs of Connacht*, Yeats *The Celtic Twilight*, Gaelic
    League f. 1893
G. Moore *Esther Waters*, Somerville and Ross *The Real Charlotte*
    1894
Moore *Celibates* 1895
G. Sigerson *Bards of the Gael and Gall*, Bram Stoker *Dracula* 1897
Shaw *Plays Pleasant and Unpleasant*, Irish Literary Theatre formed
    1898

Yeats *The Wind Among the Reeds*, Irish Texts Society founded 1899
Canon Sheehan *My New Curate* 1900
Lady Gregory *Cuchulain of Muirthemne* 1902
Poets and Dreamers, G. Moore *The Untilled Field*, Shaw *Man and Superman* 1903
Synge *Riders to the Sea*, Yeats *In the Seven Woods* 1904
G. Moore *The Lake*, Shaw *Major Barbara*, Synge *The Shadow of the Glen*, *The Well of the Saints* 1905
Joyce *Chamber Music*, Shaw *John Bull's Other Island*, Yeats *Deirdre*, Lady Gregory *The Rising of the Moon*, Synge *The Playboy of the Western World*, riots at Abbey Theatre production 1907
Yeats *Collected Works* 1908
Moore *Hail and Farewell* 1911–14
James Stephens *The Charwoman's Daughter*, *The Crock of Gold*, G. Birmingham *The Red Hand of Ulster*, Shaw *Pygmalion* 1912
G. Russell (AE) *Collected Poems* 1913
Joyce *Dubliners*, Yeats' *Responsibilities* 1914
Joyce *A Portrait of the Artist as a Young Man* 1916
Yeats *The Wild Swans at Coole* 1917
Joyce *Exiles*, Pearse *Collected Works*, Shaw *Heartbreak House*, G. O'Donovan *Waiting*, F. Ledwidge *Complete Poems* 1919
Yeats *Michael Robartes and the Dancer* 1920, *Four Plays for Dancers* 1921
Joyce *Ulysses*, Yeats *Later Poems* 1922
S. O'Casey *The Shadow of a Gunman*, Shaw *Saint Joan* 1923
D. Corkery *The Hidden Ireland*, O'Casey *Juno and the Paycock* 1924
Liam O'Flaherty *The Informer*, Somerville *The Big House at Inver* 1925
O'Casey *The Plough and the Stars* 1926
Yeats *The Tower* 1928
E. Bowen *The Last September*, Austin Clarke *Pilgrimage and Other Poems*, O'Casey *The Silver Tassie*, Yeats *The Winding Stair*, Denis Johnston *The Old Lady Says 'No!'* 1929
Frank O'Connor *Guests of the Nation* 1931
Sean O'Faolain *Midsummer Madness*, Peadar O'Donnell *The Gates Flew Open*, Yeats *Words for Music Perhaps* 1932
S. Beckett *More Pricks than Kicks* 1934
Murphy 1938

Joyce *Finnegans Wake*
Flann O'Brien *At-Swim-Two-Birds*, Yeats *Last Poems*, L. MacNeice *Autumn Journal* 1939, S. O'Faolain founds the magazine *The Bell* 1940.

Griffith founds Sinn Fein 1905
Home Rule Bill and Ulster Rebellion 1912
The Great Lockout in Dublin 1913
First World War, the Easter Rebellion and executions 1916
Russian Revolution 1917
Sinn Fein electoral triumph 1918
Anglo-Irish War 1919–21
Anglo-Irish Treaty 1921–2
Civil War 1922–3
partition confirmed 1925
de Valera founds Fianna Fail 1926, forms government 1932
new constitution 1937
neutrality in Second World War 1939–45.

England, USA and Europe
Literary events
Kipling *Barrack-Room Ballads*, Ibsen *The Master-Builder*, G. Hauptmann *The Weavers* 1892
Housman *A Shropshire Lad* 1896
Conrad *The Nigger of the Narcissus*, James *What Maisie Knew*, Wells, *The Invisible Man* 1897
Freud *The Interpretation of Dreams*, Tolstoy *Resurrection* 1899
Conrad *Lord Jim*, Chekhov *Uncle Vanya* 1900
Mann *Buddenbrooks*, Strindberg *Dance of Death*, Chekhov *Three Sisters* 1901
James *The Wings of the Dove*, Gide *L'Immoraliste* 1902
Butler *The Way of All Flesh*, James *The Ambassadors* 1903
James *The Golden Bowl*, Conrad *Nostromo*, Chekhov *The Cherry Orchard* 1904
Conrad *The Secret Agent* 1907
Forster *Howards End*, Claudel *Cinq Grands Odes* 1910
Alain-Fournier, *Le Grand Meaulnes*, Lawrence *Sons and Lovers*, Mann *Death in Venice*, Proust *A La Recherche du Temps Perdu* (begins) 1913
Ford *The Good Soldier*, Lawrence *The Rainbow*, Frost *North of Boston* 1915

T. S. Eliot *Prufrock and Other Observations*, Valery *La Jeune Parque*, Edward Thomas *Poems* 1917
G. M. Hopkins *Poems* (posth.), Strachey *Eminent Victorians* 1918
Hardy *Collected Poems*, Sassoon *War Poems* 1919
Lawrence *Women in Love*, Pound *Hugh Selwyn Mauberley*, Eliot *The Sacred Wood* 1920
The Waste Land 1922
Forster *A Passage to India*, Mann *The Magic Mountain* 1924
Kafka *The Trial*, Scott Fitzgerald *The Great Gatsby*, V. Woolf *Mrs. Dalloway* 1925
Kafka *The Castle*, Gide *Les Faux-Monnayeurs*, Hemingway *The Sun Also Rises* 1926
Woolf *To The Lighthouse*, Hesse *Steppenwolf*, Mauriac *Thérèse Desqueyroux* 1927
Faulkner *The Sound and the Fury*, Graves *Goodbye to All That*, Hemingway *A Farewell to Arms*, Sholokhov *And Quiet Flows the Don* (begins) 1929
V. Woolf *The Waves* 1931
A. Huxley *Brave New World*, A. de Saint-Exupéry *Vol de Nuit* 1932
Lorca *Blood Wedding*, Malraux *La Condition Humaine* 1933
Waugh *A Handful of Dust*, Cocteau, *La Machine Infernale* 1934
Auden and Isherwood *The Ascent of F6* 1936
Greene *Brighton Rock*, Sartre *La Nausée* 1938
E. O'Neill *Long Day's Journey Into Night*, Greene *The Power and the Glory*, R. Chandler *Farewell My Lovely*, Koestler *Darkness at Noon* 1940.

Ireland 1941–80

Flann O'Brien *An Béal Bocht* (*The Poor Mouth*), Kate O'Brien *The Land of Spices*, F. O'Connor *Dutch Interior*, O'Casey *The Star Turns Red* 1941
P. Kavanagh *The Great Hunger*, M. Lavin *Tales from Bective Bridge* 1942
Joyce Cary *The Horse's Mouth*, Joyce *Stephen Hero* (posth.) 1944
M. Wall *The Unfortunate Fursey*, D. Devlin *Lough Derg* 1946
P. Kavanagh *Tarry Flynn*, F. Stuart *A Pillar of Cloud* 1948
MacNeice *Collected Poems*, J. Cary *A Fearful Joy*, E. Bowen *The Heat of the Day*
Beckett *Molloy, Malone Meurt*, Dolmen Press f. 1951
Beckett *En attendant Godot* 1952

Clarke *Ancient Lights*, Brian Moore *Judith Hearne*, J. Plunkett *The Trusting and the Maimed* 1955
T. Kinsella *Poems*, B. Behan *The Quare Fellow* 1956
O'Faolain *Finest Stories*, Kinsella *Another September* 1958
Kavanagh *Come Dance With Kitty Stobling*, Sam Thompson *Over the Bridge*, B. Moore *The Luck of Ginger Coffey* 1960
Clarke *Later Poems*, Montague *Poisoned Lands*, Tom Murphy *Whistle in the Dark* 1961
Kinsella *Downstream* 1962
J. McGahern *The Barracks*, M. Farrell *Thy Tears Might Cease* 1963
B. Friel *Philadelphia Here I Come*, O'Faolain *Vive Moi*, Kavanagh *Collected Poems*, A. Cronin *The Life of Riley*, F. O'Brien *The Dalkey Archive*, W. Trevor *The Old Boys*, F. O'Connor *An Only Child*, Devlin *Collected Poems* 1964
McGahern *The Dark*, Moore *The Emperor of Ice-Cream* 1965
J. Boyd *The Flats*, S. Heaney *Death of a Naturalist*, A. Higgins *Langrishe Go Down*
Montague *A Chosen Light*, F. O'Brien *The Third Policeman* 1967
J. Hewitt *Collected Poems*, Moore *I am Mary Dunne*, Beckett *Breath*, Friel *Lovers*, Kinsella *Nightwalker and Other Poems*, Heaney *Door Into The Dark*, D. Mahon *Night-Crossing*, J. Simmons f. *The Honest Ulsterman* 1968
M. Longley *No Continuing City*, J. Plunkett *Strumpet City*, R. Power *The Hungry Grass*, T. Kilroy *The Death and Resurrection of Mr. Roche* 1969
Friel *Crystal and Fox*, Montague *Tides*, J. Banville *Long Lankin*, 1970
T. Kilroy *The Big Chapel*, M. Lavin *Collected Stories*, F. Stuart *Black List, Section H*, T. Murphy *The Morning After Optimism* 1971
Moore *Catholics*, Heaney *Wintering Out*, J. Johnston *The Captains and the Kings*, Montague *The Rough Field*, Mahon *Lives*, 1972
Longley *An Exploded View*, Kinsella *Notes From the Land of the Dead*, Muldoon *New Weather*, Banville *Birchwood*, Friel *The Freedom of the City*, McGahern *Nightlines* 1973
Padraic Fallon *Poems*, R. Murphy *High Island*, Kinsella *One*, Johnston *How Many Miles to Babylon* 1974
Montague *A Slow Dance*, Heaney *North*, Mahon *The Snow Party*, Friel *Volunteers*, *Living Quarters*, Moore *The Great Victorian Collection* 1975
W. Trevor *The Children of Dynmouth*, Kinsella *A Technical*

Supplement, Longley *Man Lying On A Wall*, Simmons *Judy Garland and the Cold War*, Cronin *Dead As Doornails*, Banville *Dr. Copernicus* 1976

Muldoon *Mules*, F. Stuart *A Hole in the Head* 1977

Kinsella *Song of the Night and Other Poems, The Messenger*, Montague *The Great Cloak* 1978

McGahern *The Pornographer*, Kilroy *Talbot's Box*, Moore *The Managan Inheritance*, Cronin *Identity Papers*, Johnston *The Old Jest*, Heaney *Field Work*, Friel *Aristocrats*, Murphy *Selected Poems* 1979

Muldoon *Why Brownlee Left*, T. Paulin *The Strange Museum*, Kinsella *Poems 1956–73* 1980.

Republic of Ireland declared 1948

IRA campaign in North 1956–62

Lemass and O'Neill, prime ministers of South and North, meet 1965

Economic advance in the Republic 1965–70

Northern Ireland breaks down in violence 1968–

Ireland enters Common Market, 1973

economic recession North and South 1973– .

Index